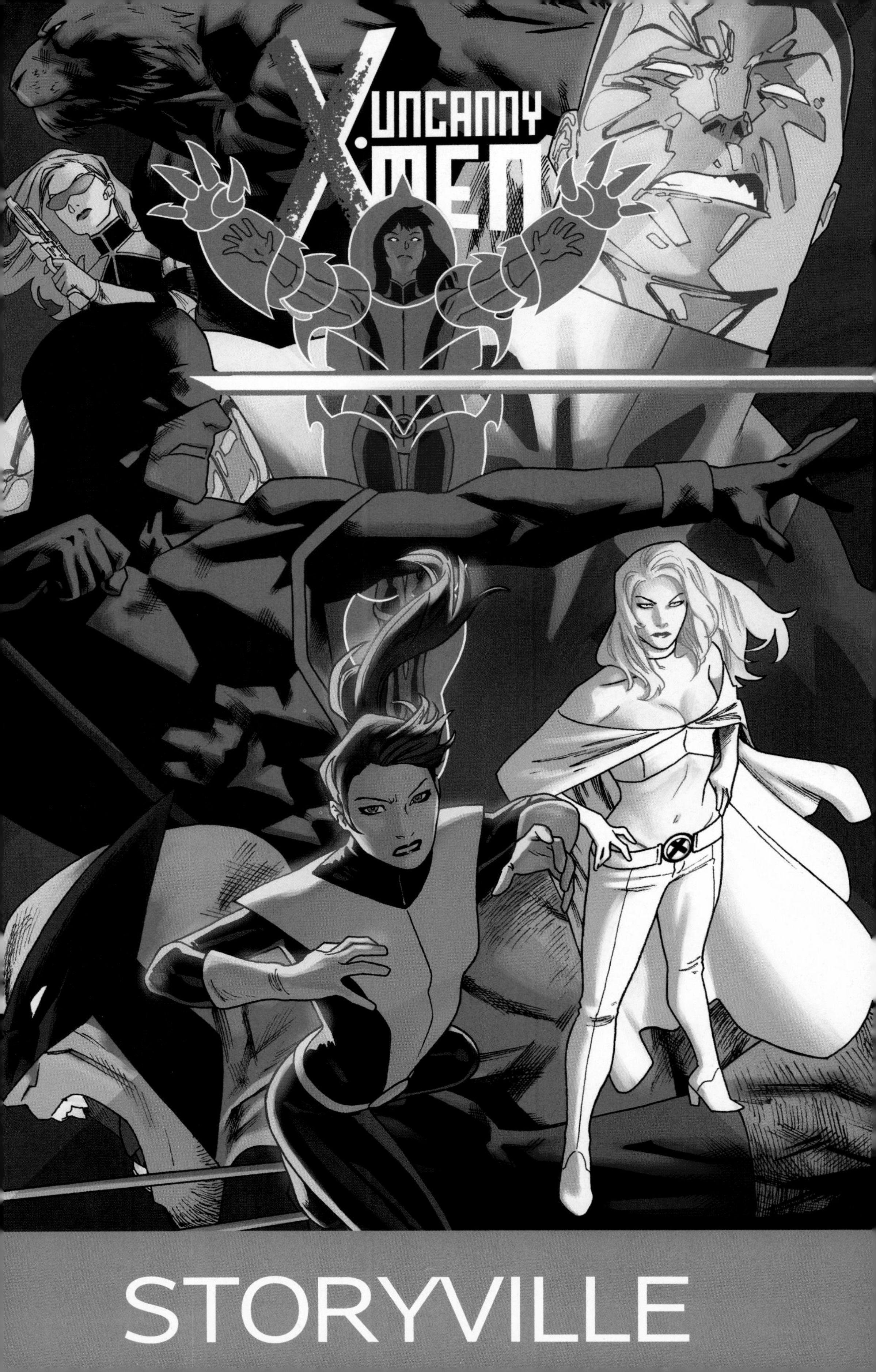
UNCANNY X-MEN

STORYVILLE

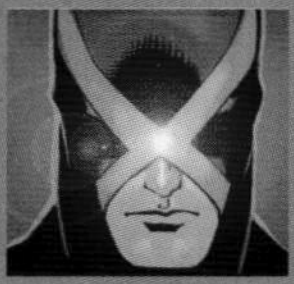

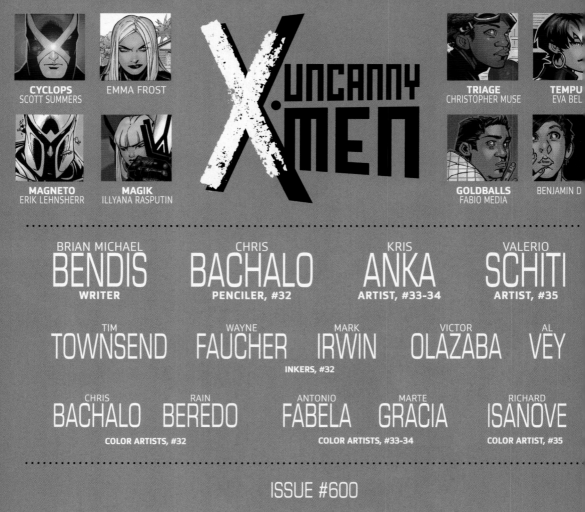

CYCLOPS
SCOTT SUMMERS

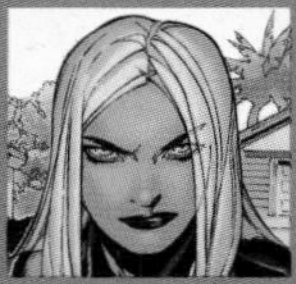

EMMA FROST

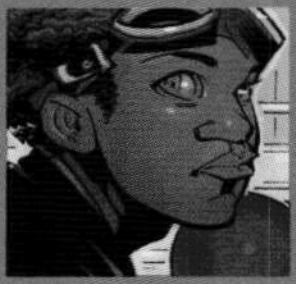

TRIAGE
CHRISTOPHER MUSE

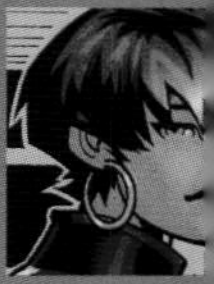

TEMPU
EVA BEL

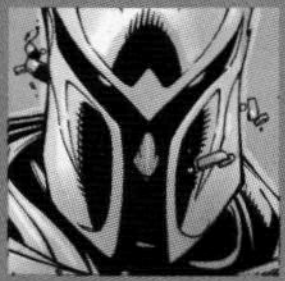

MAGNETO
ERIK LEHNSHERR

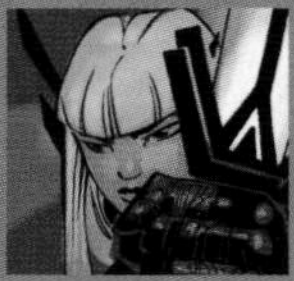

MAGIK
ILLYANA RASPUTIN

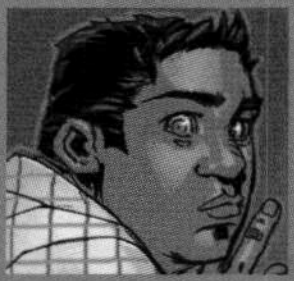

GOLDBALLS
FABIO MEDIA

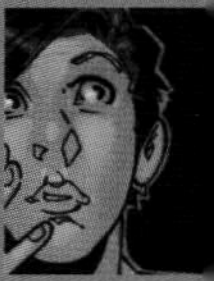

BENJAMIN D

UNCANNY X-MEN

BRIAN MICHAEL **BENDIS**
WRITER

CHRIS **BACHALO**
PENCILER, #32

KRIS **ANKA**
ARTIST, #33-34

VALERIO **SCHITI**
ARTIST, #35

TIM **TOWNSEND** · WAYNE **FAUCHER** · MARK **IRWIN** · VICTOR **OLAZABA** · AL **VEY**
INKERS, #32

CHRIS **BACHALO** · RAIN **BEREDO**
COLOR ARTISTS, #32

ANTONIO **FABELA** · MARTE **GRACIA**
COLOR ARTISTS, #33-34

RICHARD **ISANOVE**
COLOR ARTIST, #35

ISSUE #600

PENCILERS: **SARA PICHELLI, MAHMUD ASRAR, STUART IMMONEN, KRIS ANKA, CHRIS BACHALO, DAVID MARQUEZ** & **FRAZER IRVING**
INKERS: **WADE VON GRAWBADGER, TIM TOWNSEND** & **MARK IRWIN**
COLOR ARTISTS: **MARTE GRACIA, JASON KEITH, CHRIS BACHALO** & **FRAZER IRVING**

COVER ART: **CHRIS BACHALO** & **TIM TOWNSEND** (#32, #600) AND **KRIS ANKA** (#33-35)
LETTERER: **VC's JOE CARAMAGNA** ASSISTANT EDITORS: **XANDER JAROWEY** & **CHRISTINA HARRINGTON**
EDITORS: **MIKE MARTS** & **MARK PANICCIA**

X-MEN CREATED BY **STAN LEE** & **JACK KIRBY**

COLLECTION EDITOR: **JENNIFER GRÜNWALD** ASSISTANT EDITOR: **SARAH BRUNSTAD**
ASSOCIATE MANAGING EDITOR: **ALEX STARBUCK** EDITOR, SPECIAL PROJECTS: **MARK D. BEAZLEY**
SENIOR EDITOR, SPECIAL PROJECTS: **JEFF YOUNGQUIST** SVP PRINT, SALES & MARKETING: **DAVID GABRIEL**
BOOK DESIGNER: **ADAM DEL RE**

EDITOR IN CHIEF: **AXEL ALONSO** CHIEF CREATIVE OFFICER: **JOE QUESADA**
PUBLISHER: **DAN BUCKLEY** EXECUTIVE PRODUCER: **ALAN FINE**

UNCANNY X-MEN VOL. 6: STORYVILLE. Contains material originally published in magazine form as UNCANNY X-MEN #32-35 and #600. First printing 2015. ISBN# 978-0-7851-9230-5. Published by M WORLDWIDE, INC., a subsidiary of MARVEL ENTERTAINMENT, LLC. OFFICE OF PUBLICATION: 135 West 50th Street, New York, NY 10020. Copyright © 2015 MARVEL No similarity between any of the names, cha persons, and/or institutions in this magazine with those of any living or dead person or institution is intended, and any such similarity which may exist is purely coincidental. **Printed in the U.S.A.** ALAN FINE, Pre Marvel Entertainment; DAN BUCKLEY, President, TV, Publishing and Brand Management; JOE QUESADA, Chief Creative Officer; TOM BREVOORT, SVP of Publishing; DAVID BOGART, SVP of Operations & Procur Publishing; C.B. CEBULSKI, VP of International Development & Brand Management; DAVID GABRIEL, SVP Print, Sales & Marketing; JIM O'KEEFE, VP of Operations & Logistics; DAN CARR, Executive Director of Pub Technology; SUSAN CRESPI, Editorial Operations Manager; ALEX MORALES, Publishing Operations Manager; STAN LEE, Chairman Emeritus. For information regarding advertising in Marvel Comics or on Marv please contact Jonathan Rheingold, VP of Custom Solutions & Ad Sales, at jrheingold@marvel.com. For Marvel subscription inquiries, please call 800-217-9158. **Manufactured between 9/4/2015 and 10/19/2**

Born with genetic mutations that gave them abilities beyond those of normal humans, mutants are the next stage in evolution. As such, they are feared and hated by humanity. A group of mutants known as the X-Men fight for peaceful coexistence between mutants and humankind. But not all mutants see peaceful coexistence as a reality.

Cyclops is the public face for what he calls "the new mutant revolution." Vowing to protect the mutant race, he's begun to gather and train a new generation of mutants.

When Charles Xavier died at the hands of a phoenix-possessed Scott Summers, the reading of his last will and testament brought to light the existence of a mutant of immense power whom Xavier had kept hidden. With thousands of lives being lost as the mutant lost control of his abilities, Eva Bell traveled back in time and used the help of a younger Xavier to ensure the mutant was never born. In doing this, she erased the deaths caused by the mutant, also changing Xavier's will to now read that all that he owned should be left to Scott Summers. Racked by guilt, Scott was unable to accept his surrogate father's gifts, and relinquished the ownership of the school to Storm, walking away from his father's legacy.

Meanwhile, his brother Alex, a.k.a. Havok, finding that his beliefs no longer fell in line with the Avengers' mission, left the Uncanny Avengers to join his brother.

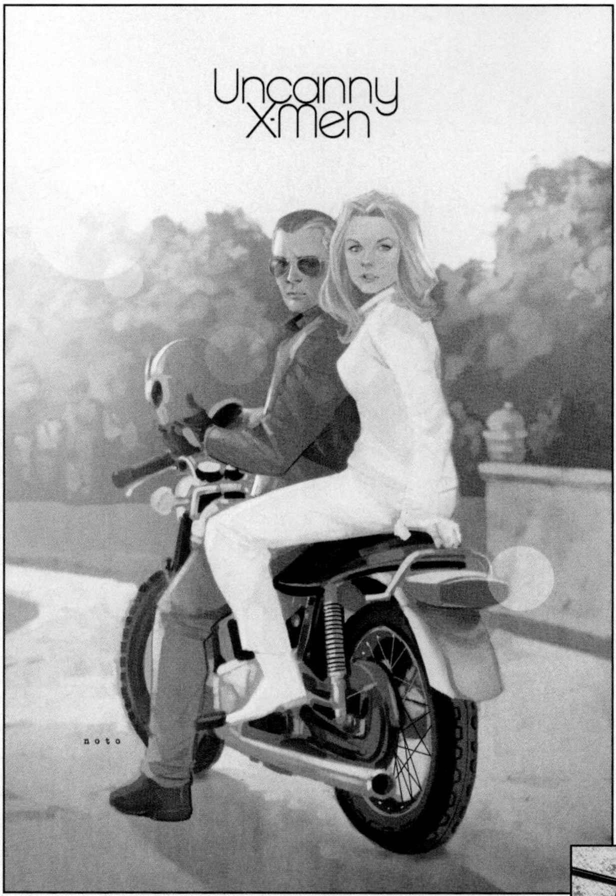
Uncanny X-Men
noto

UNCANNY X-MEN #32 VARIANT
BY PHIL NOTO

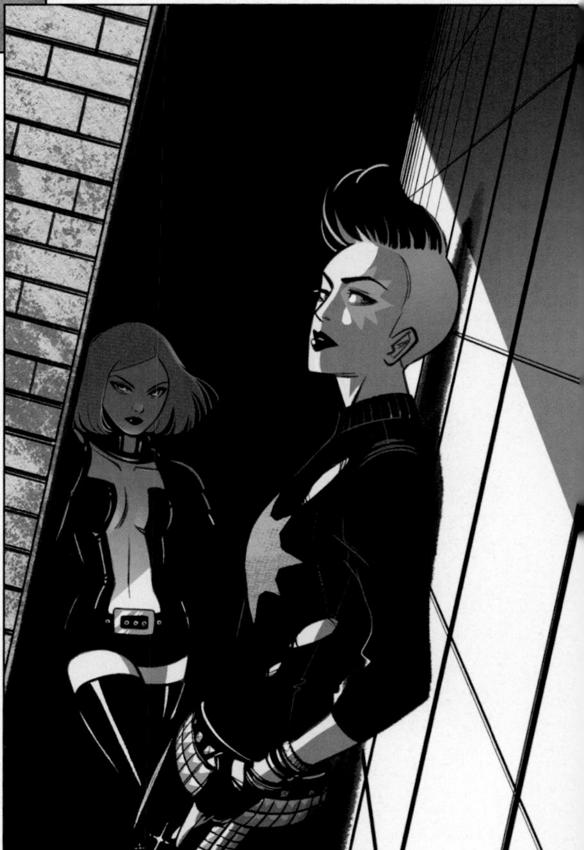

UNCANNY X-MEN #33 WOMEN OF MARVEL VARIA
BY STACEY LEE

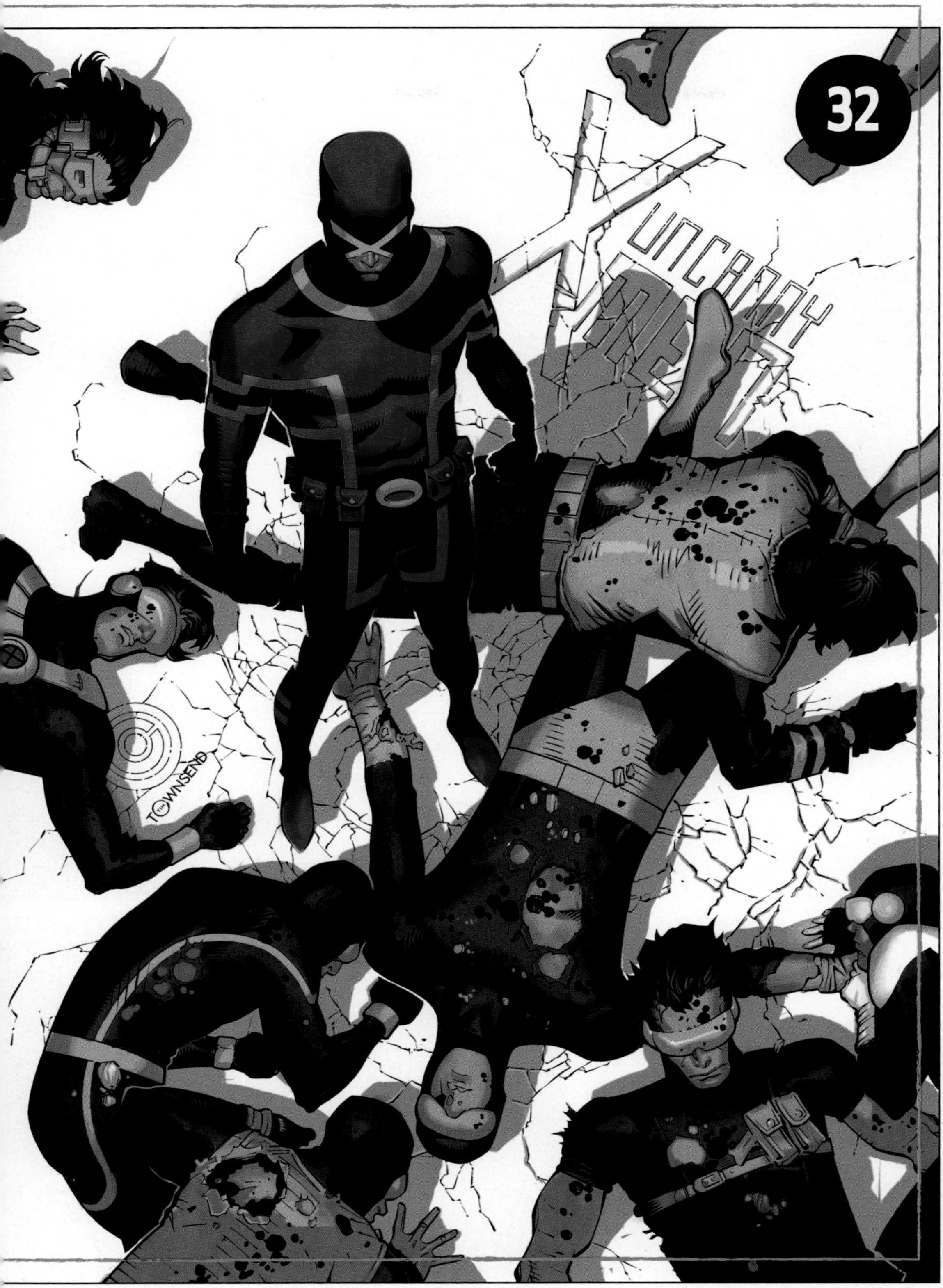
32
UNCANNY
X-MEN
TOWNSEND

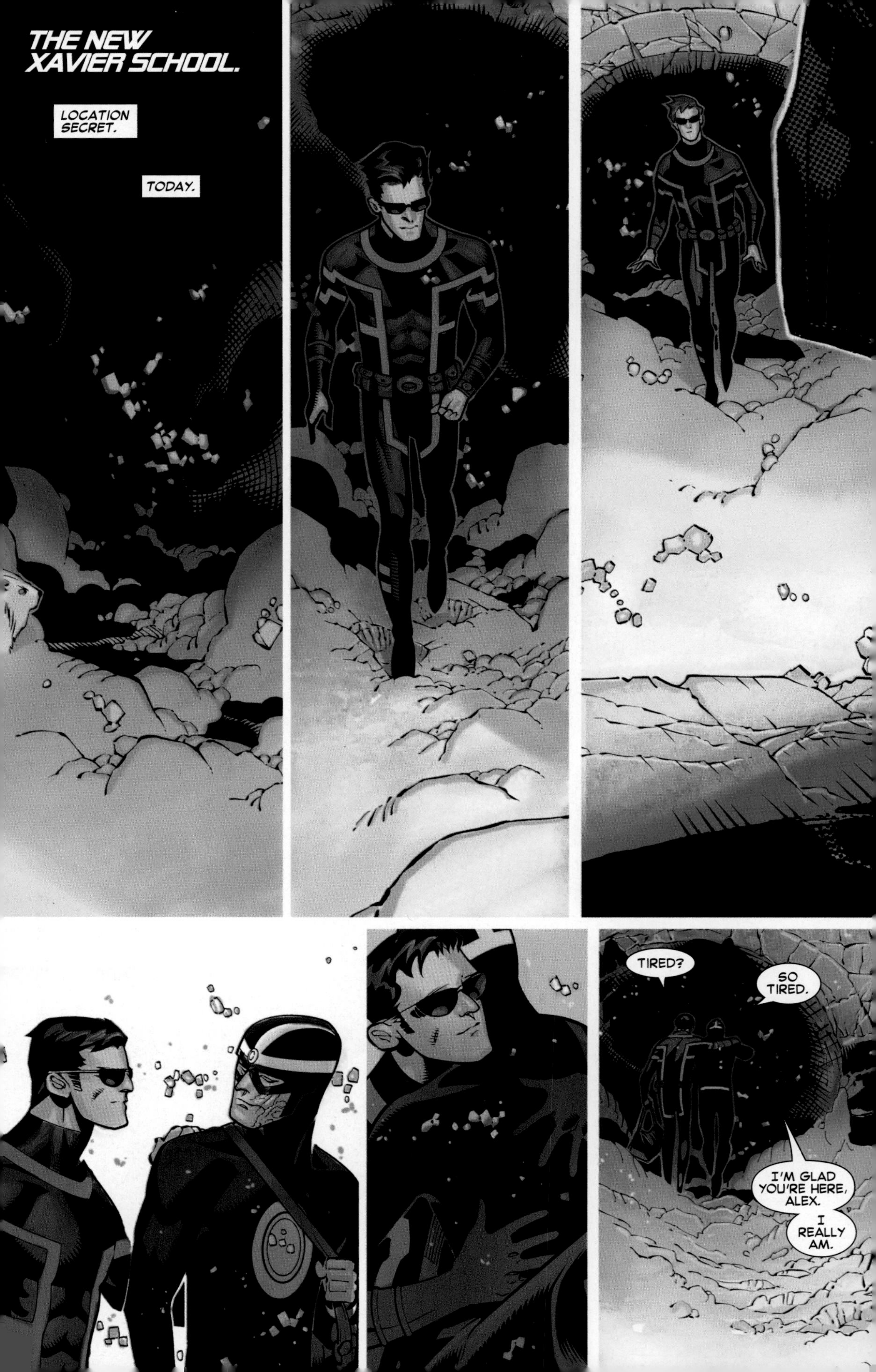
THE NEW XAVIER SCHOOL.
LOCATION SECRET.
TODAY.
TIRED?
SO TIRED.
I'M GLAD YOU'RE HERE, ALEX.
I REALLY AM.

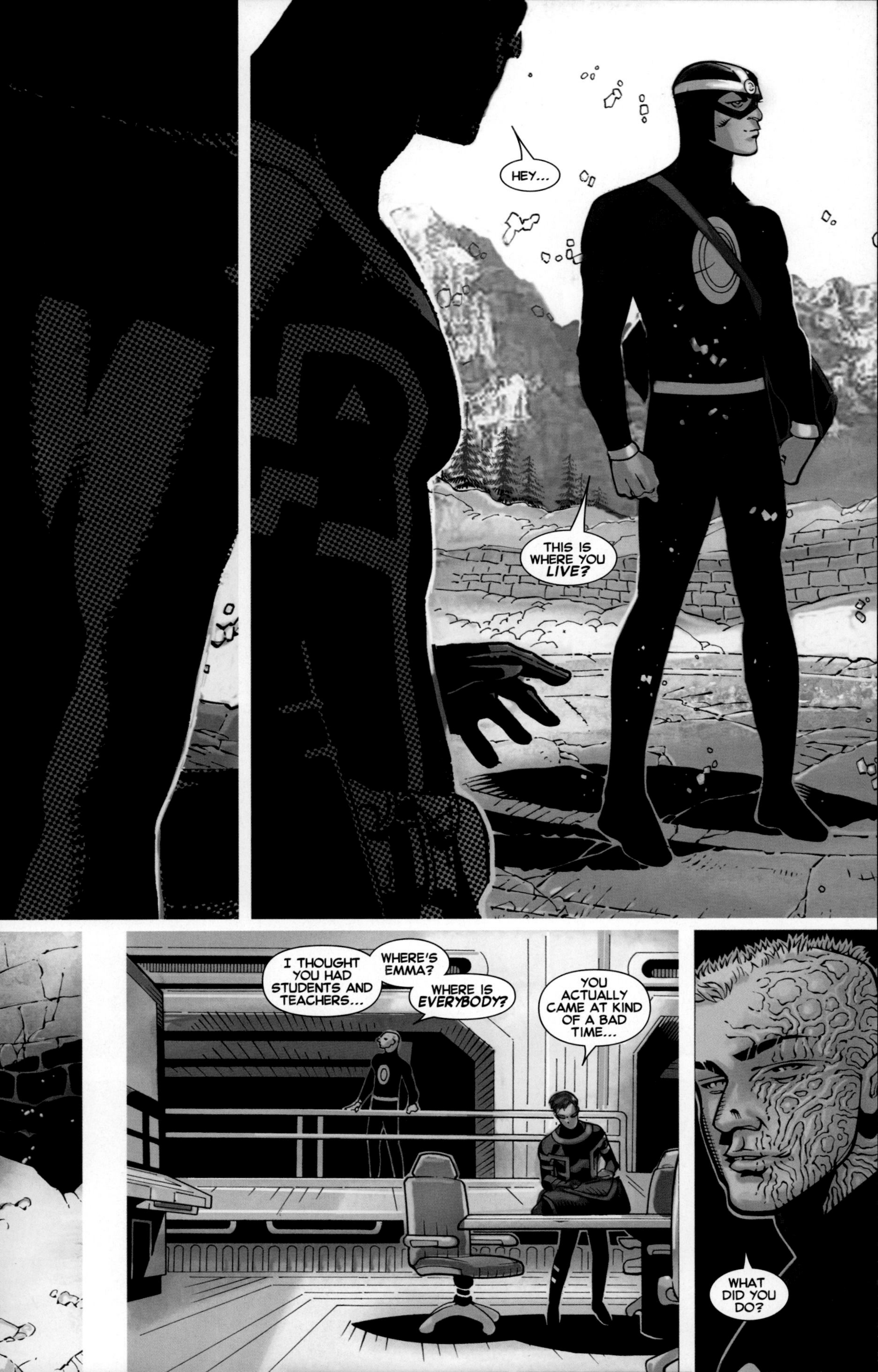
HEY...
THIS IS WHERE YOU *LIVE?*
I THOUGHT YOU HAD STUDENTS AND TEACHERS...
WHERE'S EMMA?
WHERE IS *EVERYBODY?*
YOU ACTUALLY CAME AT KIND OF A BAD TIME...
WHAT DID YOU DO?

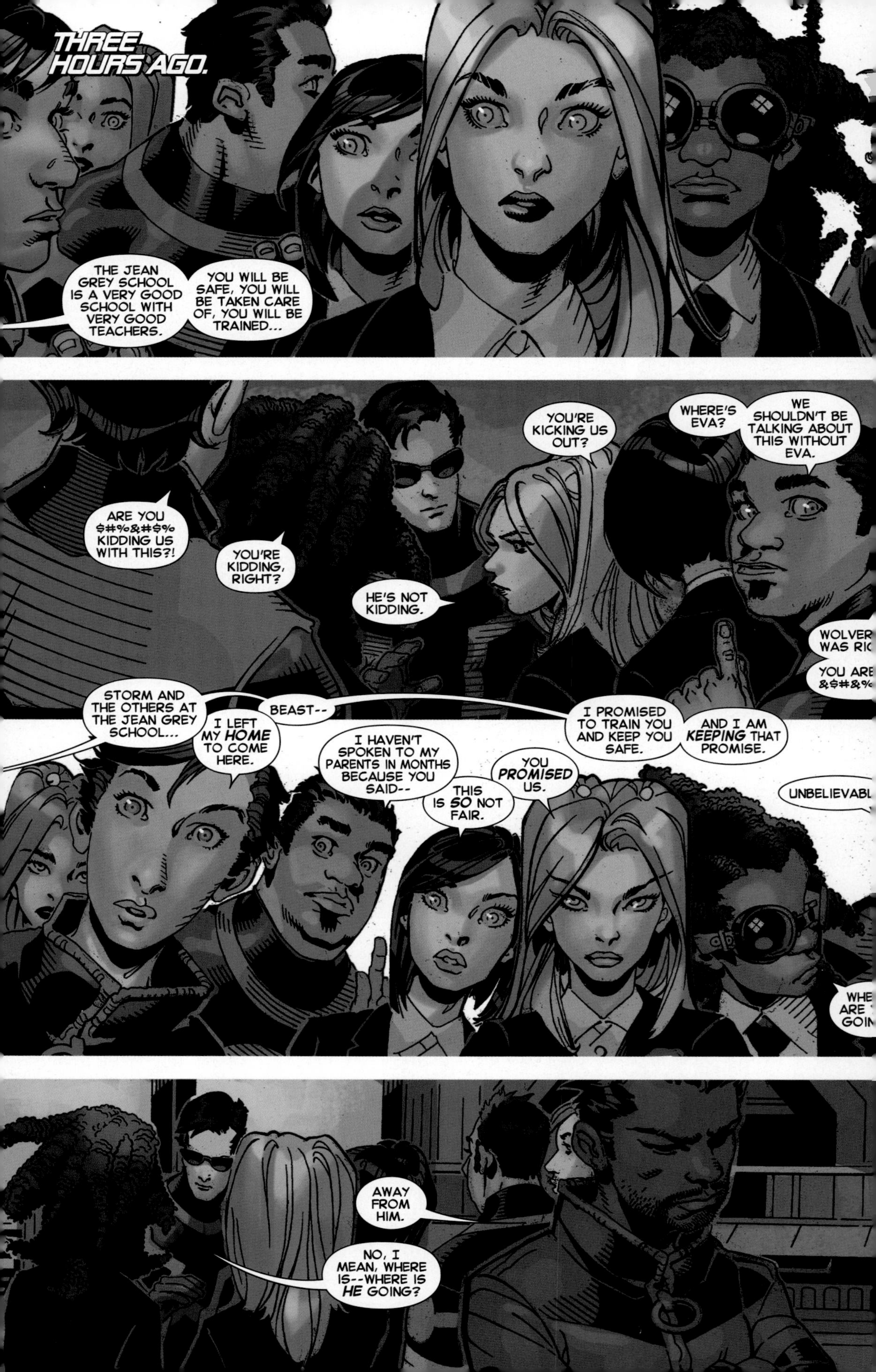
THREE HOURS AGO.
THE JEAN GREY SCHOOL IS A VERY GOOD SCHOOL WITH VERY GOOD TEACHERS.
YOU WILL BE SAFE, YOU WILL BE TAKEN CARE OF, YOU WILL BE TRAINED...
ARE YOU $#%&#$% KIDDING US WITH THIS?!
YOU'RE KIDDING, RIGHT?
HE'S NOT KIDDING.
YOU'RE KICKING US OUT?
WHERE'S EVA?
WE SHOULDN'T BE TALKING ABOUT THIS WITHOUT EVA.
STORM AND THE OTHERS AT THE JEAN GREY SCHOOL...
BEAST--
I PROMISED TO TRAIN YOU AND KEEP YOU SAFE.
AND I AM KEEPING THAT PROMISE.
I LEFT MY HOME TO COME HERE.
I HAVEN'T SPOKEN TO MY PARENTS IN MONTHS BECAUSE YOU SAID--
THIS IS SO NOT FAIR.
YOU PROMISED US.
AWAY FROM HIM.
NO, I MEAN, WHERE IS--WHERE IS HE GOING?

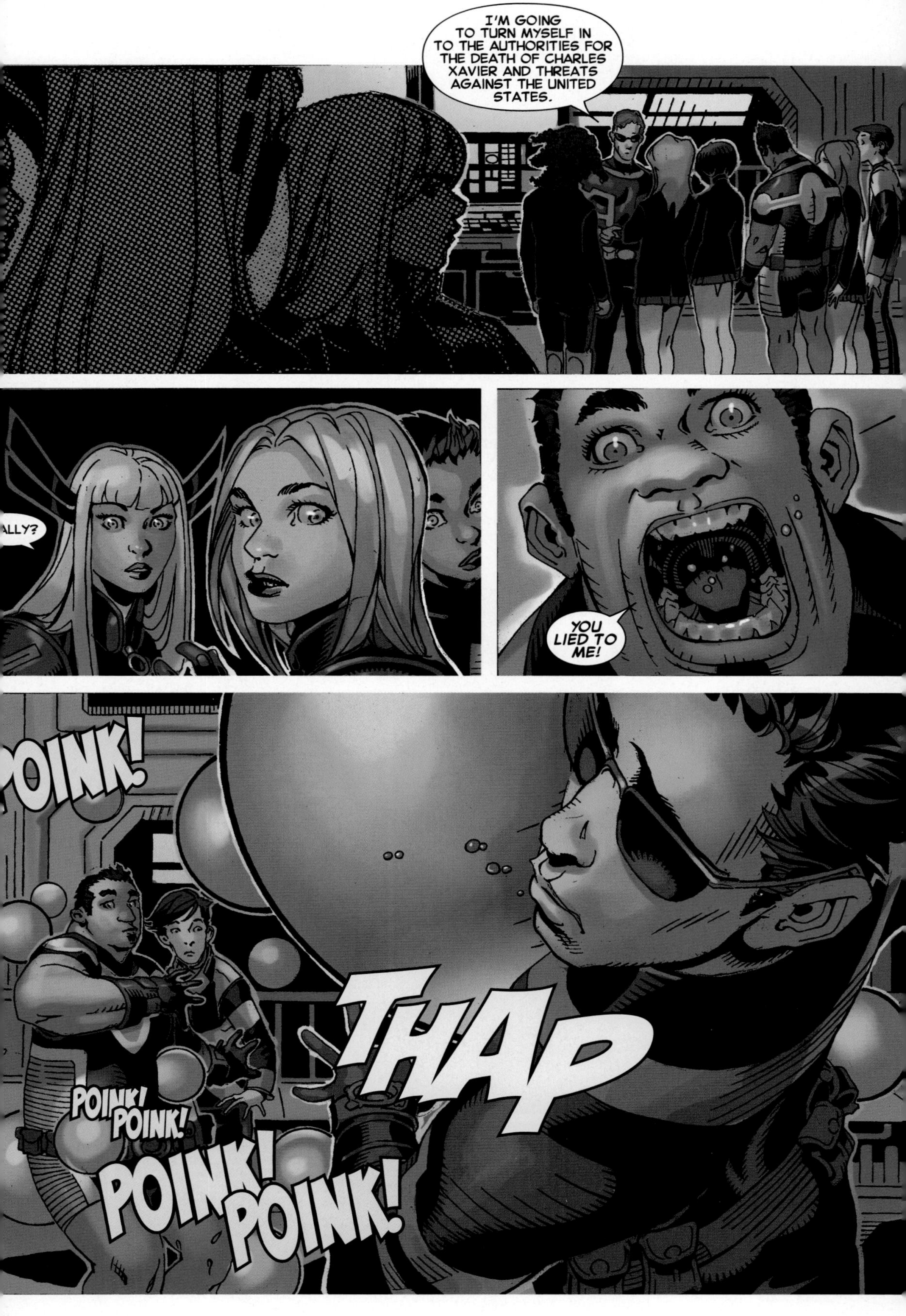
I'M GOING TO TURN MYSELF IN TO THE AUTHORITIES FOR THE DEATH OF CHARLES XAVIER AND THREATS AGAINST THE UNITED STATES.
ALLY?
YOU LIED TO ME!
POINK!
THAP
POINK! POINK!
POINK! POINK!

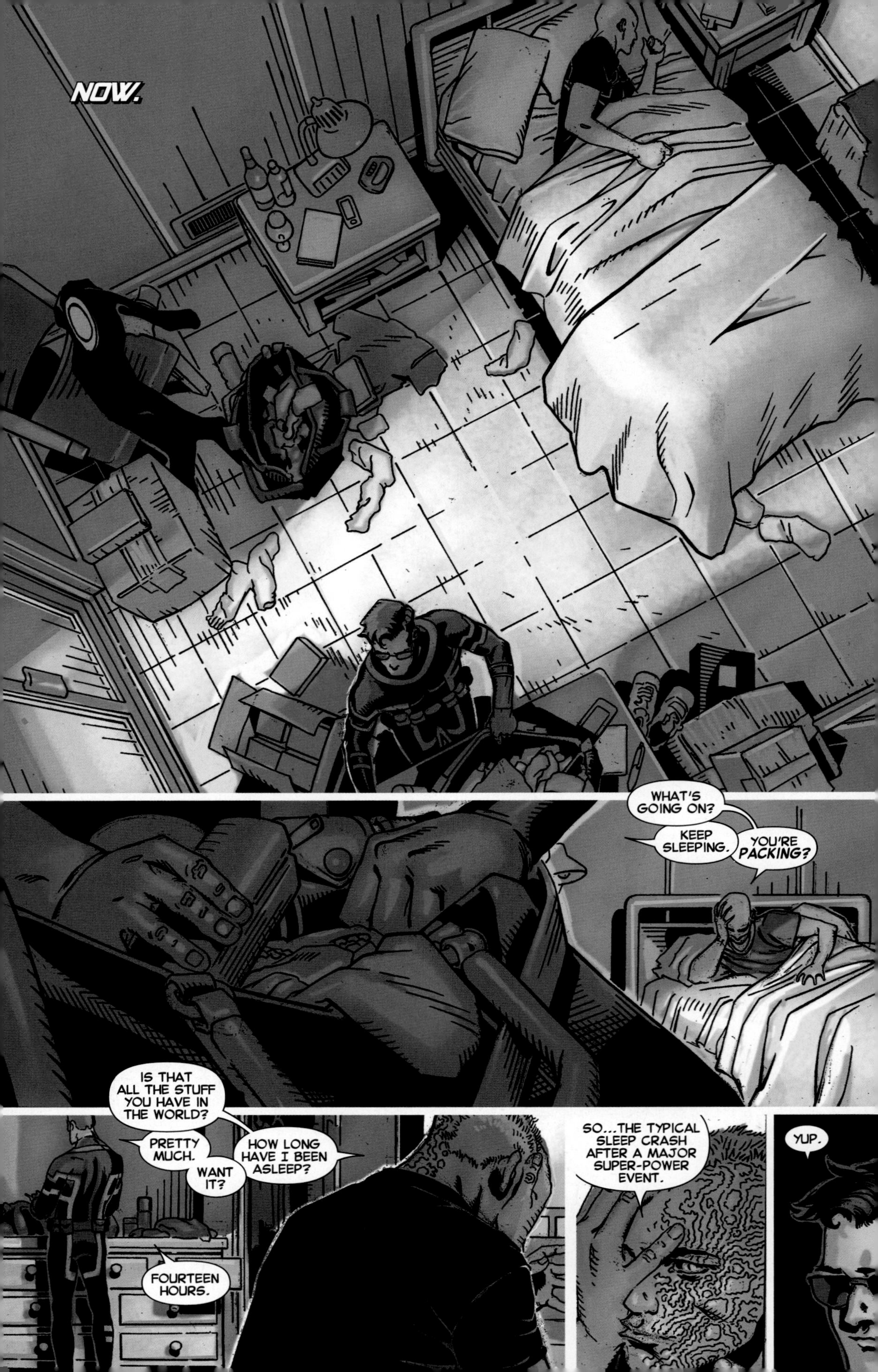

NOW.
WHAT'S GOING ON?
KEEP SLEEPING.
YOU'RE PACKING?
IS THAT ALL THE STUFF YOU HAVE IN THE WORLD?
PRETTY MUCH.
WANT IT?
HOW LONG HAVE I BEEN ASLEEP?
FOURTEEN HOURS.
SO...THE TYPICAL SLEEP CRASH AFTER A MAJOR SUPER-POWER EVENT.
YUP.

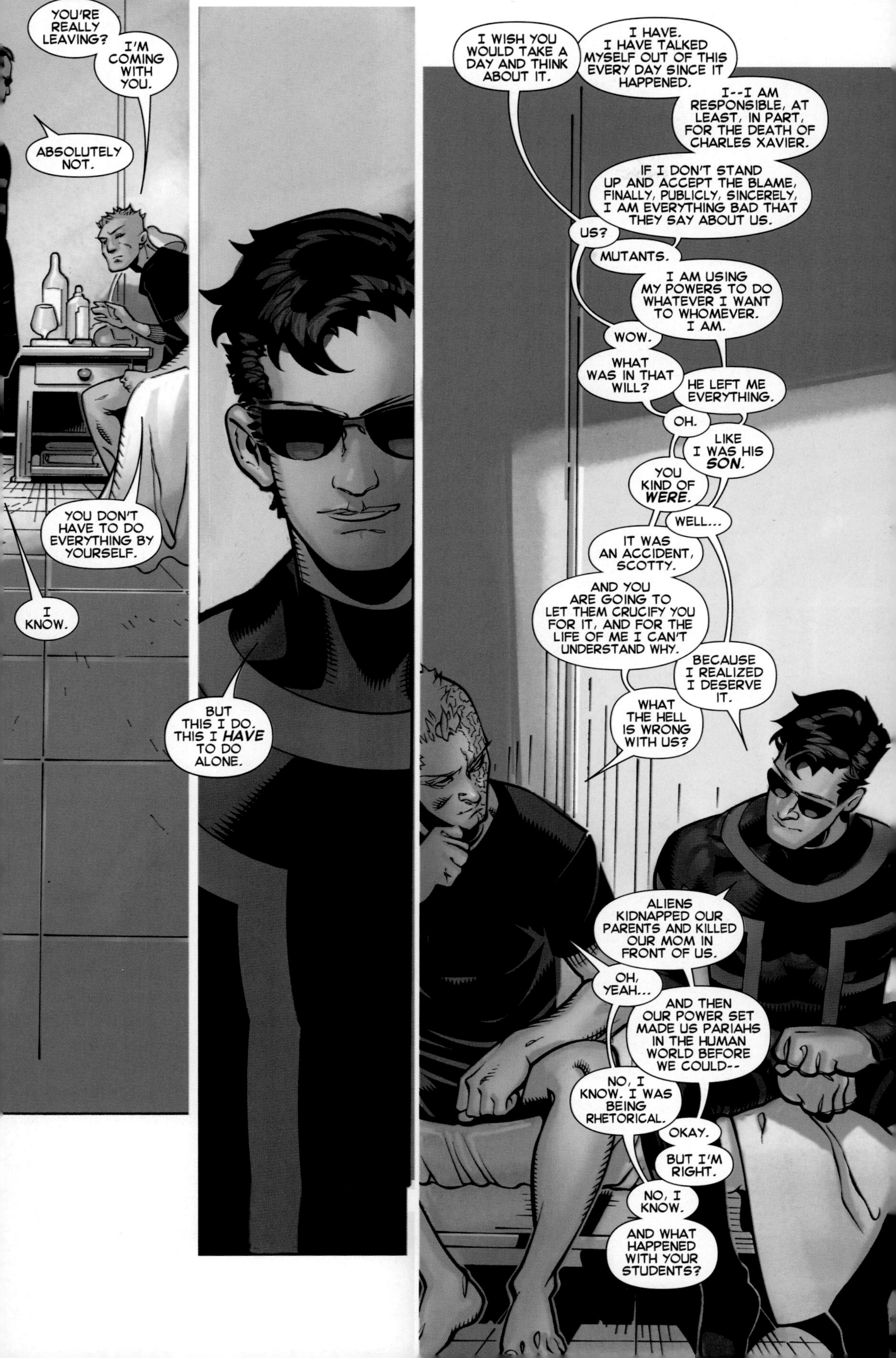
YOU'RE REALLY LEAVING?
I'M COMING WITH YOU.
ABSOLUTELY NOT.
YOU DON'T HAVE TO DO EVERYTHING BY YOURSELF.
I KNOW.
BUT THIS I DO. THIS I *HAVE* TO DO ALONE.
I WISH YOU WOULD TAKE A DAY AND THINK ABOUT IT.
I HAVE. I HAVE TALKED MYSELF OUT OF THIS EVERY DAY SINCE IT HAPPENED.
I--I AM RESPONSIBLE, AT LEAST, IN PART, FOR THE DEATH OF CHARLES XAVIER.
IF I DON'T STAND UP AND ACCEPT THE BLAME, FINALLY, PUBLICLY, SINCERELY, I AM EVERYTHING BAD THAT THEY SAY ABOUT US.
US?
MUTANTS.
I AM USING MY POWERS TO DO WHATEVER I WANT TO WHOMEVER. I AM.
WOW.
WHAT WAS IN THAT WILL?
HE LEFT ME EVERYTHING.
OH.
LIKE I WAS HIS *SON*.
YOU KIND OF *WERE*.
WELL...
IT WAS AN ACCIDENT, SCOTTY.
AND YOU ARE GOING TO LET THEM CRUCIFY YOU FOR IT, AND FOR THE LIFE OF ME I CAN'T UNDERSTAND WHY.
BECAUSE I REALIZED I DESERVE IT.
WHAT THE HELL IS WRONG WITH US?
ALIENS KIDNAPPED OUR PARENTS AND KILLED OUR MOM IN FRONT OF US.
OH, YEAH...
AND THEN OUR POWER SET MADE US PARIAHS IN THE HUMAN WORLD BEFORE WE COULD--
NO, I KNOW. I WAS BEING RHETORICAL.
OKAY.
BUT I'M RIGHT.
NO, I KNOW.
AND WHAT HAPPENED WITH YOUR STUDENTS?

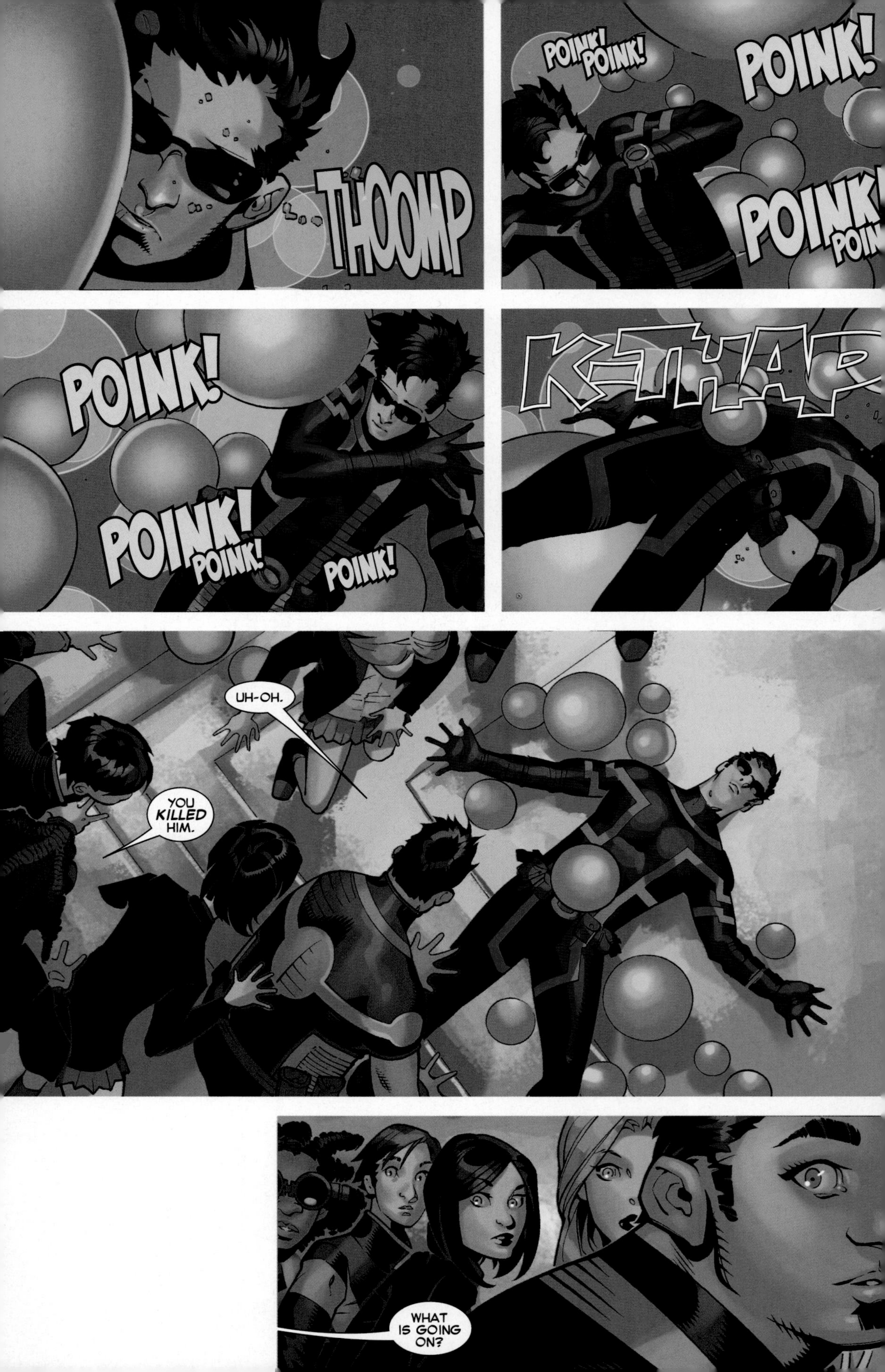
THOOMP
POINK! POINK!
POINK!
POINK!
POIN
POINK!
POINK! POINK!
POINK!
K-THAP
UH-OH.
YOU KILLED HIM.
WHAT IS GOING ON?

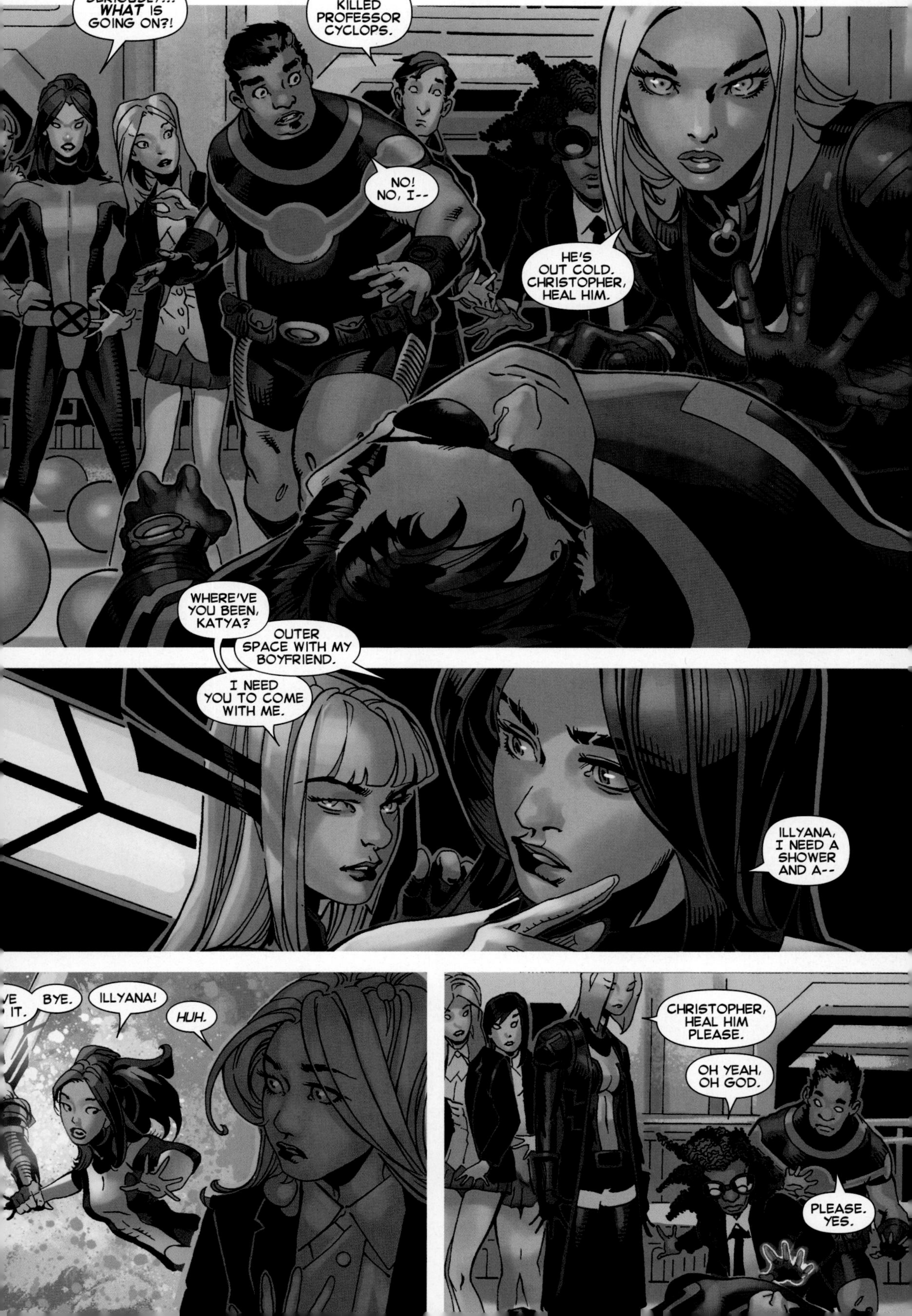
SERIOUSLY... WHAT IS GOING ON?!
FABIO KILLED PROFESSOR CYCLOPS.
NO! NO, I--
HE'S OUT COLD. CHRISTOPHER, HEAL HIM.
WHERE'VE YOU BEEN, KATYA?
OUTER SPACE WITH MY BOYFRIEND.
I NEED YOU TO COME WITH ME.
ILLYANA, I NEED A SHOWER AND A--
BYE.
ILLYANA!
HUH.
CHRISTOPHER, HEAL HIM PLEASE.
OH YEAH, OH GOD.
PLEASE. YES.

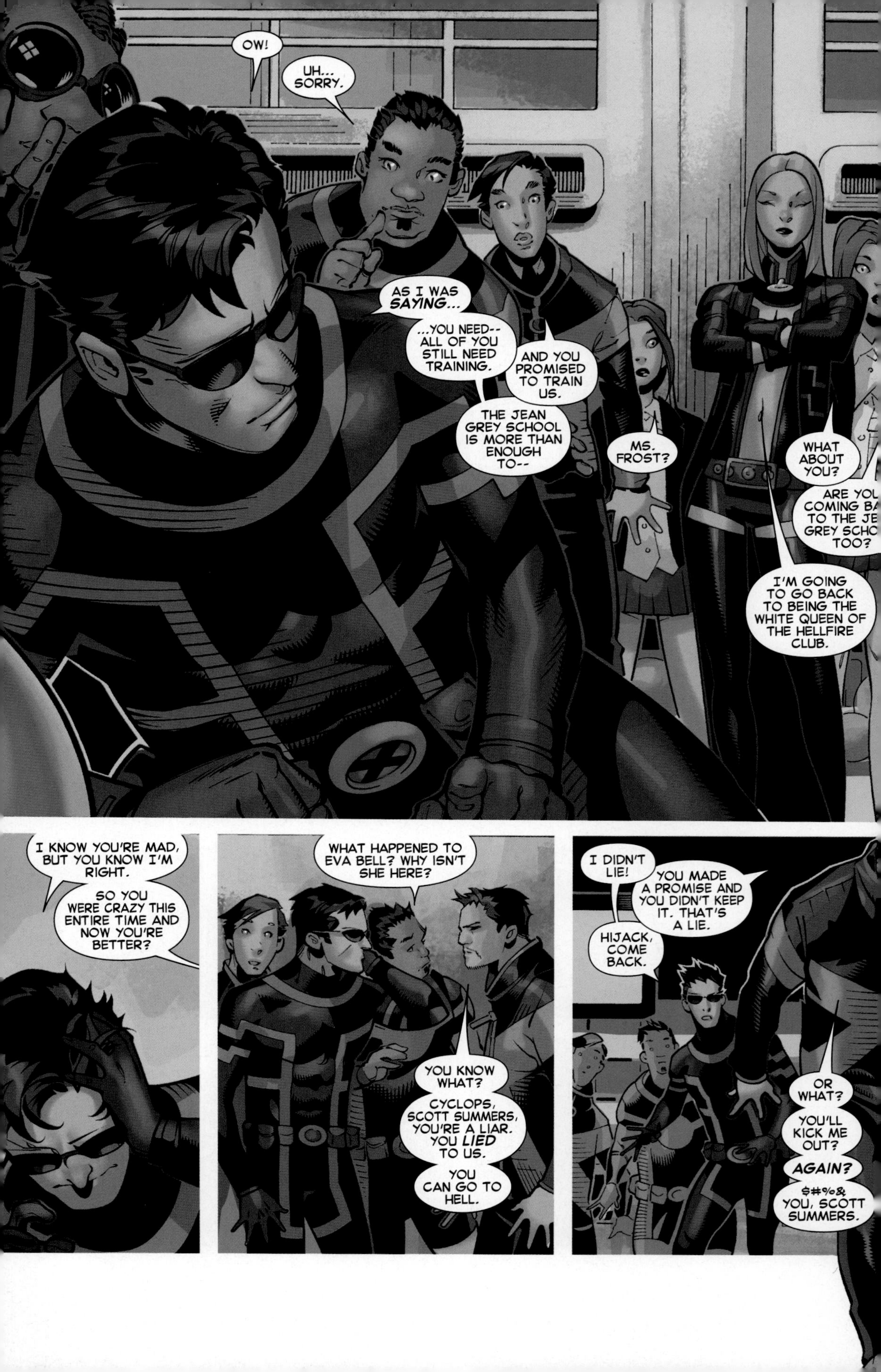
OW!
UH... SORRY.
AS I WAS SAYING...
...YOU NEED-- ALL OF YOU STILL NEED TRAINING.
AND YOU PROMISED TO TRAIN US.
THE JEAN GREY SCHOOL IS MORE THAN ENOUGH TO--
MS. FROST?
WHAT ABOUT YOU?
I'M GOING TO GO BACK TO BEING THE WHITE QUEEN OF THE HELLFIRE CLUB.
I KNOW YOU'RE MAD, BUT YOU KNOW I'M RIGHT.
SO YOU WERE CRAZY THIS ENTIRE TIME AND NOW YOU'RE BETTER?
WHAT HAPPENED TO EVA BELL? WHY ISN'T SHE HERE?
YOU KNOW WHAT?
CYCLOPS, SCOTT SUMMERS, YOU'RE A LIAR. YOU LIED TO US.
YOU CAN GO TO HELL.
I DIDN'T LIE!
YOU MADE A PROMISE AND YOU DIDN'T KEEP IT. THAT'S A LIE.
HIJACK, COME BACK.
OR WHAT?
YOU'LL KICK ME OUT?
AGAIN?
$#%& YOU, SCOTT SUMMERS.

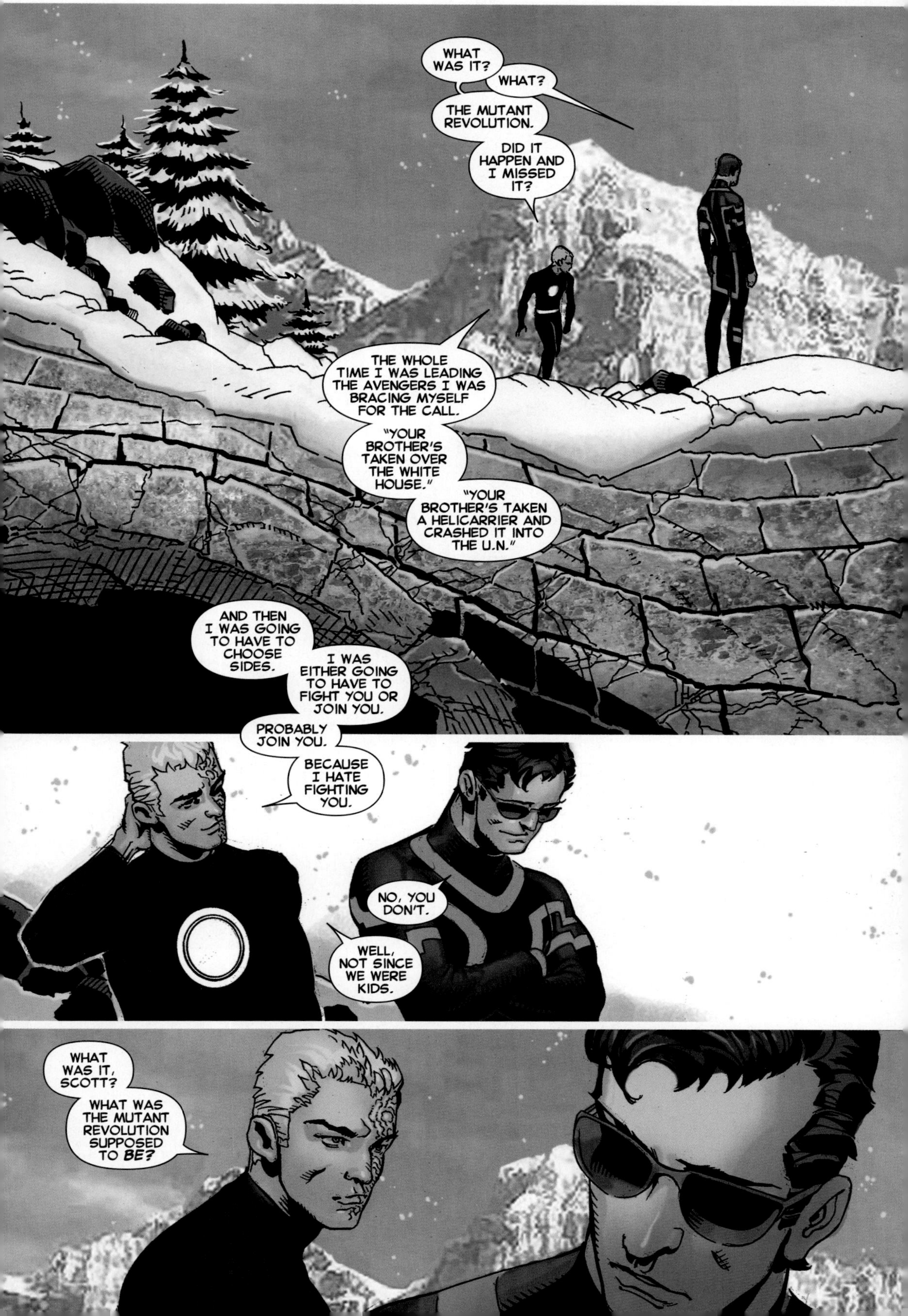
WHAT WAS IT?
WHAT?
THE MUTANT REVOLUTION.
DID IT HAPPEN AND I MISSED IT?
THE WHOLE TIME I WAS LEADING THE AVENGERS I WAS BRACING MYSELF FOR THE CALL.
"YOUR BROTHER'S TAKEN OVER THE WHITE HOUSE."
"YOUR BROTHER'S TAKEN A HELICARRIER AND CRASHED IT INTO THE U.N."
AND THEN I WAS GOING TO HAVE TO CHOOSE SIDES.
I WAS EITHER GOING TO HAVE TO FIGHT YOU OR JOIN YOU.
PROBABLY JOIN YOU.
BECAUSE I HATE FIGHTING YOU.
NO, YOU DON'T.
WELL, NOT SINCE WE WERE KIDS.
WHAT WAS IT, SCOTT?
WHAT WAS THE MUTANT REVOLUTION SUPPOSED TO *BE?*

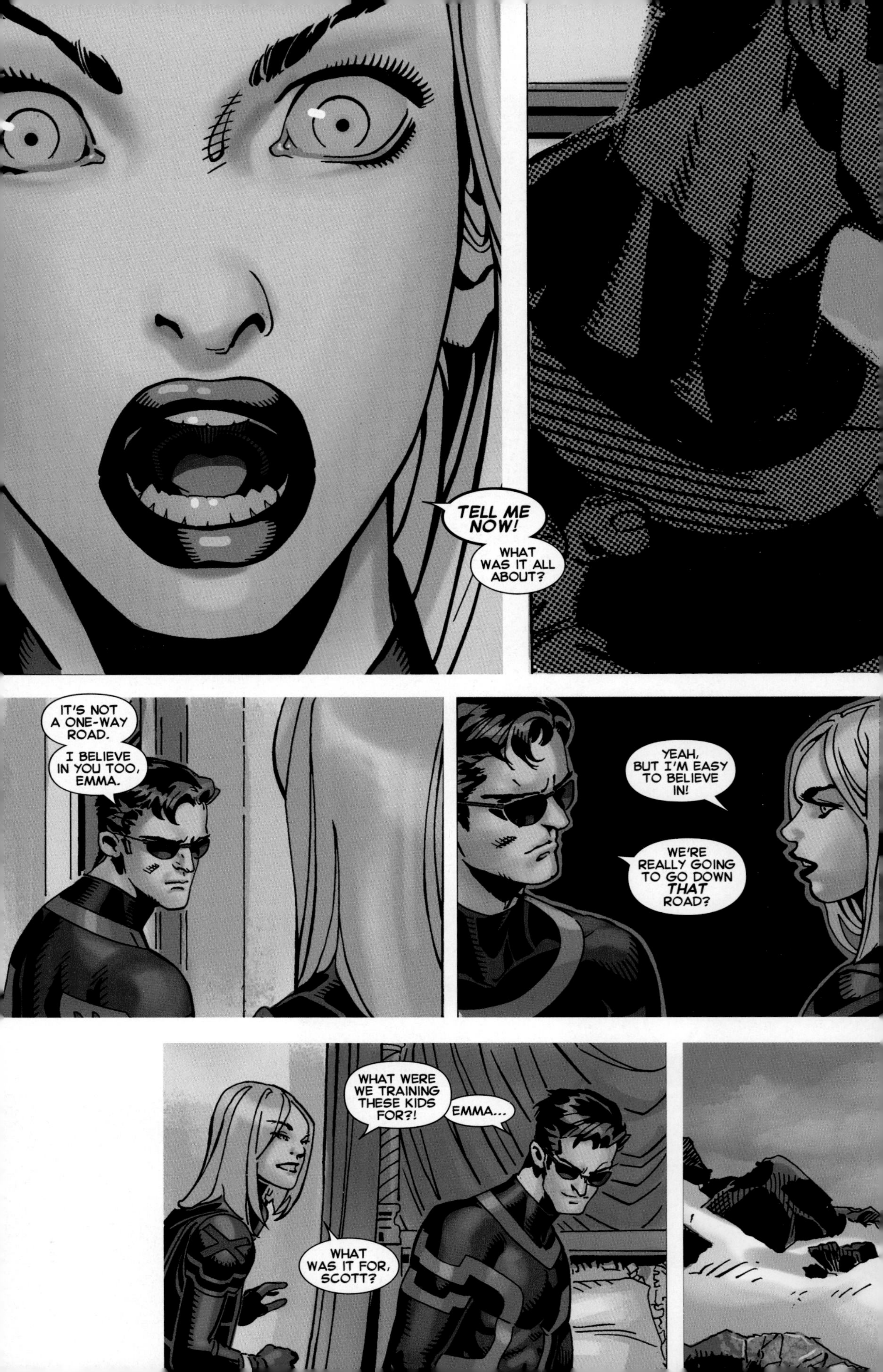
TELL ME NOW!
WHAT WAS IT ALL ABOUT?
IT'S NOT A ONE-WAY ROAD.
I BELIEVE IN YOU TOO, EMMA.
YEAH, BUT I'M EASY TO BELIEVE IN!
WE'RE REALLY GOING TO GO DOWN THAT ROAD?
WHAT WERE WE TRAINING THESE KIDS FOR?!
EMMA...
WHAT WAS IT FOR, SCOTT?

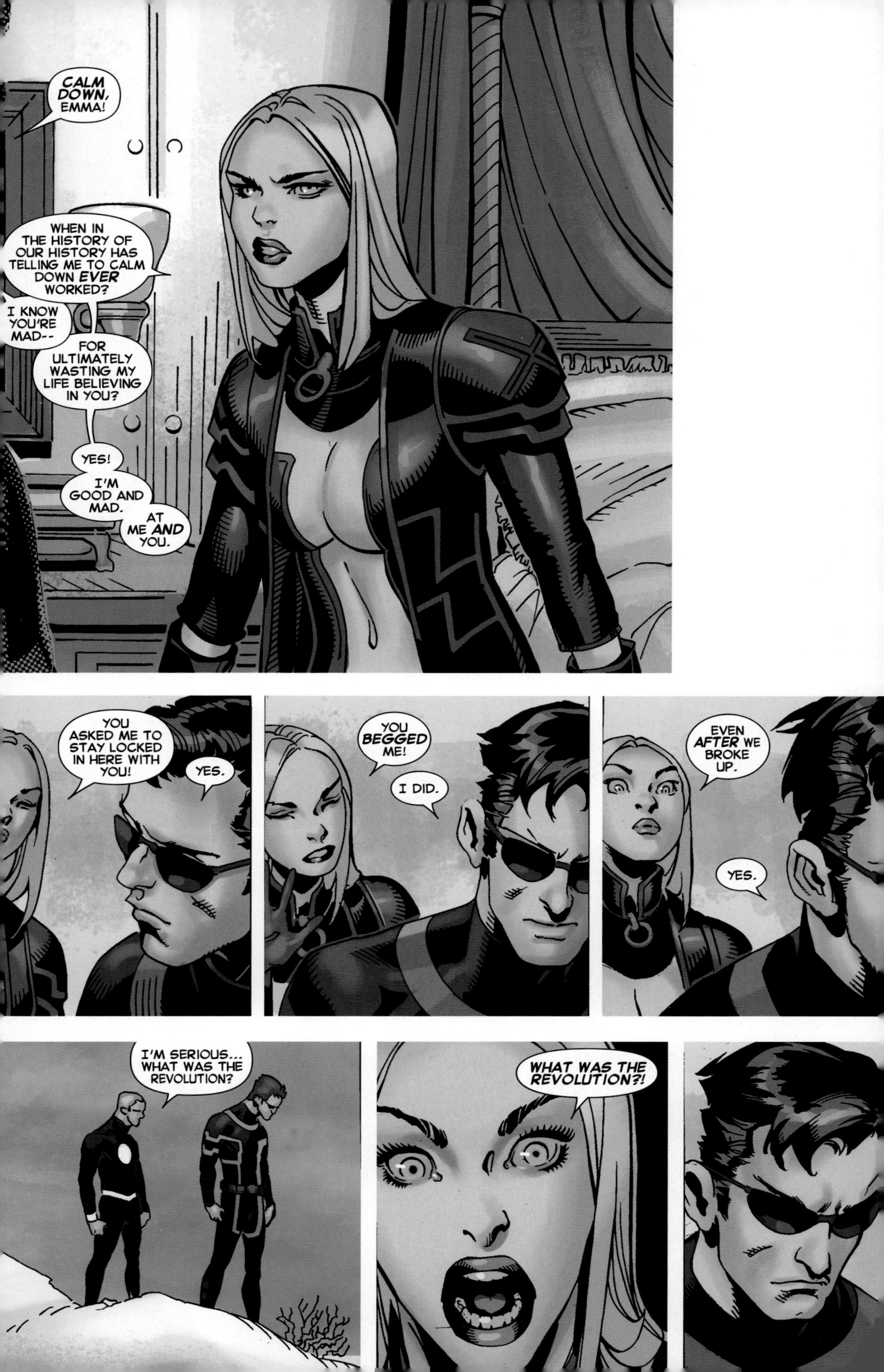
CALM DOWN, EMMA!
WHEN IN THE HISTORY OF OUR HISTORY HAS TELLING ME TO CALM DOWN EVER WORKED?
I KNOW YOU'RE MAD--
FOR ULTIMATELY WASTING MY LIFE BELIEVING IN YOU?
YES!
I'M GOOD AND MAD.
AT ME AND YOU.
YOU ASKED ME TO STAY LOCKED IN HERE WITH YOU!
YES.
YOU BEGGED ME!
I DID.
EVEN AFTER WE BROKE UP.
YES.
I'M SERIOUS... WHAT WAS THE REVOLUTION?
WHAT WAS THE REVOLUTION?!

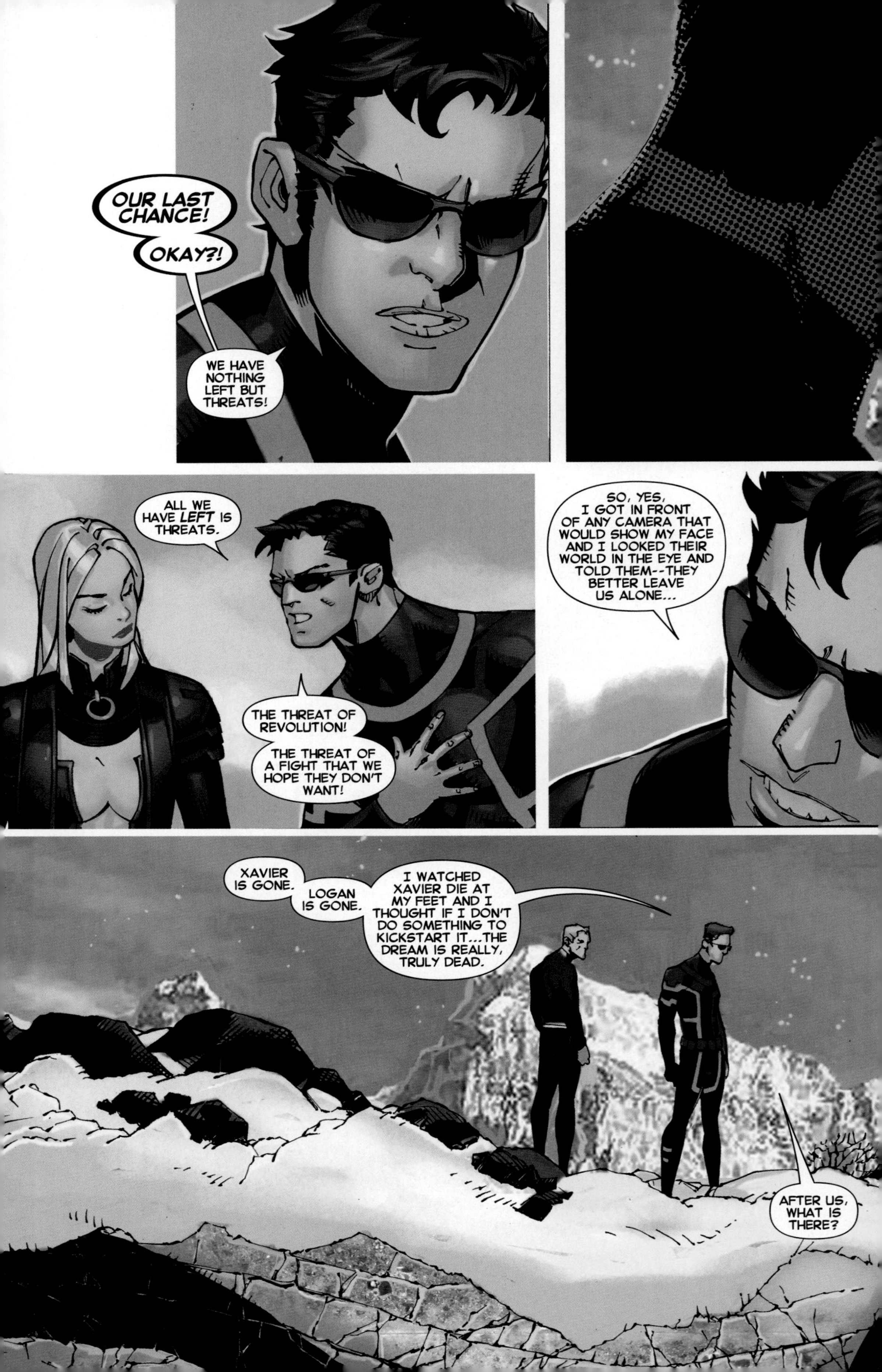
OUR LAST CHANCE!
OKAY?!
WE HAVE NOTHING LEFT BUT THREATS!
ALL WE HAVE LEFT IS THREATS.
THE THREAT OF REVOLUTION!
THE THREAT OF A FIGHT THAT WE HOPE THEY DON'T WANT!
SO, YES, I GOT IN FRONT OF ANY CAMERA THAT WOULD SHOW MY FACE AND I LOOKED THEIR WORLD IN THE EYE AND TOLD THEM--THEY BETTER LEAVE US ALONE...
XAVIER IS GONE.
LOGAN IS GONE.
I WATCHED XAVIER DIE AT MY FEET AND I THOUGHT IF I DON'T DO SOMETHING TO KICKSTART IT...THE DREAM IS REALLY, TRULY DEAD.
AFTER US, WHAT IS THERE?

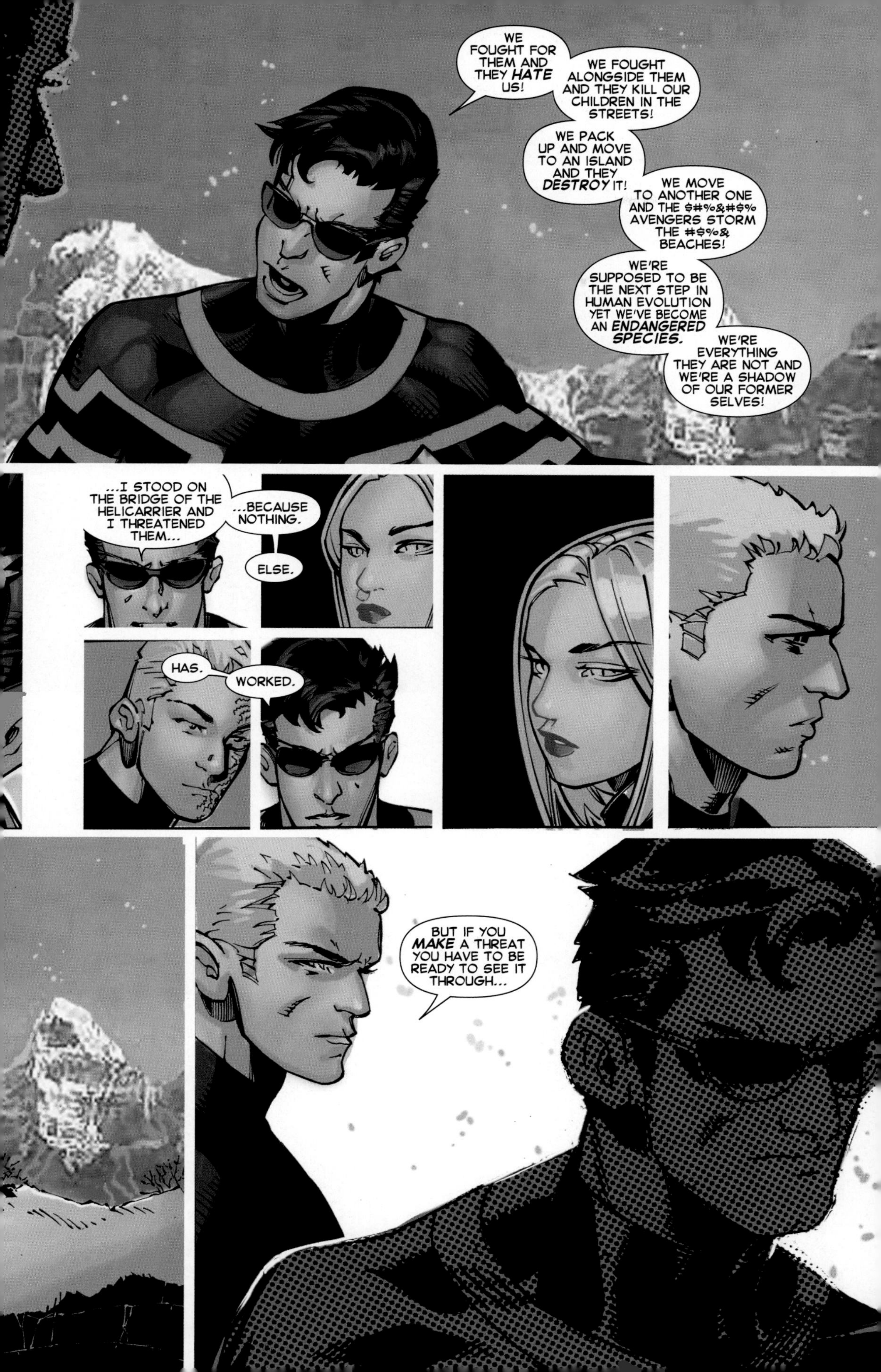
WE FOUGHT FOR THEM AND THEY HATE US!
WE FOUGHT ALONGSIDE THEM AND THEY KILL OUR CHILDREN IN THE STREETS!
WE PACK UP AND MOVE TO AN ISLAND AND THEY DESTROY IT!
WE MOVE TO ANOTHER ONE AND THE $#%&#$% AVENGERS STORM THE #$%& BEACHES!
WE'RE SUPPOSED TO BE THE NEXT STEP IN HUMAN EVOLUTION YET WE'VE BECOME AN ENDANGERED SPECIES.
WE'RE EVERYTHING THEY ARE NOT AND WE'RE A SHADOW OF OUR FORMER SELVES!
...I STOOD ON THE BRIDGE OF THE HELICARRIER AND I THREATENED THEM...
...BECAUSE NOTHING.
ELSE.
HAS.
WORKED.
BUT IF YOU MAKE A THREAT YOU HAVE TO BE READY TO SEE IT THROUGH...

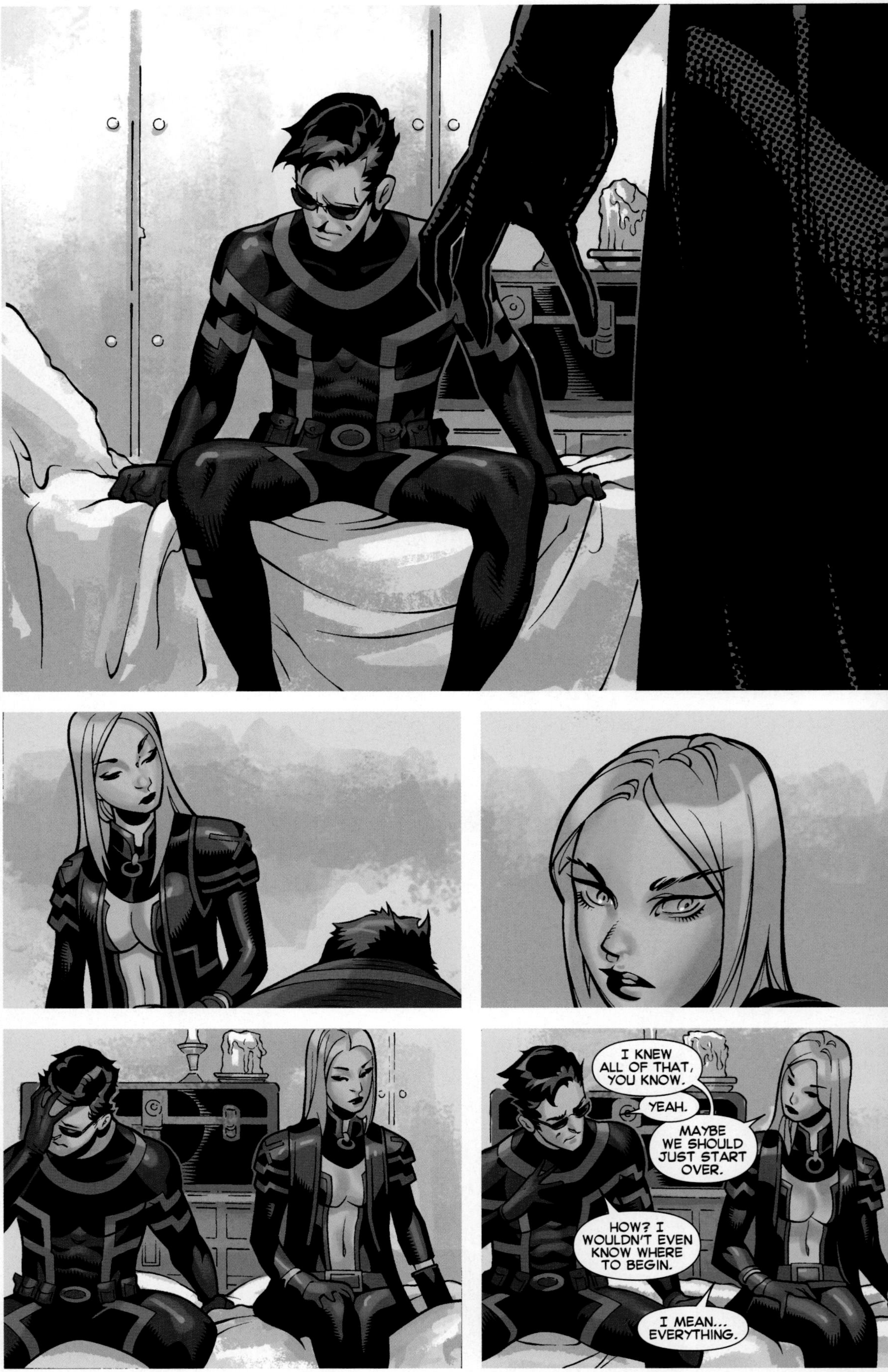
I KNEW ALL OF THAT, YOU KNOW.
YEAH.
MAYBE WE SHOULD JUST START OVER.
HOW? I WOULDN'T EVEN KNOW WHERE TO BEGIN.
I MEAN... EVERYTHING.

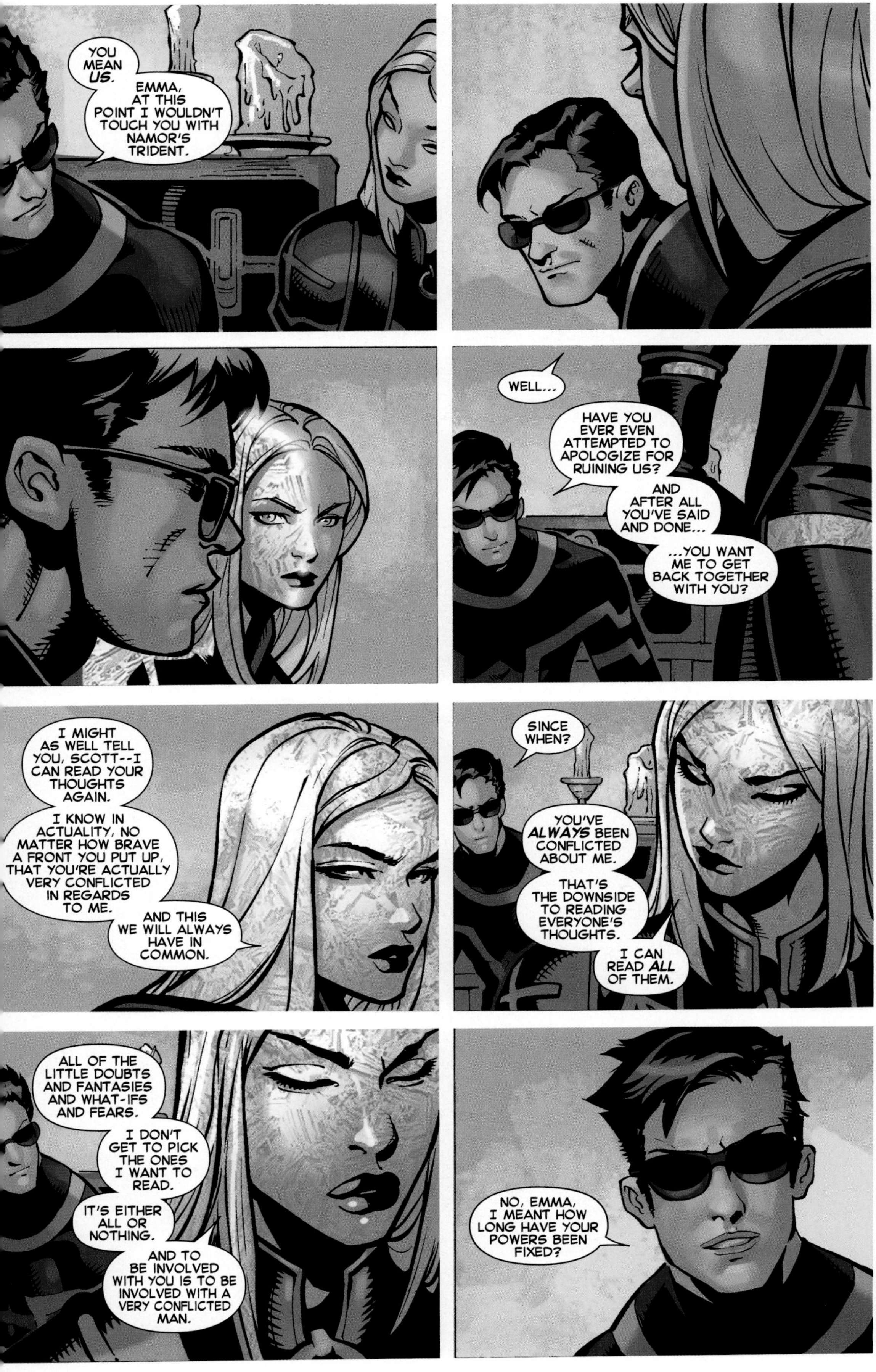

YOU MEAN *US*.
EMMA, AT THIS POINT I WOULDN'T TOUCH YOU WITH NAMOR'S TRIDENT.
WELL...
HAVE YOU EVER EVEN ATTEMPTED TO APOLOGIZE FOR RUINING US?
AND AFTER ALL YOU'VE SAID AND DONE...
...YOU WANT ME TO GET BACK TOGETHER WITH YOU?
I MIGHT AS WELL TELL YOU, SCOTT--I CAN READ YOUR THOUGHTS AGAIN.
I KNOW IN ACTUALITY, NO MATTER HOW BRAVE A FRONT YOU PUT UP, THAT YOU'RE ACTUALLY VERY CONFLICTED IN REGARDS TO ME.
AND THIS WE WILL ALWAYS HAVE IN COMMON.
SINCE WHEN?
YOU'VE *ALWAYS* BEEN CONFLICTED ABOUT ME.
THAT'S THE DOWNSIDE TO READING EVERYONE'S THOUGHTS.
I CAN READ *ALL* OF THEM.
ALL OF THE LITTLE DOUBTS AND FANTASIES AND WHAT-IFS AND FEARS.
I DON'T GET TO PICK THE ONES I WANT TO READ.
IT'S EITHER ALL OR NOTHING.
AND TO BE INVOLVED WITH YOU IS TO BE INVOLVED WITH A VERY CONFLICTED MAN.
NO, EMMA, I MEANT HOW LONG HAVE YOUR POWERS BEEN FIXED?

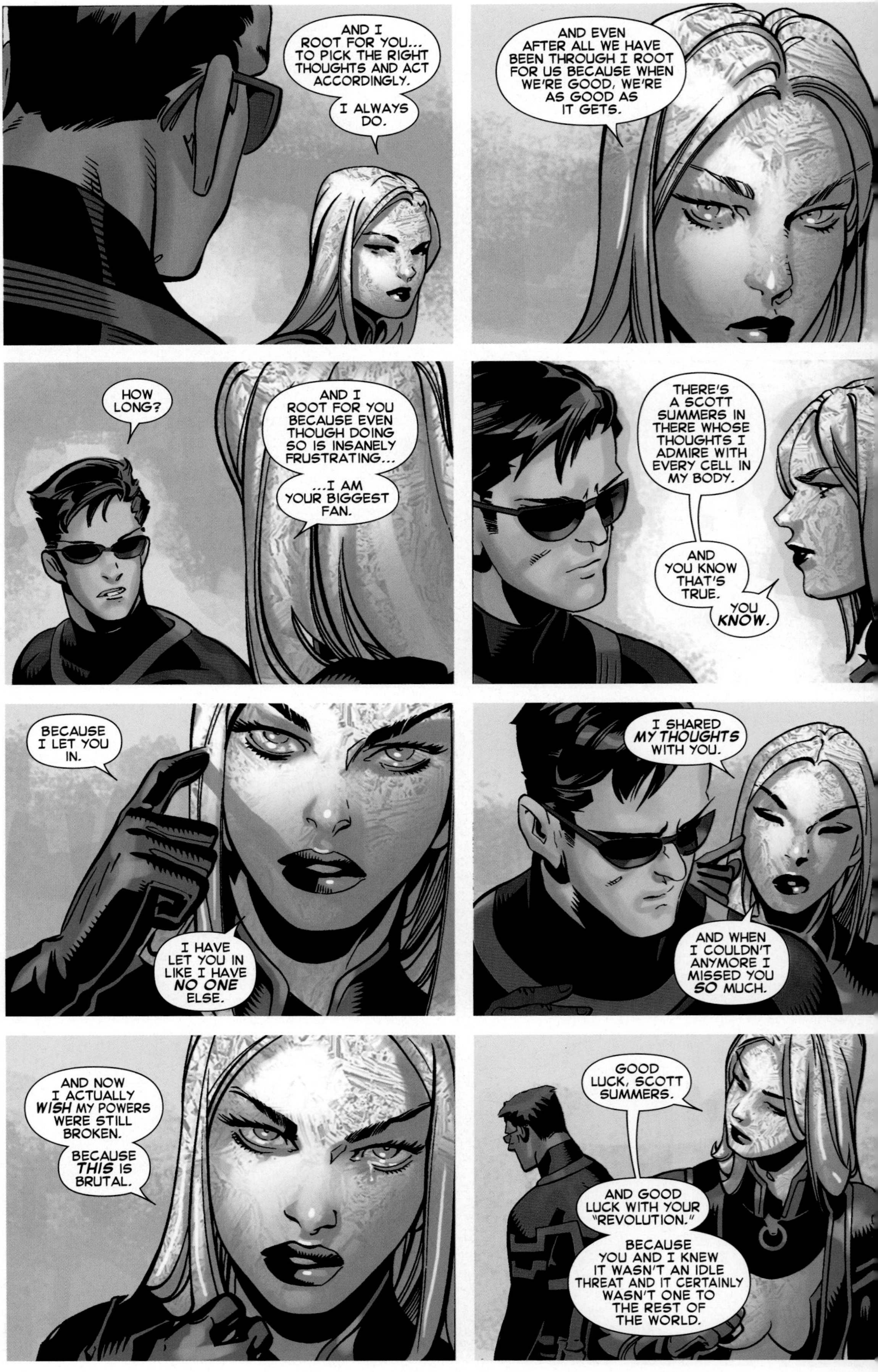
AND I ROOT FOR YOU... TO PICK THE RIGHT THOUGHTS AND ACT ACCORDINGLY.
I ALWAYS DO.
AND EVEN AFTER ALL WE HAVE BEEN THROUGH I ROOT FOR US BECAUSE WHEN WE'RE GOOD, WE'RE AS GOOD AS IT GETS.
HOW LONG?
AND I ROOT FOR YOU BECAUSE EVEN THOUGH DOING SO IS INSANELY FRUSTRATING...
...I AM YOUR BIGGEST FAN.
THERE'S A SCOTT SUMMERS IN THERE WHOSE THOUGHTS I ADMIRE WITH EVERY CELL IN MY BODY.
AND YOU KNOW THAT'S TRUE.
YOU KNOW.
BECAUSE I LET YOU IN.
I HAVE LET YOU IN LIKE I HAVE NO ONE ELSE.
I SHARED MY THOUGHTS WITH YOU.
AND WHEN I COULDN'T ANYMORE I MISSED YOU SO MUCH.
AND NOW I ACTUALLY WISH MY POWERS WERE STILL BROKEN.
BECAUSE THIS IS BRUTAL.
GOOD LUCK, SCOTT SUMMERS.
AND GOOD LUCK WITH YOUR "REVOLUTION."
BECAUSE YOU AND I KNEW IT WASN'T AN IDLE THREAT AND IT CERTAINLY WASN'T ONE TO THE REST OF THE WORLD.

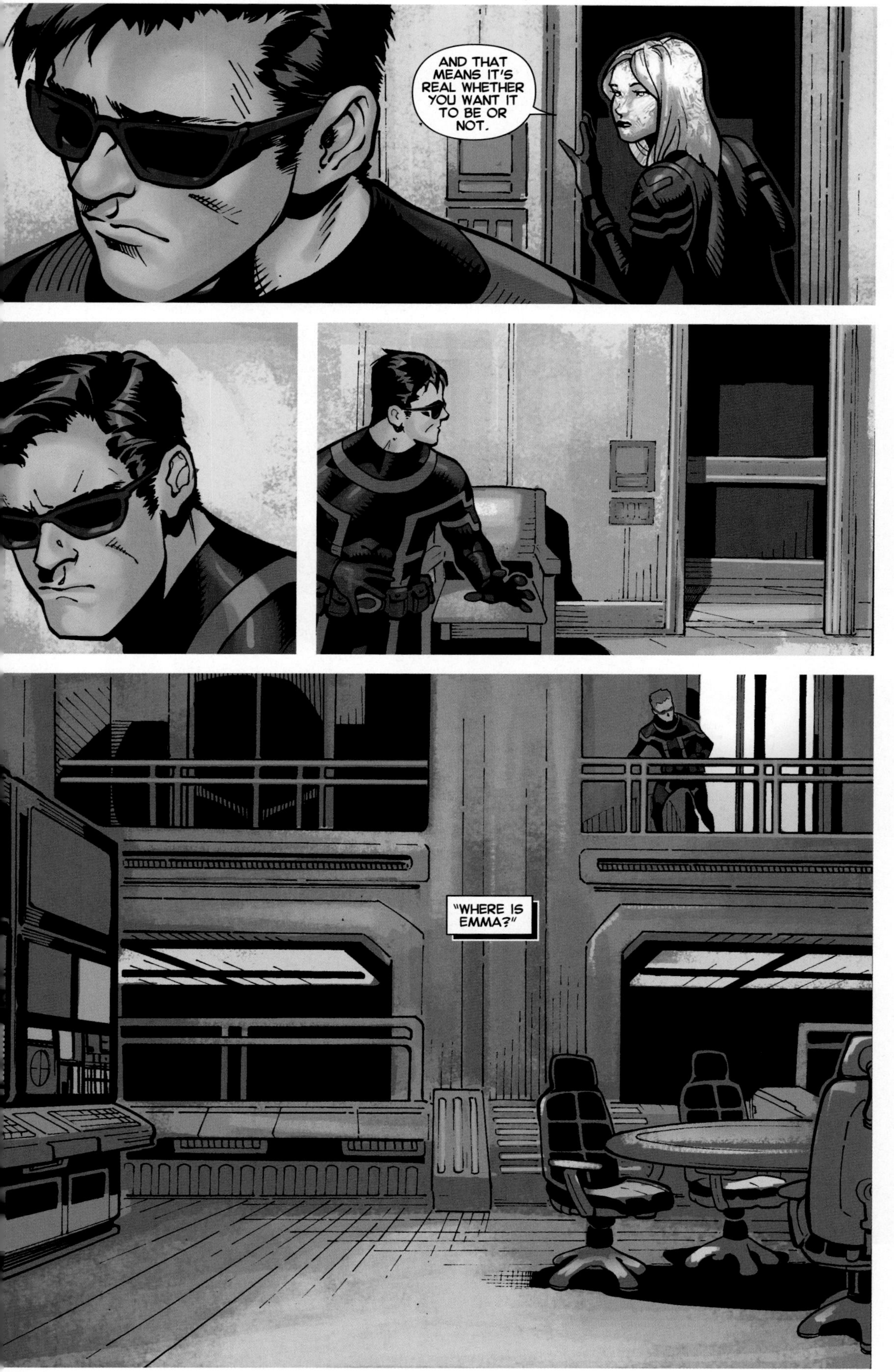
AND THAT MEANS IT'S REAL WHETHER YOU WANT IT TO BE OR NOT.
"WHERE IS EMMA?"

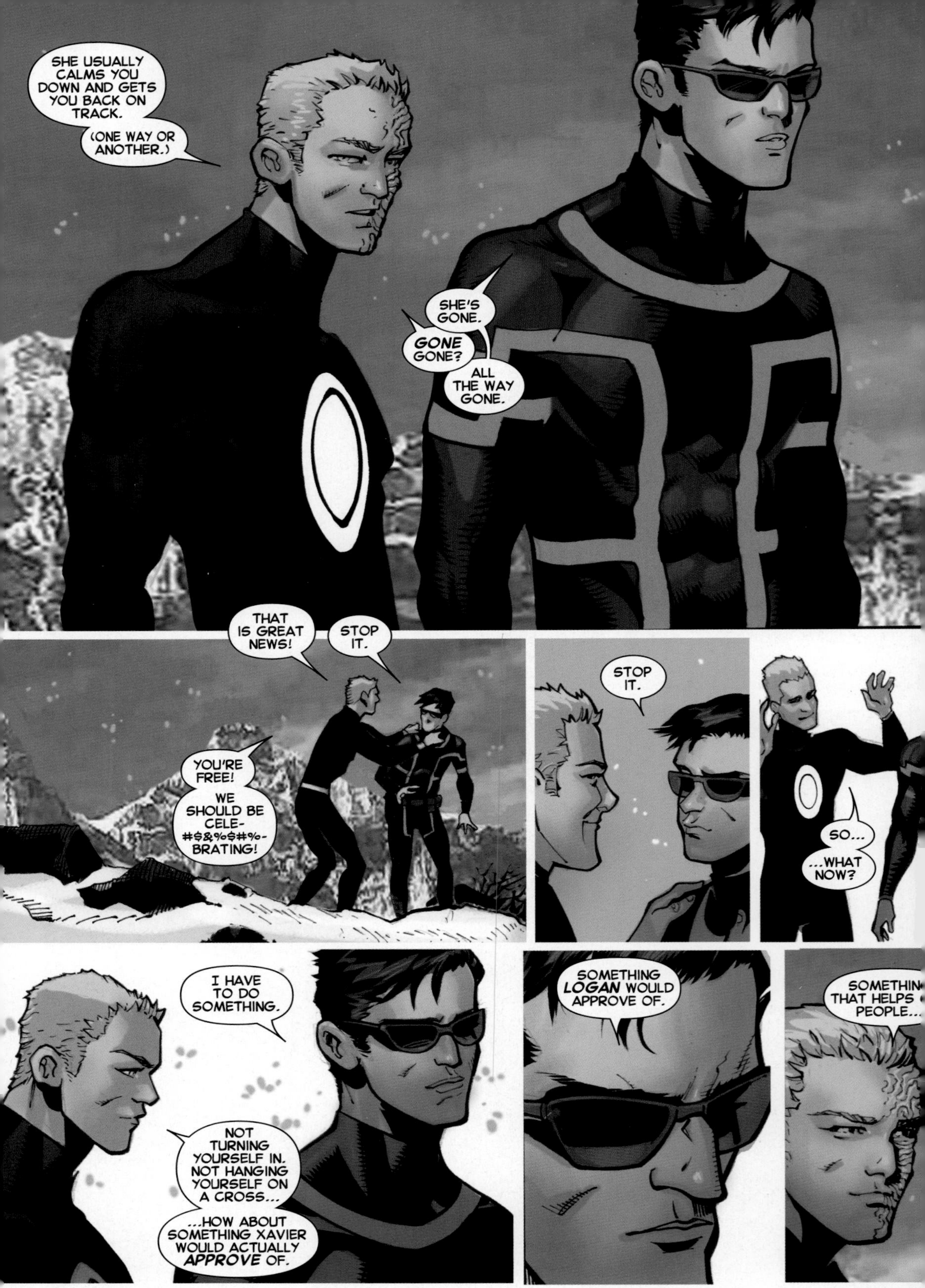
SHE USUALLY CALMS YOU DOWN AND GETS YOU BACK ON TRACK.
(ONE WAY OR ANOTHER.)
SHE'S GONE.
GONE GONE?
ALL THE WAY GONE.
THAT IS GREAT NEWS!
STOP IT.
YOU'RE FREE!
WE SHOULD BE CELE-#$&%$#%-BRATING!
STOP IT.
SO...
...WHAT NOW?
I HAVE TO DO SOMETHING.
NOT TURNING YOURSELF IN. NOT HANGING YOURSELF ON A CROSS...
...HOW ABOUT SOMETHING XAVIER WOULD ACTUALLY APPROVE OF.
SOMETHING LOGAN WOULD APPROVE OF.
SOMETHIN THAT HELPS PEOPLE...

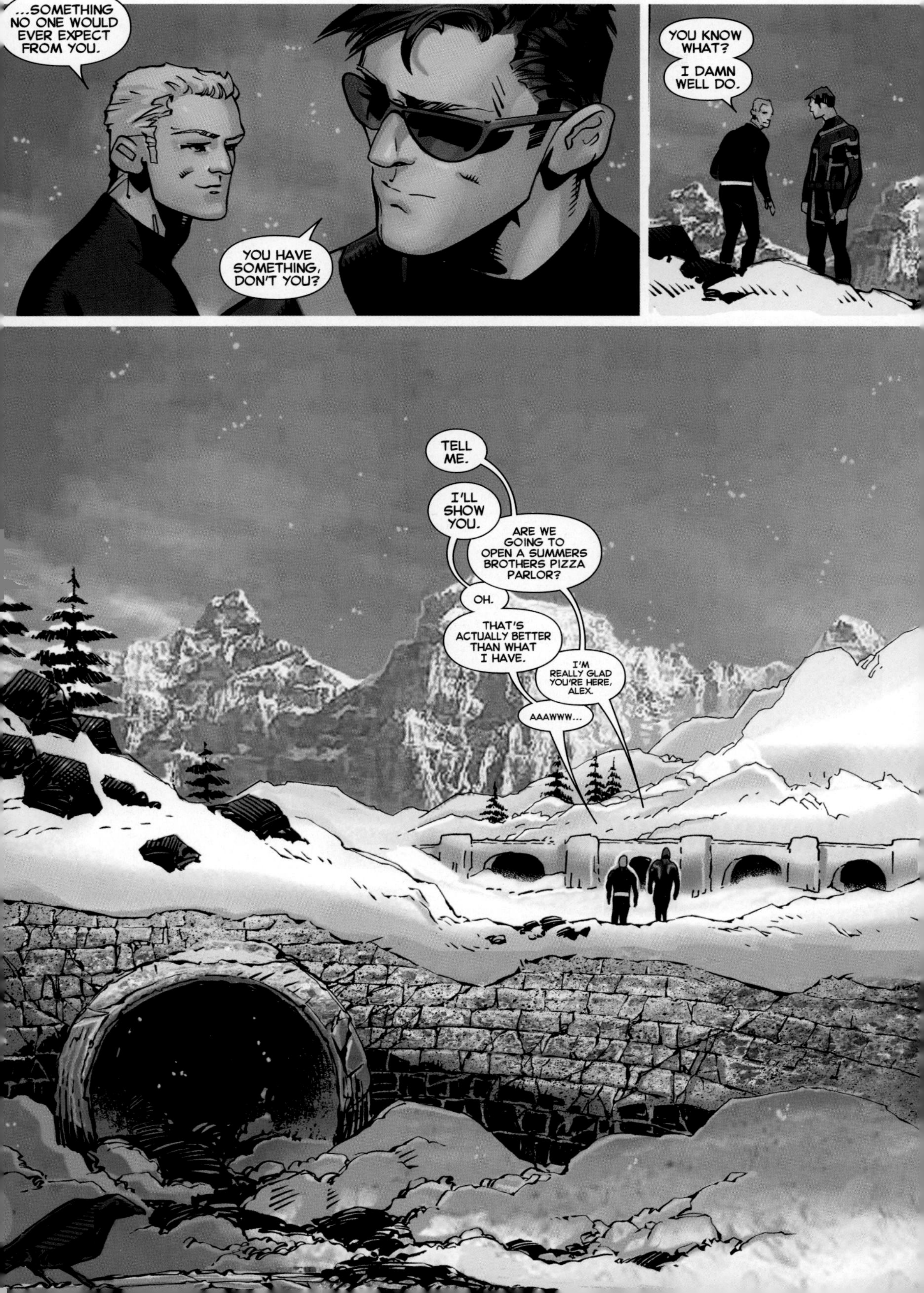
...SOMETHING NO ONE WOULD EVER EXPECT FROM YOU.
YOU HAVE SOMETHING, DON'T YOU?
YOU KNOW WHAT?
I DAMN WELL DO.
TELL ME.
I'LL SHOW YOU.
ARE WE GOING TO OPEN A SUMMERS BROTHERS PIZZA PARLOR?
OH.
THAT'S ACTUALLY BETTER THAN WHAT I HAVE.
I'M REALLY GLAD YOU'RE HERE, ALEX.
AAAWWW...

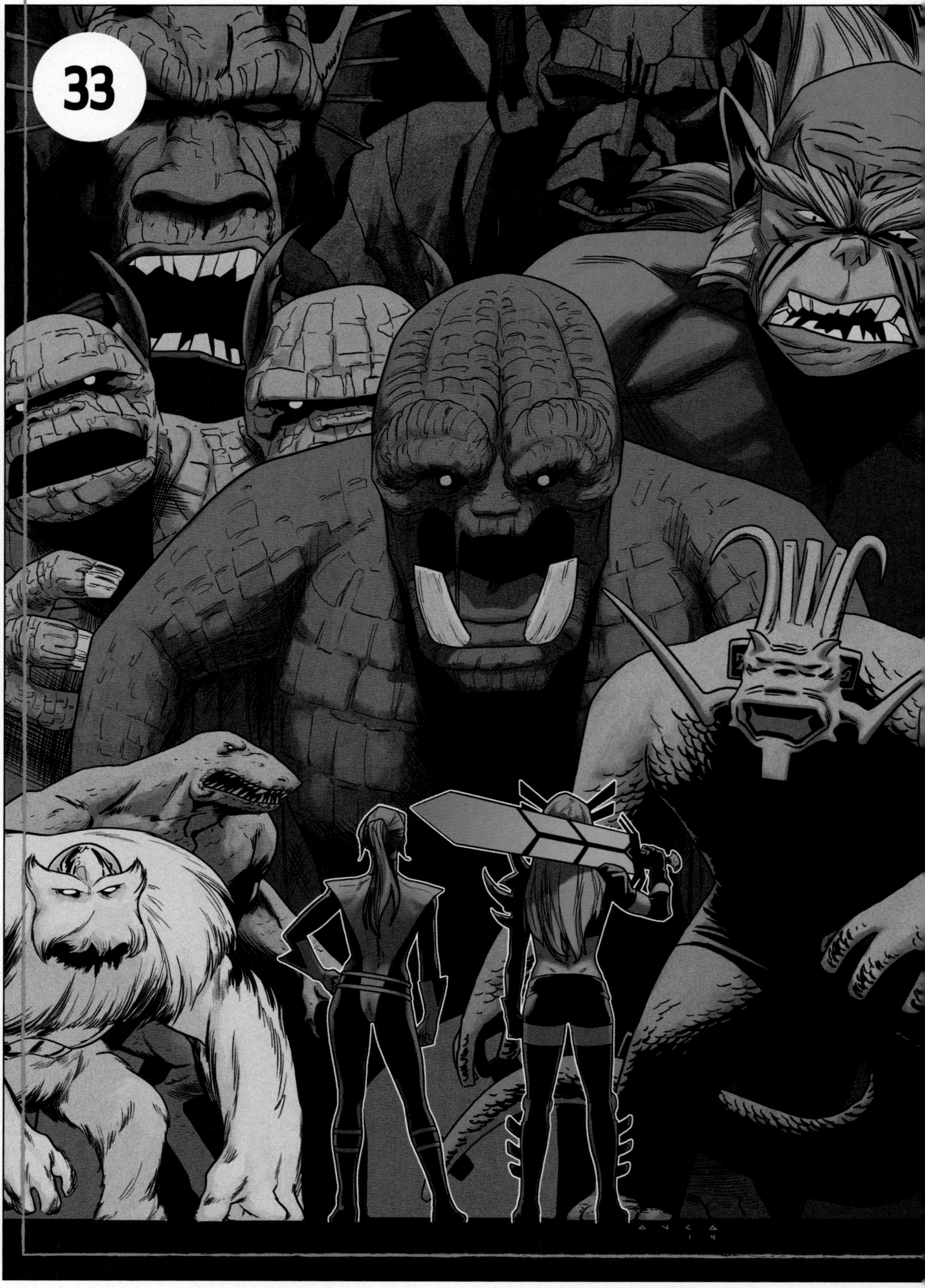
33

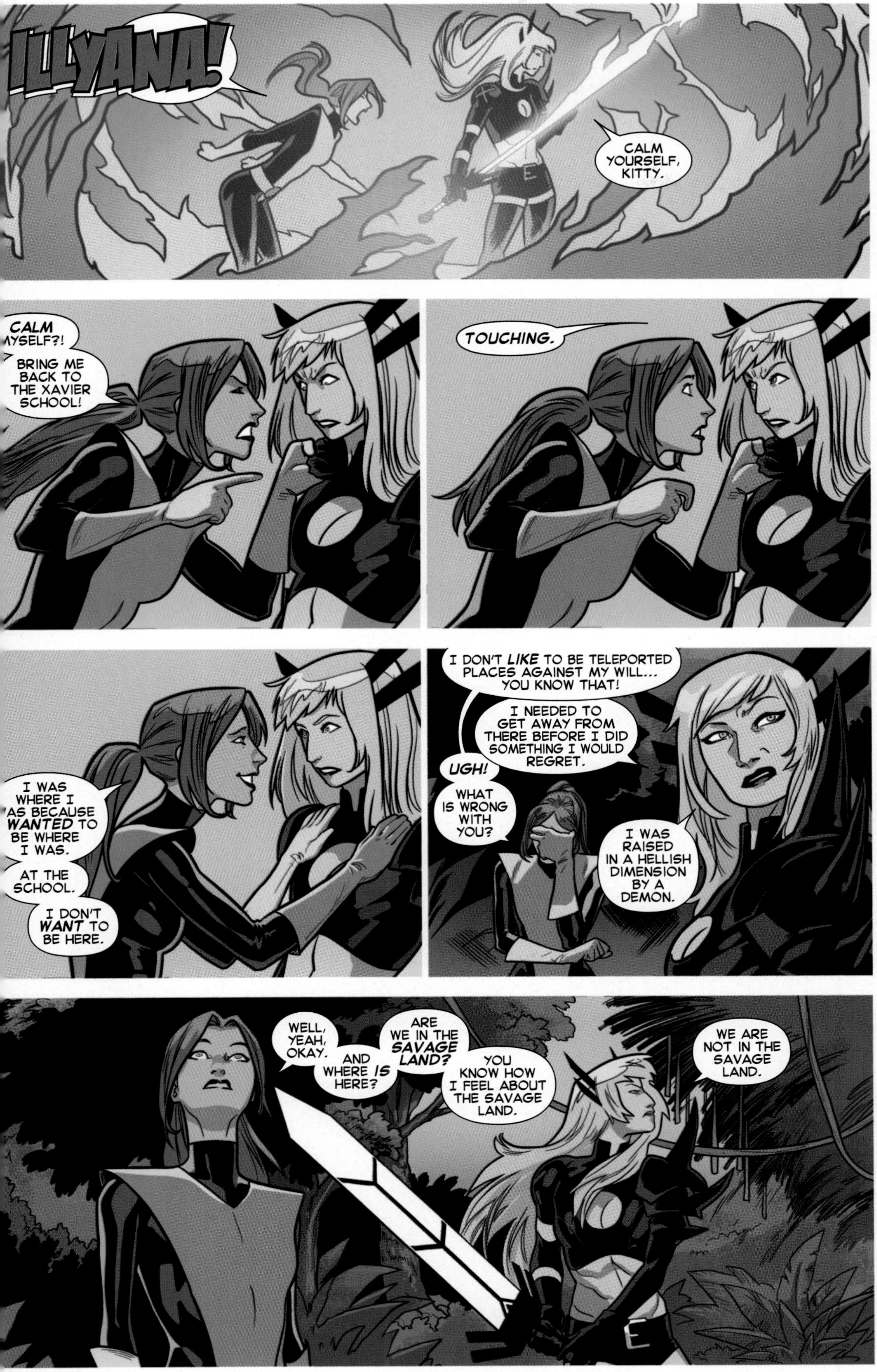

ILLYANA!
CALM YOURSELF, KITTY.
CALM MYSELF?!
BRING ME BACK TO THE XAVIER SCHOOL!
TOUCHING.
I WAS WHERE I WAS BECAUSE I WANTED TO BE WHERE I WAS.
AT THE SCHOOL.
I DON'T WANT TO BE HERE.
I DON'T LIKE TO BE TELEPORTED PLACES AGAINST MY WILL... YOU KNOW THAT!
I NEEDED TO GET AWAY FROM THERE BEFORE I DID SOMETHING I WOULD REGRET.
UGH!
WHAT IS WRONG WITH YOU?
I WAS RAISED IN A HELLISH DIMENSION BY A DEMON.
WELL, YEAH, OKAY.
AND WHERE IS HERE?
ARE WE IN THE SAVAGE LAND?
YOU KNOW HOW I FEEL ABOUT THE SAVAGE LAND.
WE ARE NOT IN THE SAVAGE LAND.

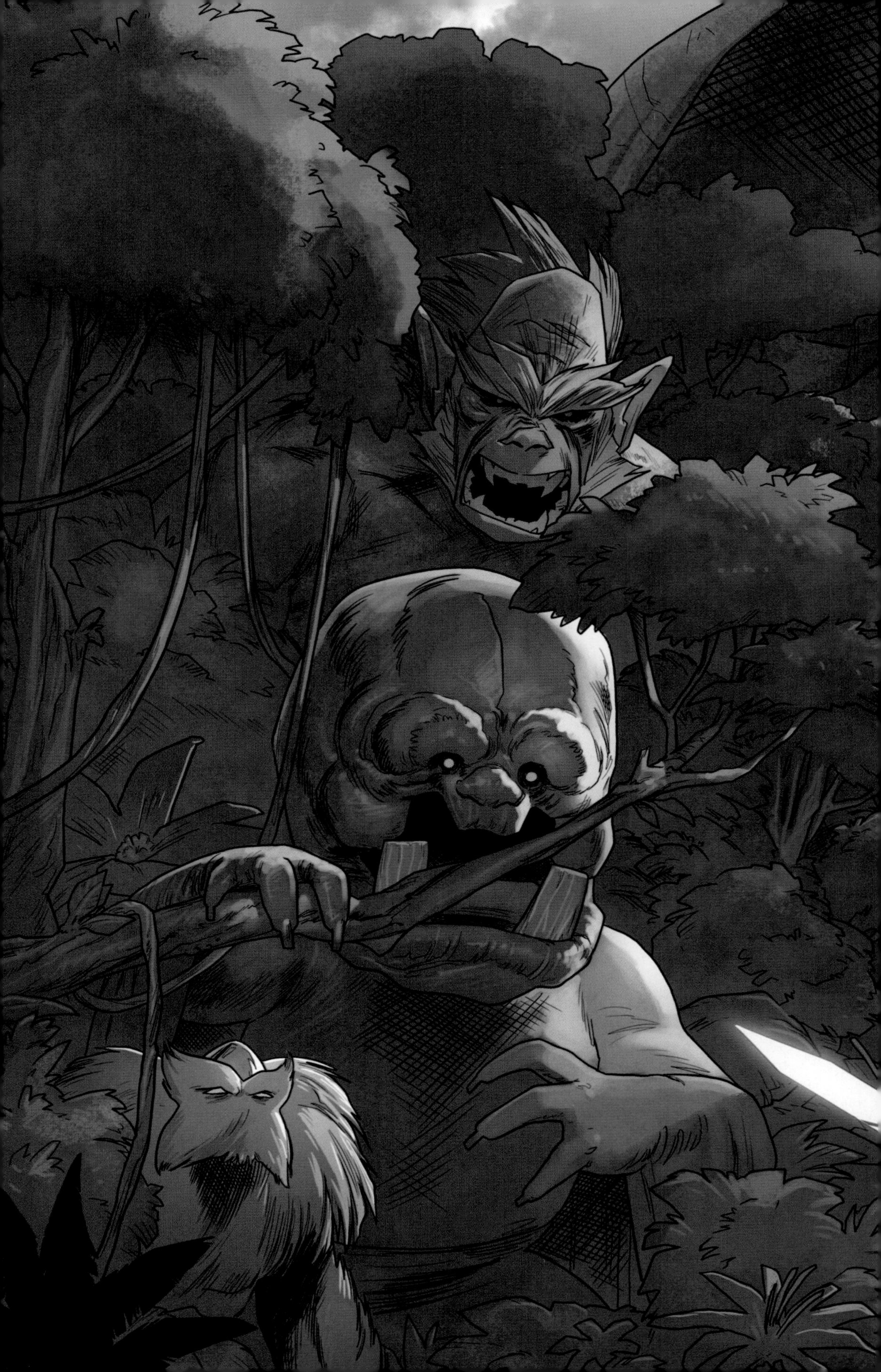

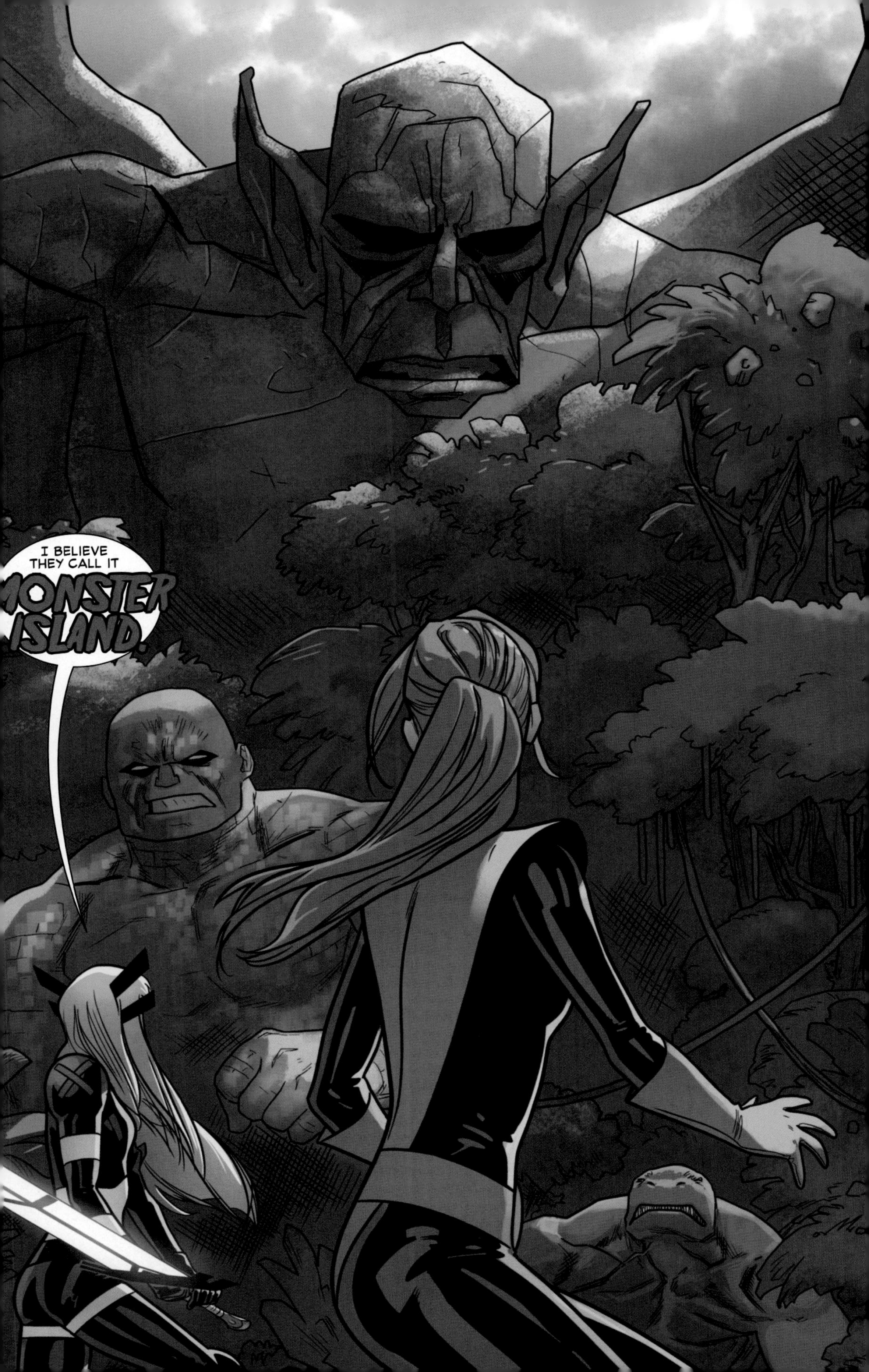
I BELIEVE THEY CALL IT MONSTER ISLAND.

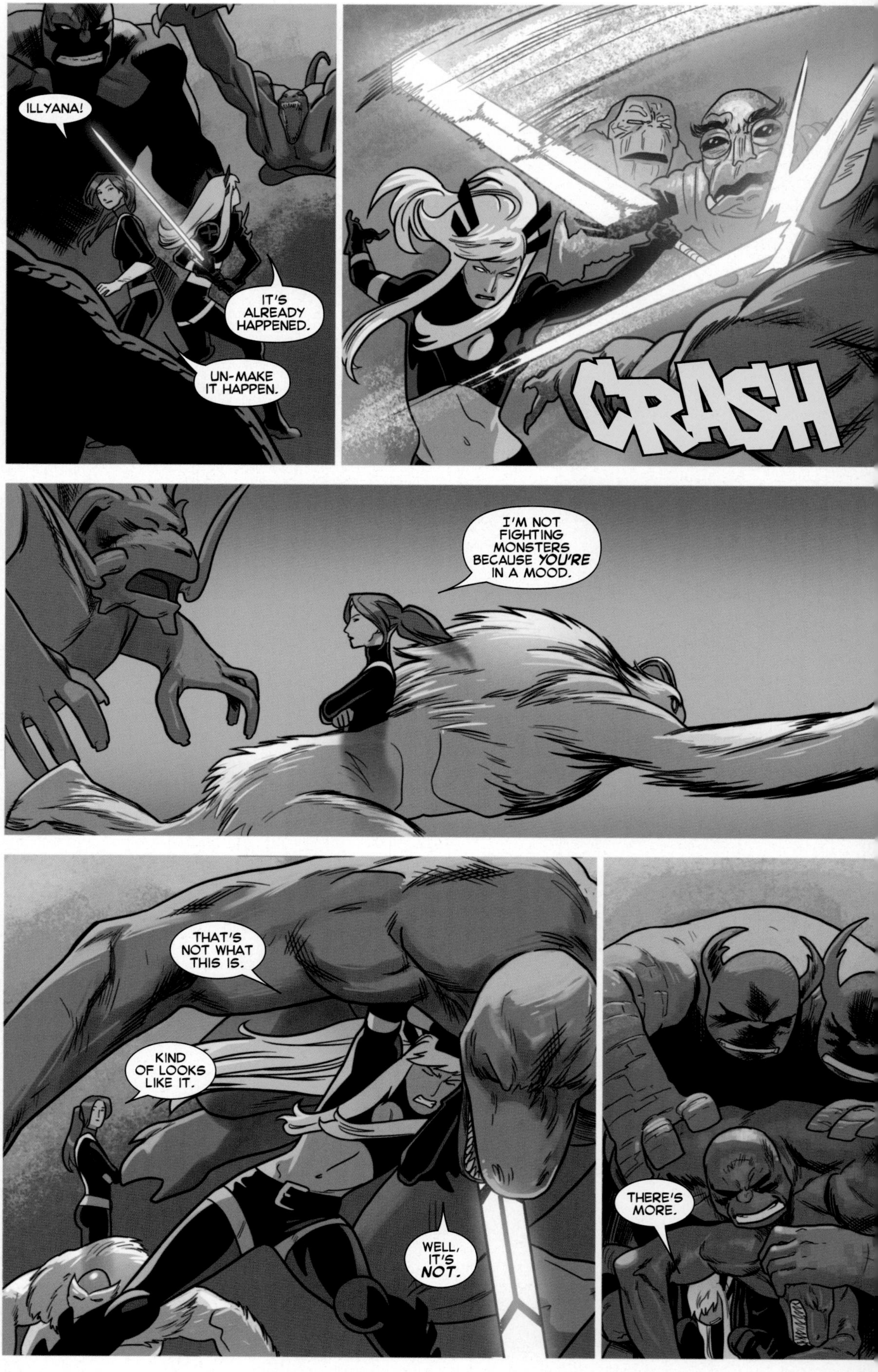
ILLYANA!
IT'S ALREADY HAPPENED.
UN-MAKE IT HAPPEN.
CRASH
I'M NOT FIGHTING MONSTERS BECAUSE YOU'RE IN A MOOD.
THAT'S NOT WHAT THIS IS.
KIND OF LOOKS LIKE IT.
WELL, IT'S NOT.
THERE'S MORE.

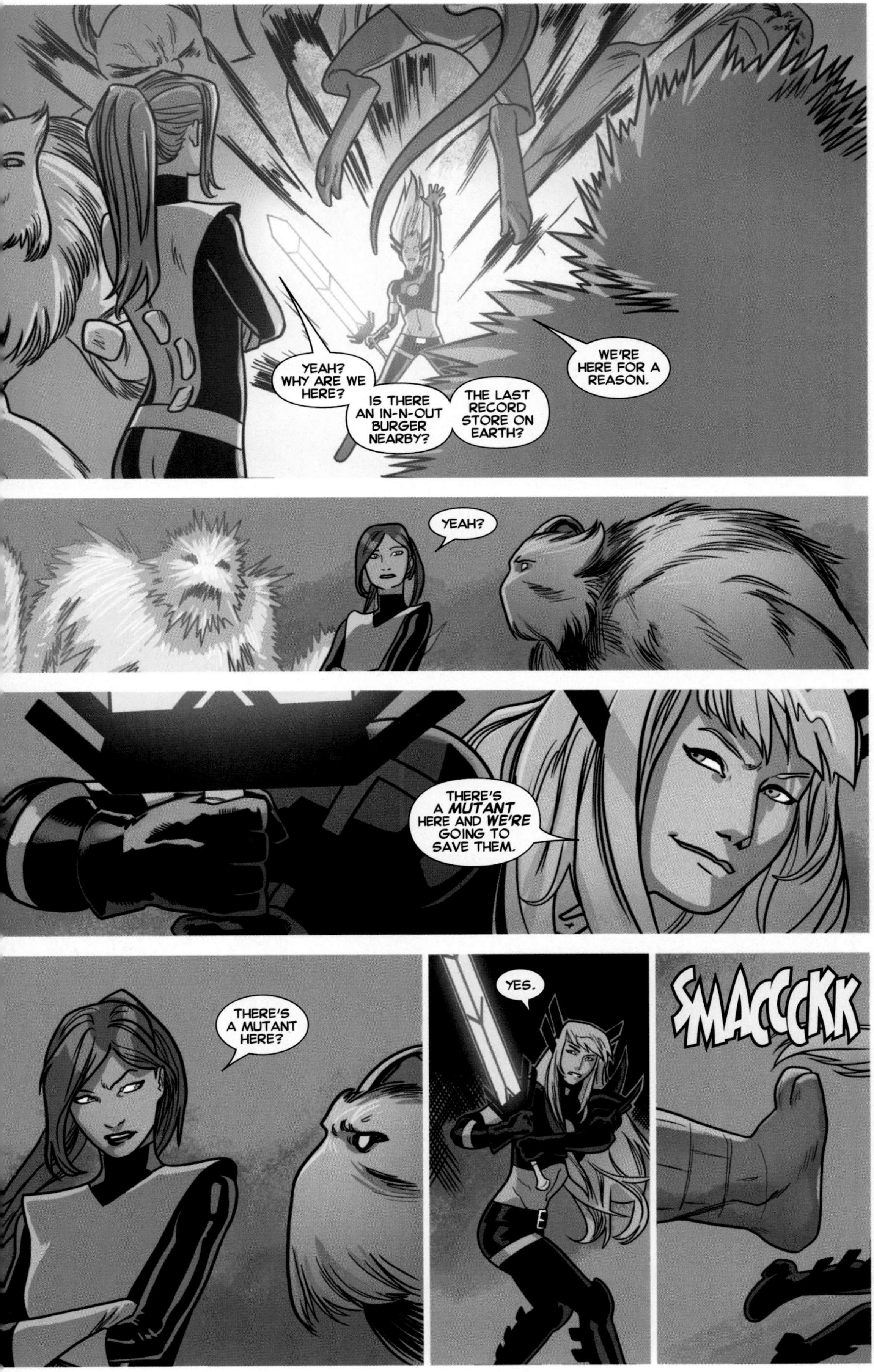
YEAH? WHY ARE WE HERE?
IS THERE AN IN-N-OUT BURGER NEARBY?
THE LAST RECORD STORE ON EARTH?
WE'RE HERE FOR A REASON.
YEAH?
THERE'S A *MUTANT* HERE AND *WE'RE* GOING TO SAVE THEM.
THERE'S A MUTANT HERE?
YES.
SMACCCKK

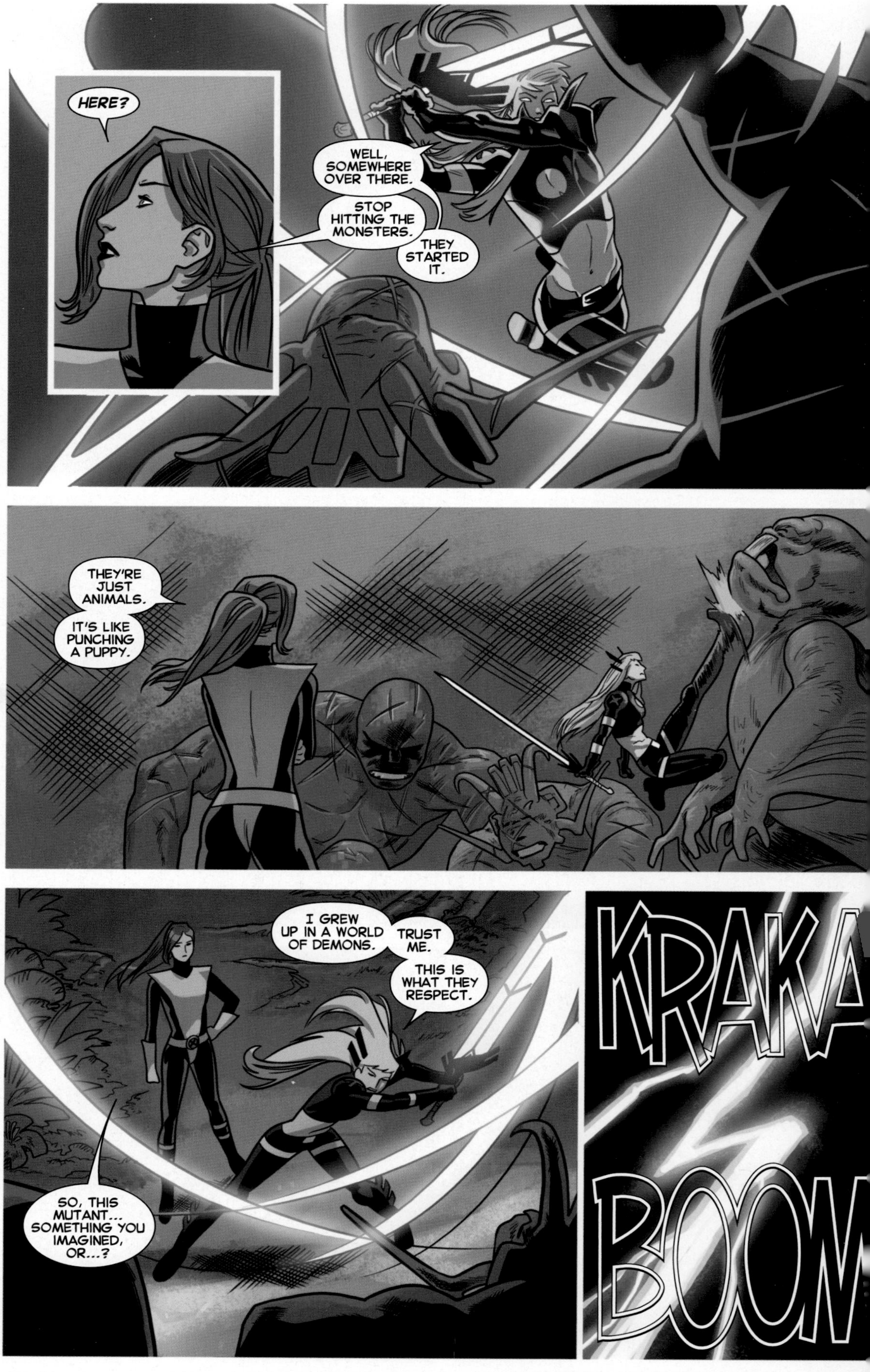
HERE?
WELL, SOMEWHERE OVER THERE.
STOP HITTING THE MONSTERS.
THEY STARTED IT.
THEY'RE JUST ANIMALS.
IT'S LIKE PUNCHING A PUPPY.
I GREW UP IN A WORLD OF DEMONS.
TRUST ME.
THIS IS WHAT THEY RESPECT.
SO, THIS MUTANT... SOMETHING YOU IMAGINED, OR...?
KRAKA
BOOM

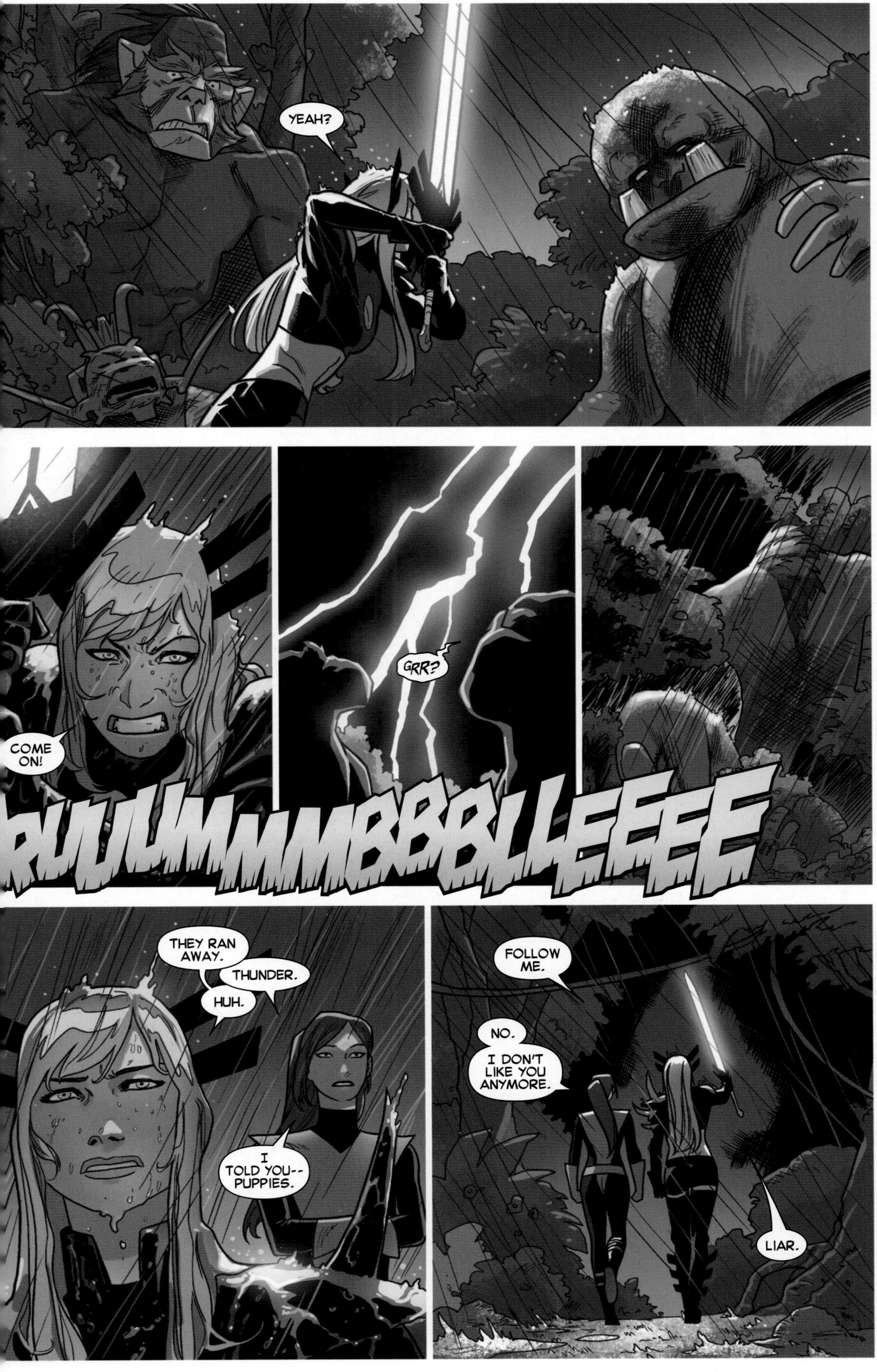
YEAH?
COME ON!
GRR?
RUUUMMMBBBLLEEEE
THEY RAN AWAY.
THUNDER.
HUH.
I TOLD YOU-- PUPPIES.
FOLLOW ME.
NO.
I DON'T LIKE YOU ANYMORE.
LIAR.

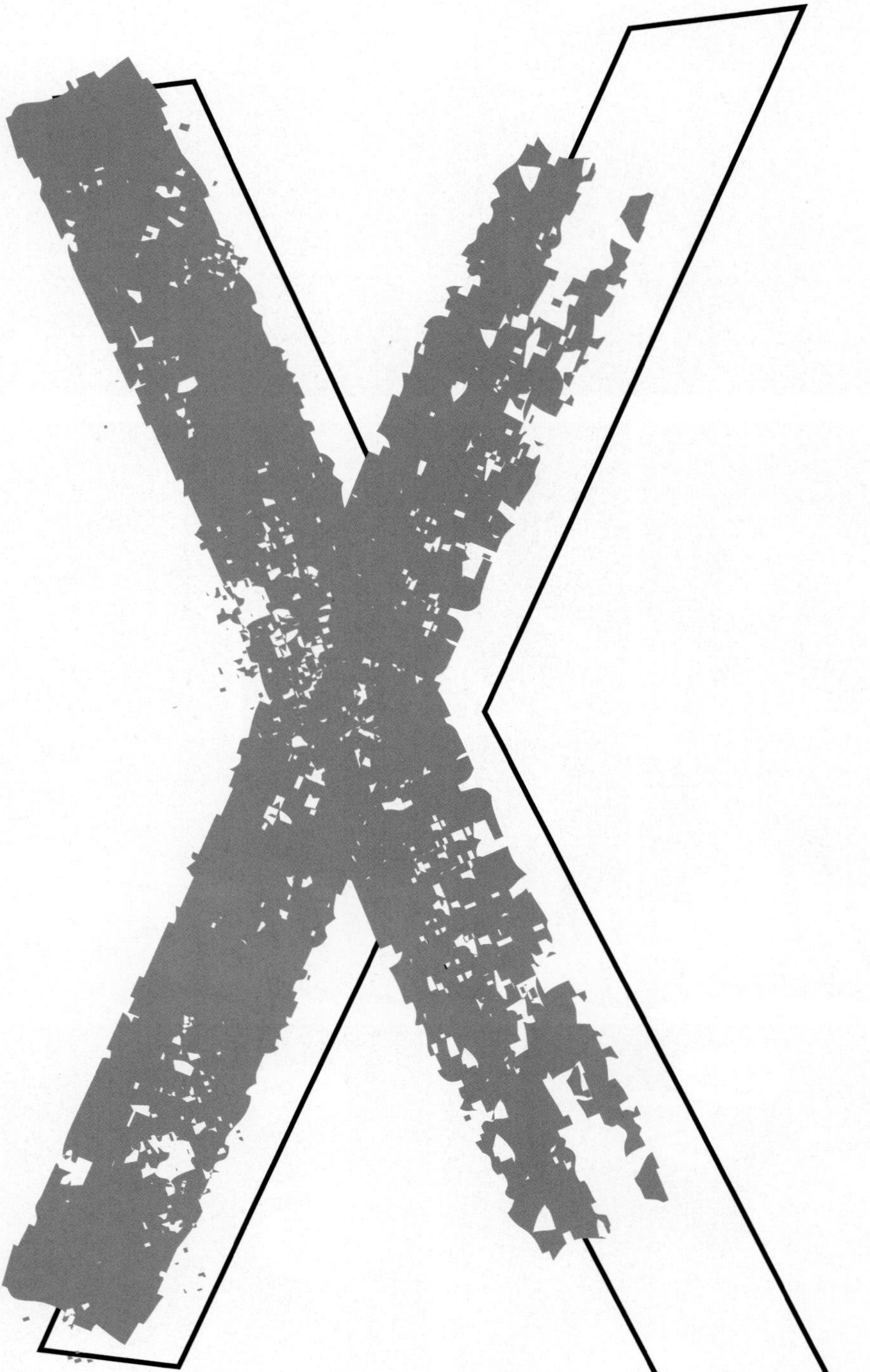

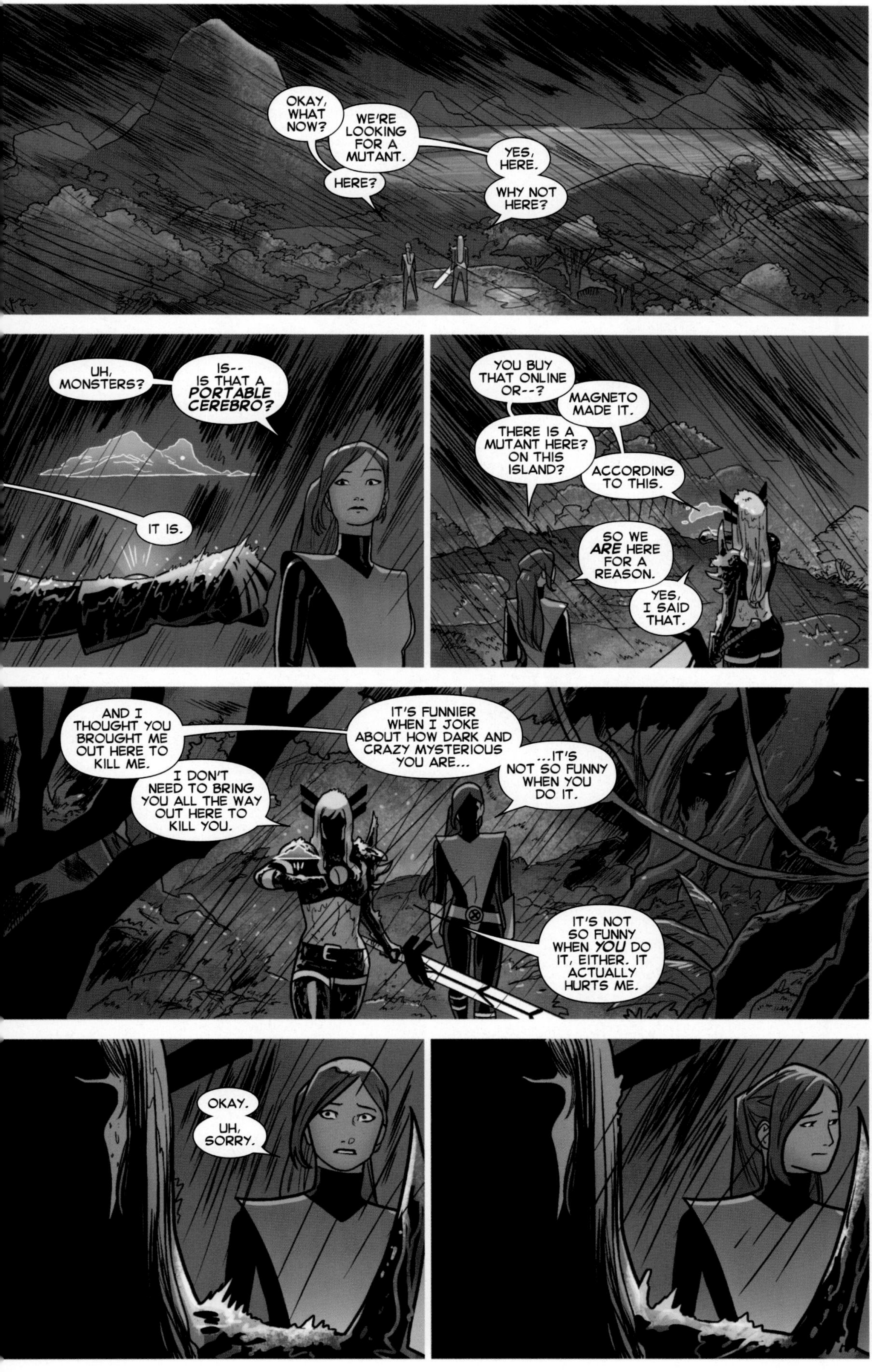
OKAY, WHAT NOW?
WE'RE LOOKING FOR A MUTANT.
YES, HERE.
HERE?
WHY NOT HERE?
UH, MONSTERS?
IS-- IS THAT A PORTABLE CEREBRO?
IT IS.
YOU BUY THAT ONLINE OR--?
MAGNETO MADE IT.
THERE IS A MUTANT HERE? ON THIS ISLAND?
ACCORDING TO THIS.
SO WE ARE HERE FOR A REASON.
YES, I SAID THAT.
AND I THOUGHT YOU BROUGHT ME OUT HERE TO KILL ME.
I DON'T NEED TO BRING YOU ALL THE WAY OUT HERE TO KILL YOU.
IT'S FUNNIER WHEN I JOKE ABOUT HOW DARK AND CRAZY MYSTERIOUS YOU ARE...
...IT'S NOT SO FUNNY WHEN YOU DO IT.
IT'S NOT SO FUNNY WHEN YOU DO IT, EITHER. IT ACTUALLY HURTS ME.
OKAY.
UH, SORRY.

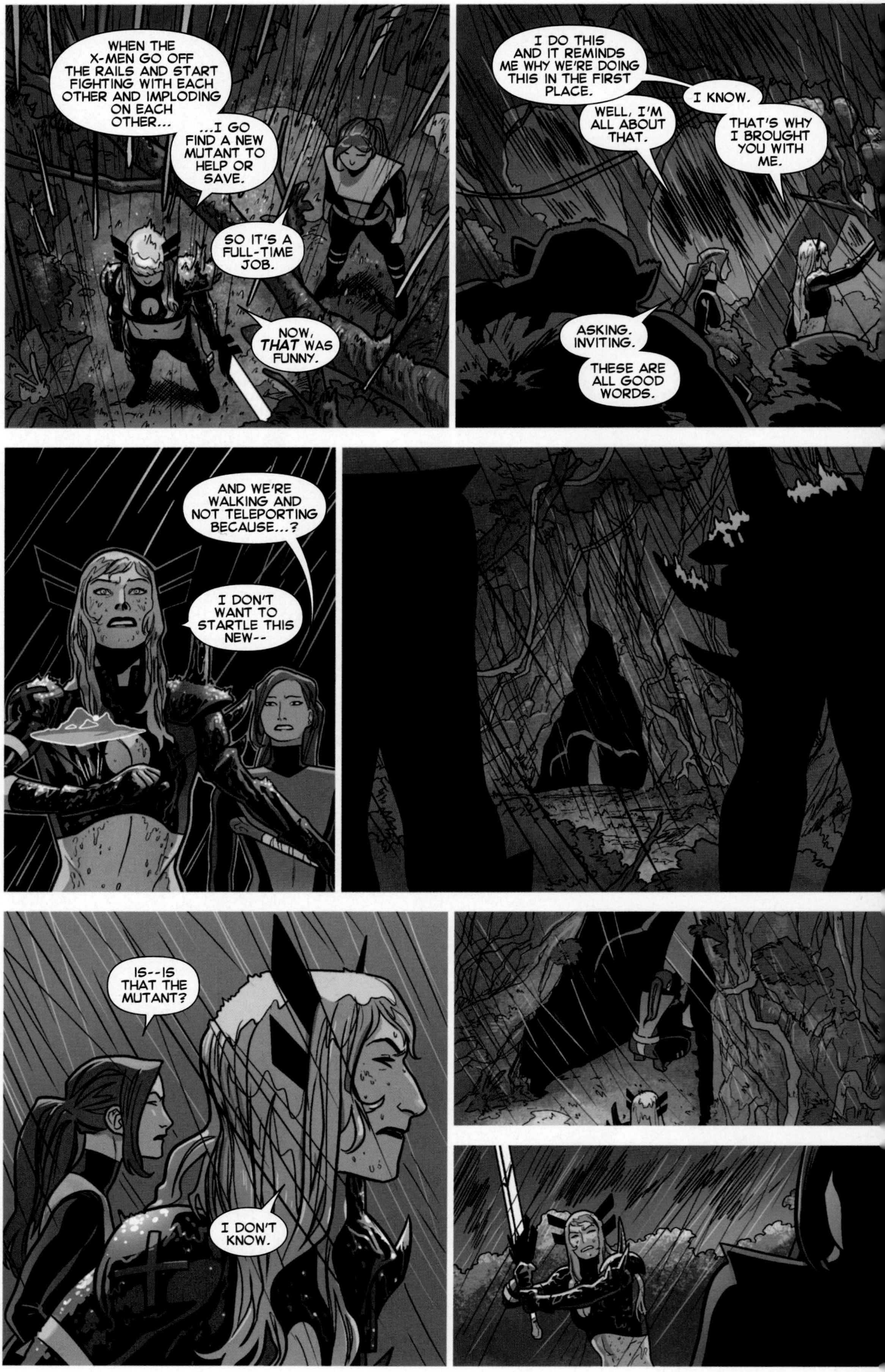
WHEN THE X-MEN GO OFF THE RAILS AND START FIGHTING WITH EACH OTHER AND IMPLODING ON EACH OTHER...
...I GO FIND A NEW MUTANT TO HELP OR SAVE.
SO IT'S A FULL-TIME JOB.
NOW, *THAT* WAS FUNNY.
I DO THIS AND IT REMINDS ME WHY WE'RE DOING THIS IN THE FIRST PLACE.
WELL, I'M ALL ABOUT THAT.
I KNOW.
THAT'S WHY I BROUGHT YOU WITH ME.
ASKING. INVITING.
THESE ARE ALL GOOD WORDS.
AND WE'RE WALKING AND NOT TELEPORTING BECAUSE...?
I DON'T WANT TO STARTLE THIS NEW--
IS--IS THAT THE MUTANT?
I DON'T KNOW.

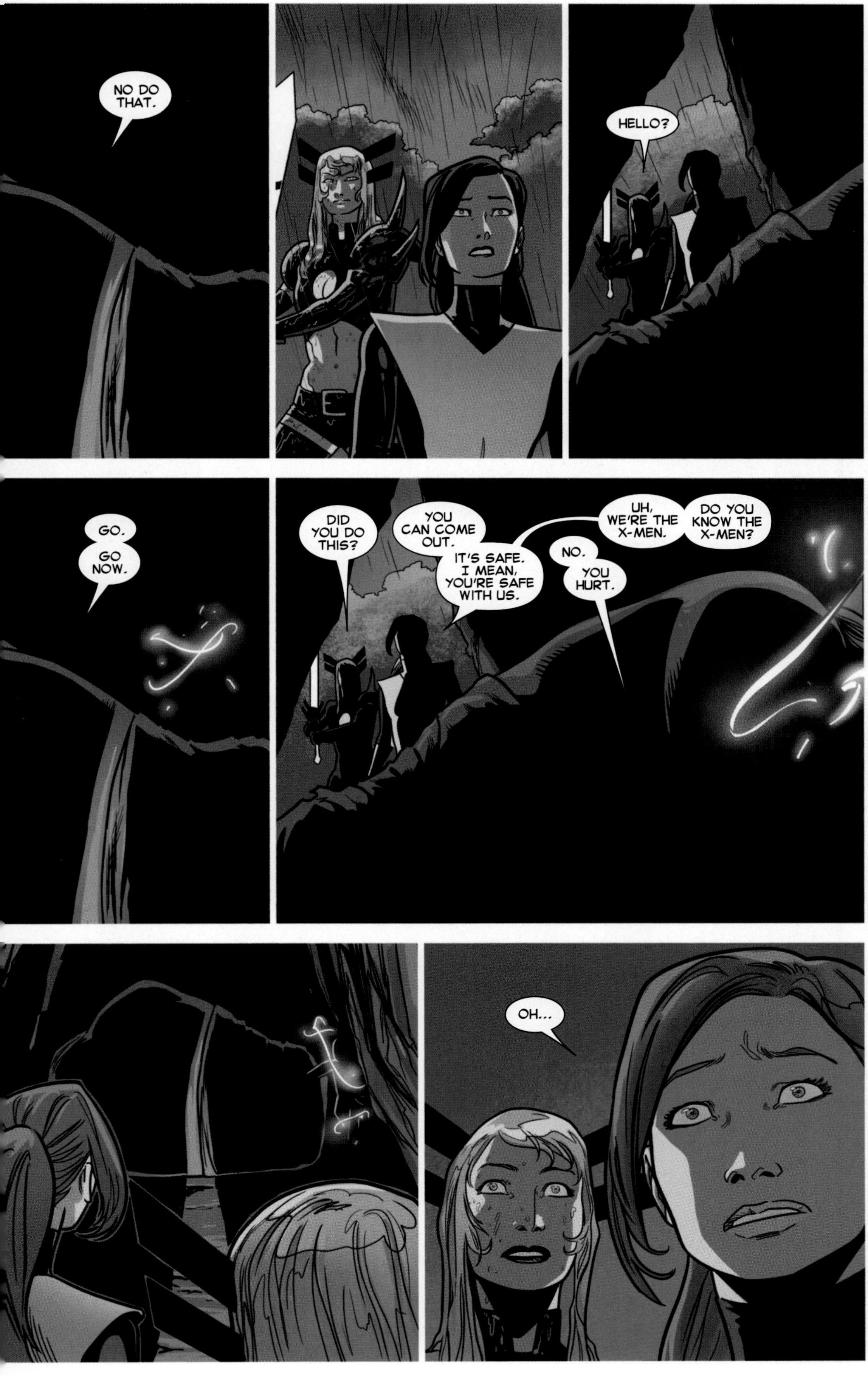
NO DO THAT.
HELLO?
GO.
GO NOW.
DID YOU DO THIS?
YOU CAN COME OUT.
IT'S SAFE. I MEAN, YOU'RE SAFE WITH US.
UH, WE'RE THE X-MEN.
DO YOU KNOW THE X-MEN?
NO.
YOU HURT.
OH...

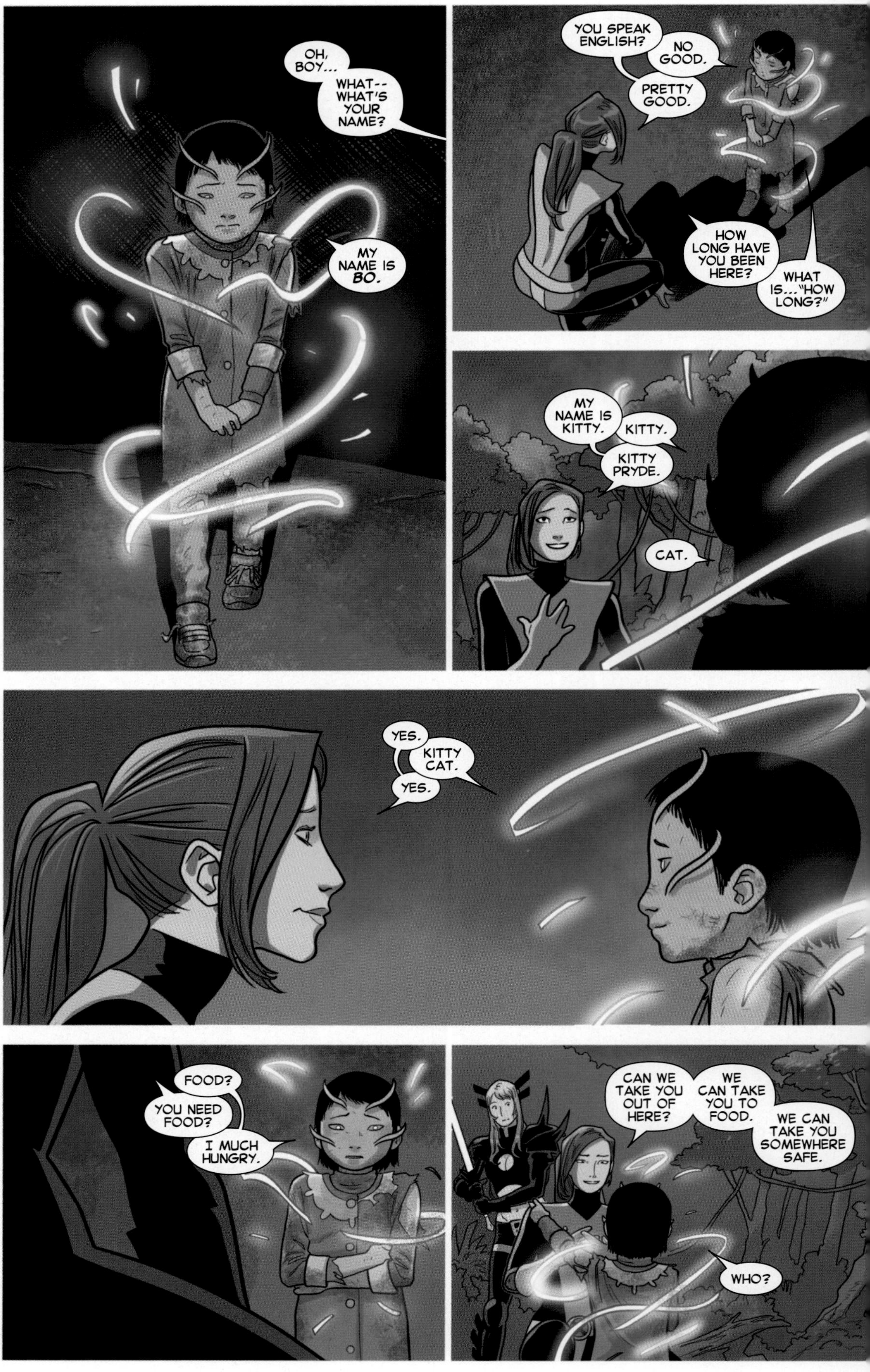
OH, BOY...
WHAT-- WHAT'S YOUR NAME?
MY NAME IS BO.
YOU SPEAK ENGLISH?
NO GOOD.
PRETTY GOOD.
HOW LONG HAVE YOU BEEN HERE?
WHAT IS..."HOW LONG?"
MY NAME IS KITTY.
KITTY.
KITTY PRYDE.
CAT.
YES.
KITTY CAT.
YES.
FOOD?
YOU NEED FOOD?
I MUCH HUNGRY.
CAN WE TAKE YOU OUT OF HERE?
WE CAN TAKE YOU TO FOOD.
WE CAN TAKE YOU SOMEWHERE SAFE.
WHO?

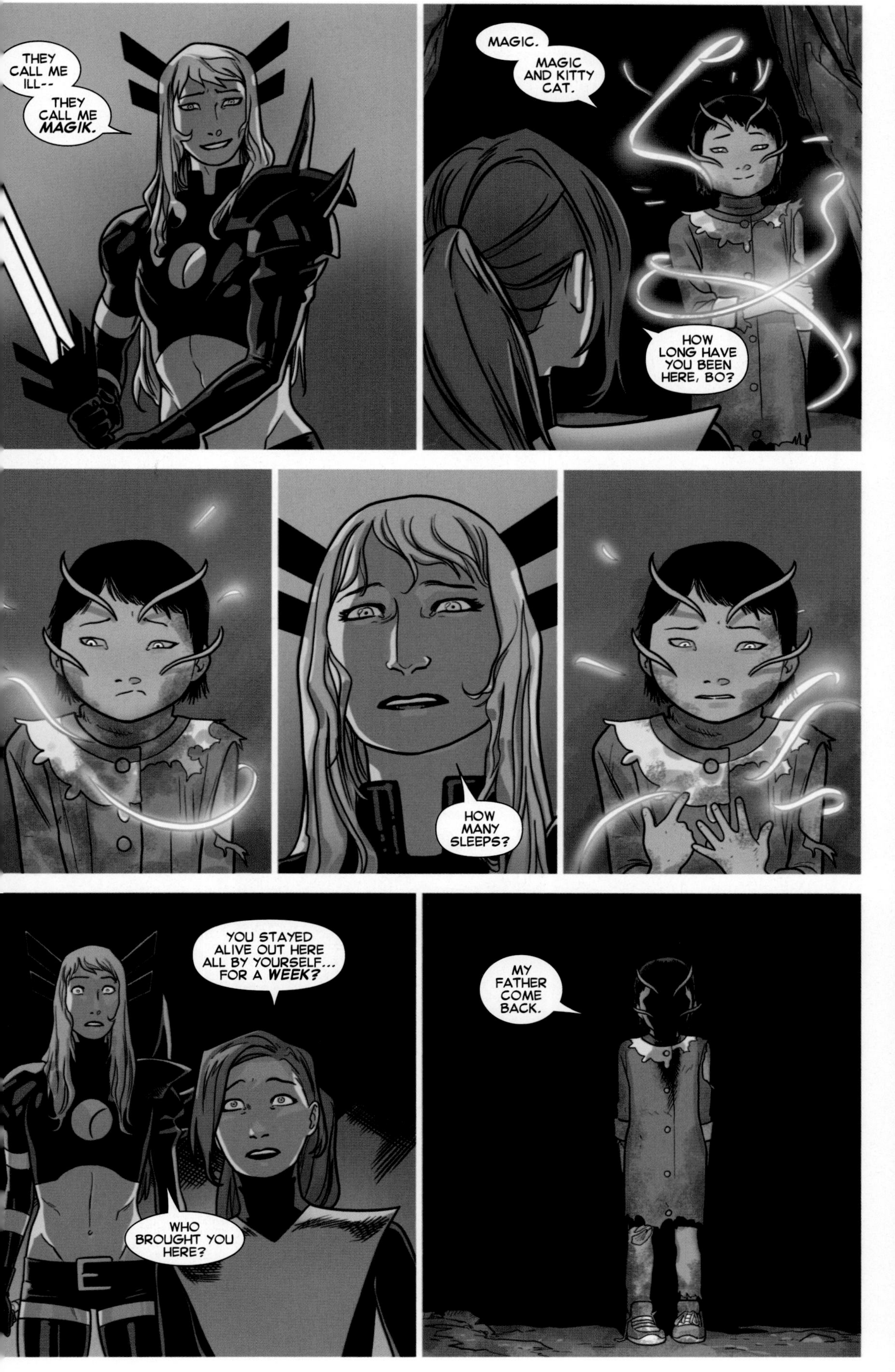
THEY CALL ME ILL--
THEY CALL ME *MAGIK.*
MAGIC.
MAGIC AND KITTY CAT.
HOW LONG HAVE YOU BEEN HERE, BO?
HOW MANY SLEEPS?
YOU STAYED ALIVE OUT HERE ALL BY YOURSELF... FOR A *WEEK?*
WHO BROUGHT YOU HERE?
MY FATHER COME BACK.

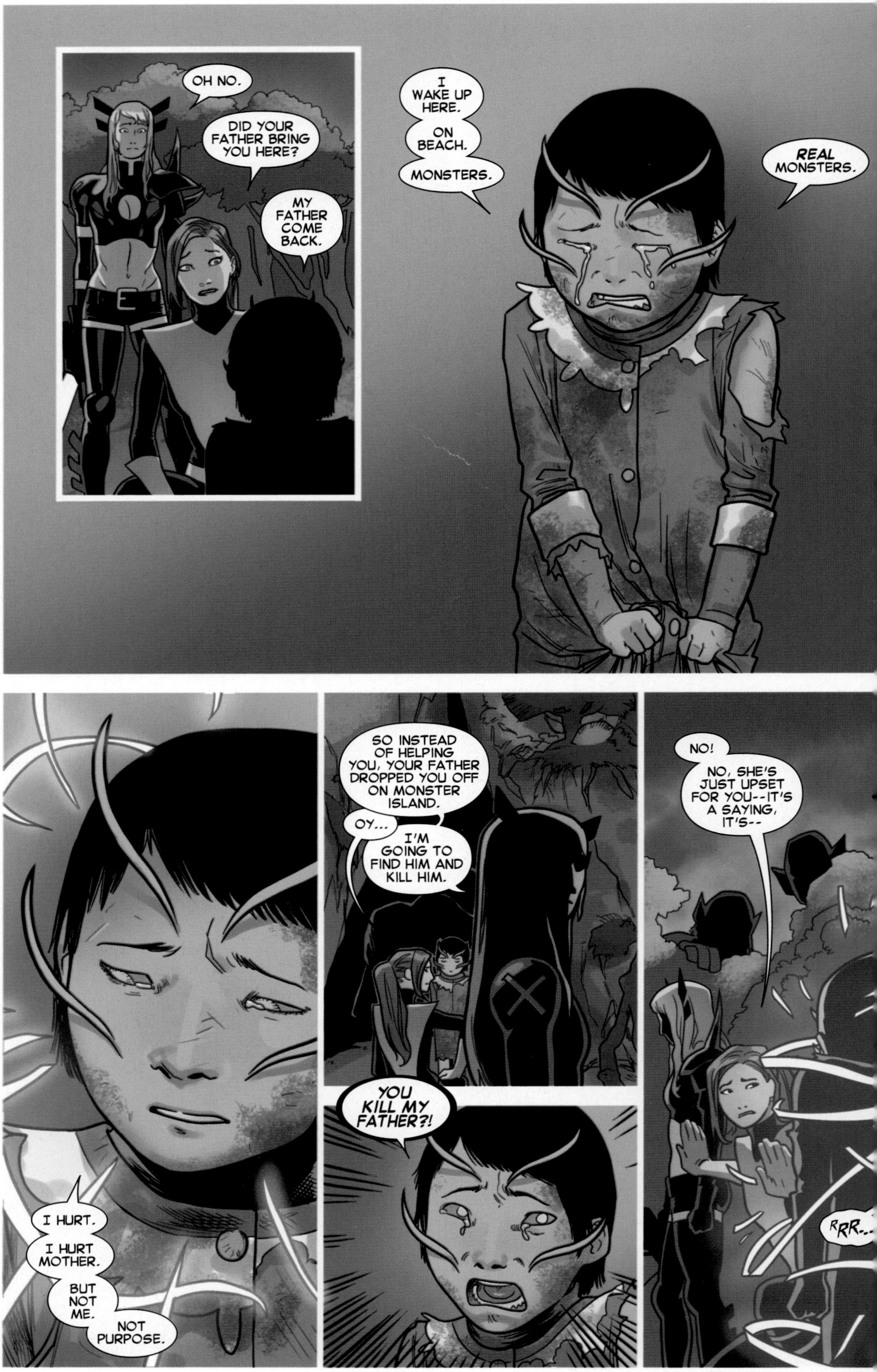

OH NO.
DID YOUR FATHER BRING YOU HERE?
MY FATHER COME BACK.
I WAKE UP HERE.
ON BEACH.
MONSTERS.
REAL MONSTERS.
I HURT.
I HURT MOTHER.
BUT NOT ME.
NOT PURPOSE.
SO INSTEAD OF HELPING YOU, YOUR FATHER DROPPED YOU OFF ON MONSTER ISLAND.
OY...
I'M GOING TO FIND HIM AND KILL HIM.
YOU KILL MY FATHER?!
NO!
NO, SHE'S JUST UPSET FOR YOU--IT'S A SAYING, IT'S--
RRR...

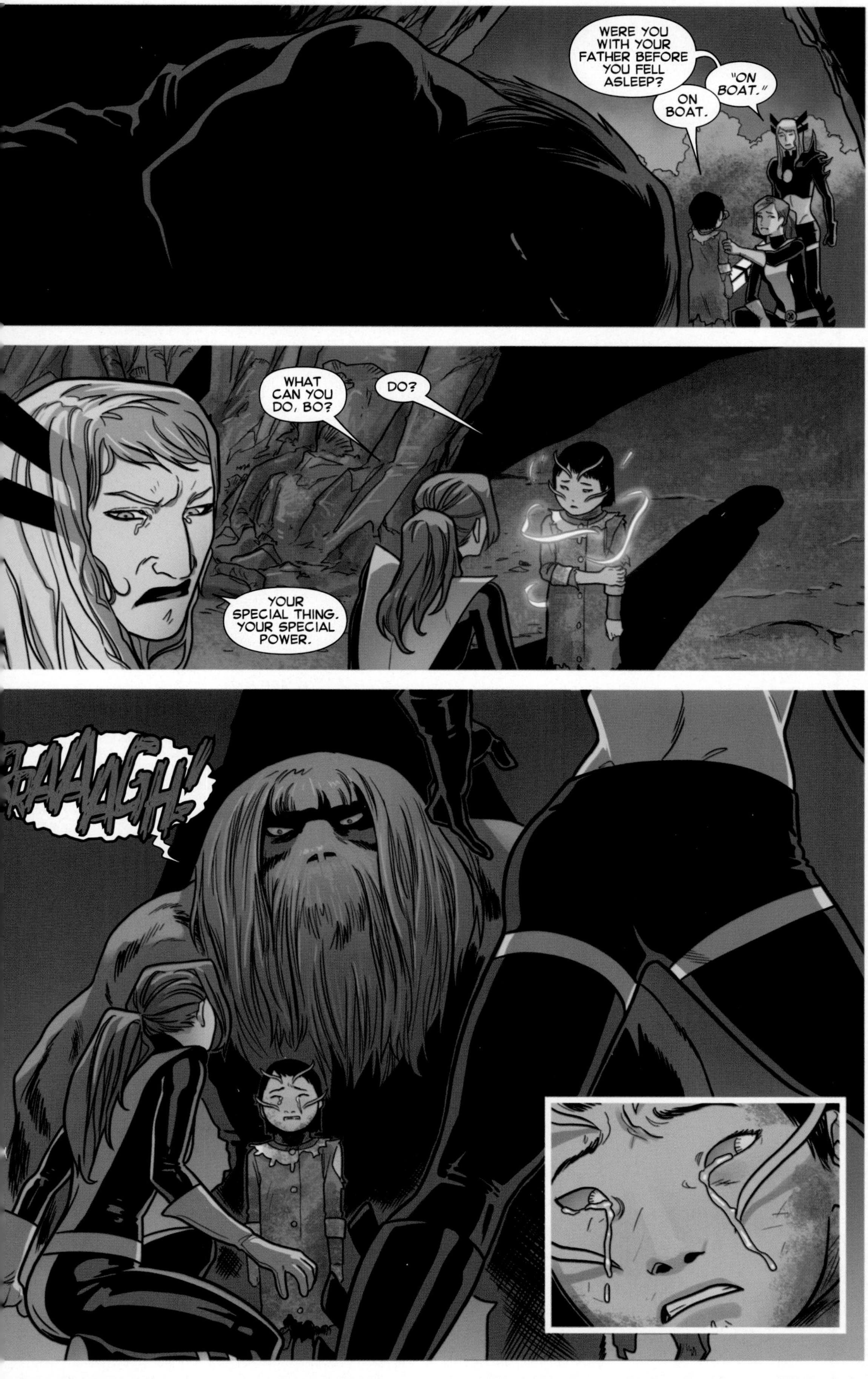
WERE YOU WITH YOUR FATHER BEFORE YOU FELL ASLEEP?
ON BOAT.
"ON BOAT."
WHAT CAN YOU DO, BO?
DO?
YOUR SPECIAL THING. YOUR SPECIAL POWER.
RAAAGH!

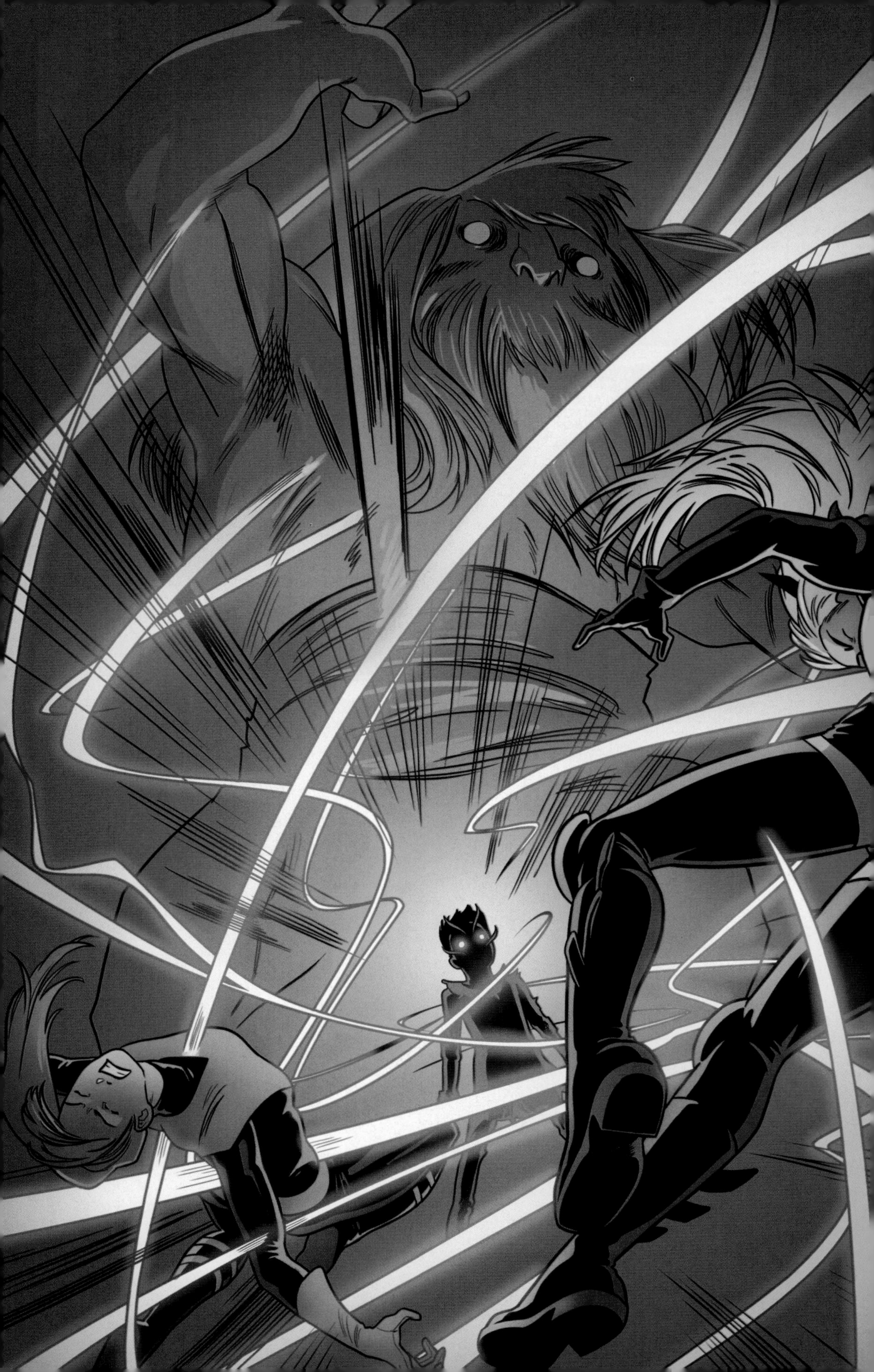

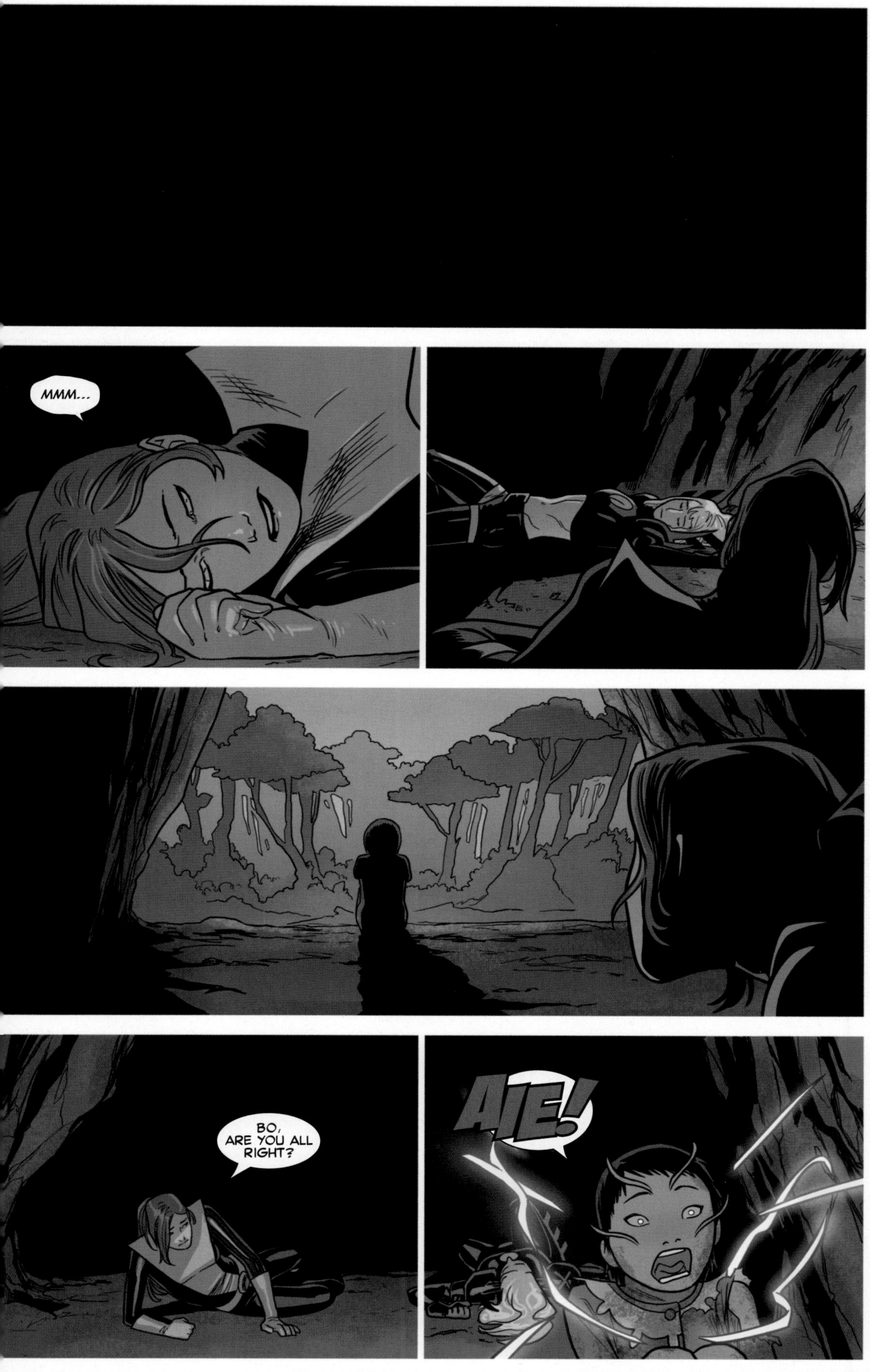
MMM...
BO, ARE YOU ALL RIGHT?
AIE!

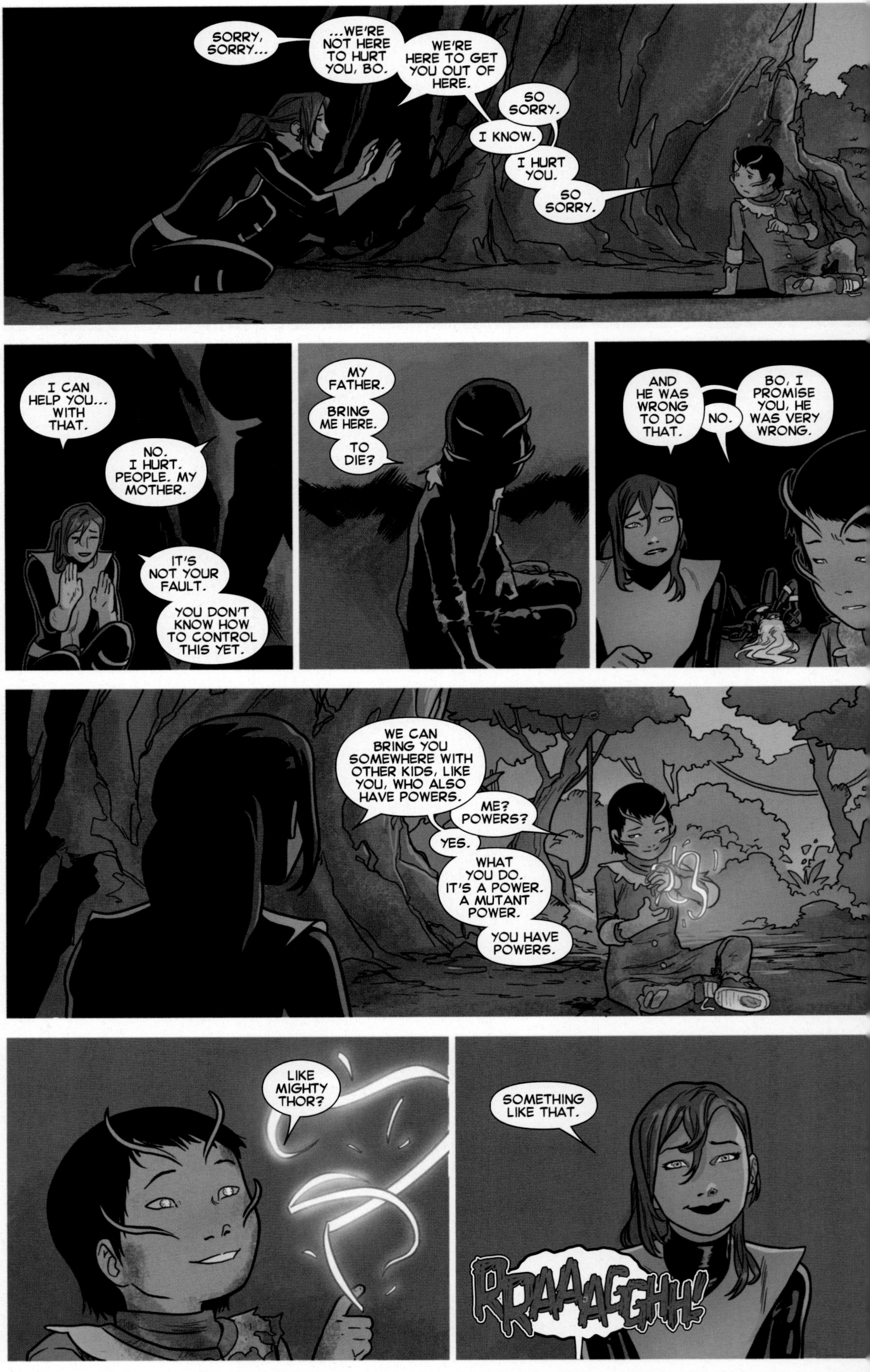
SORRY, SORRY...
...WE'RE NOT HERE TO HURT YOU, BO.
WE'RE HERE TO GET YOU OUT OF HERE.
SO SORRY.
I KNOW.
I HURT YOU.
SO SORRY.
I CAN HELP YOU... WITH THAT.
NO. I HURT. PEOPLE. MY MOTHER.
IT'S NOT YOUR FAULT.
YOU DON'T KNOW HOW TO CONTROL THIS YET.
MY FATHER.
BRING ME HERE.
TO DIE?
AND HE WAS WRONG TO DO THAT.
NO.
BO, I PROMISE YOU, HE WAS VERY WRONG.
WE CAN BRING YOU SOMEWHERE WITH OTHER KIDS, LIKE YOU, WHO ALSO HAVE POWERS.
ME? POWERS?
YES.
WHAT YOU DO. IT'S A POWER. A MUTANT POWER.
YOU HAVE POWERS.
LIKE MIGHTY THOR?
SOMETHING LIKE THAT.
RRAAAGGHH!

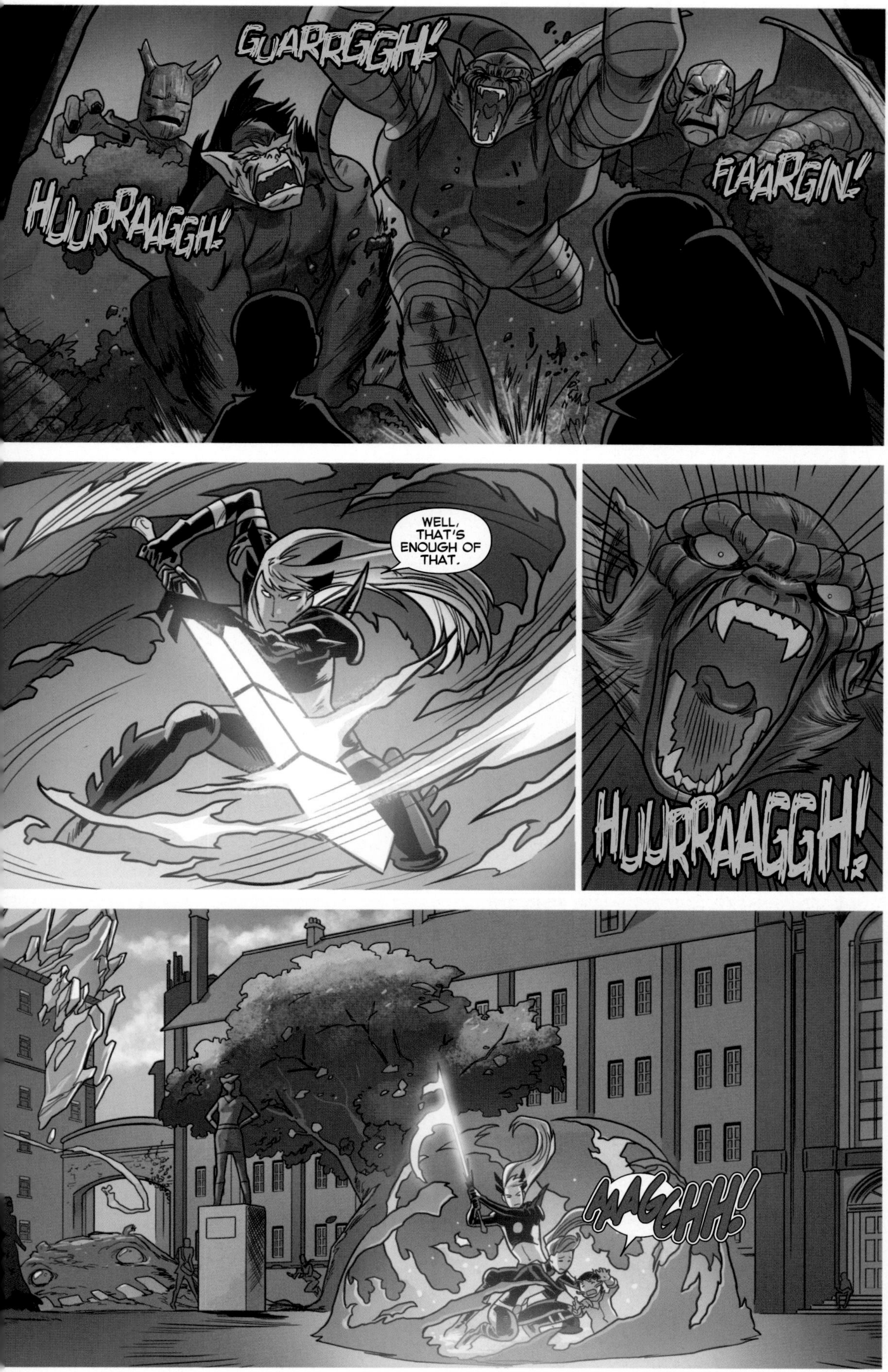
GUARRGGH!
HUURRAAGGH!
FLAARGIN!
WELL, THAT'S ENOUGH OF THAT.
HUURRAAGGH!
AAAGGHH!

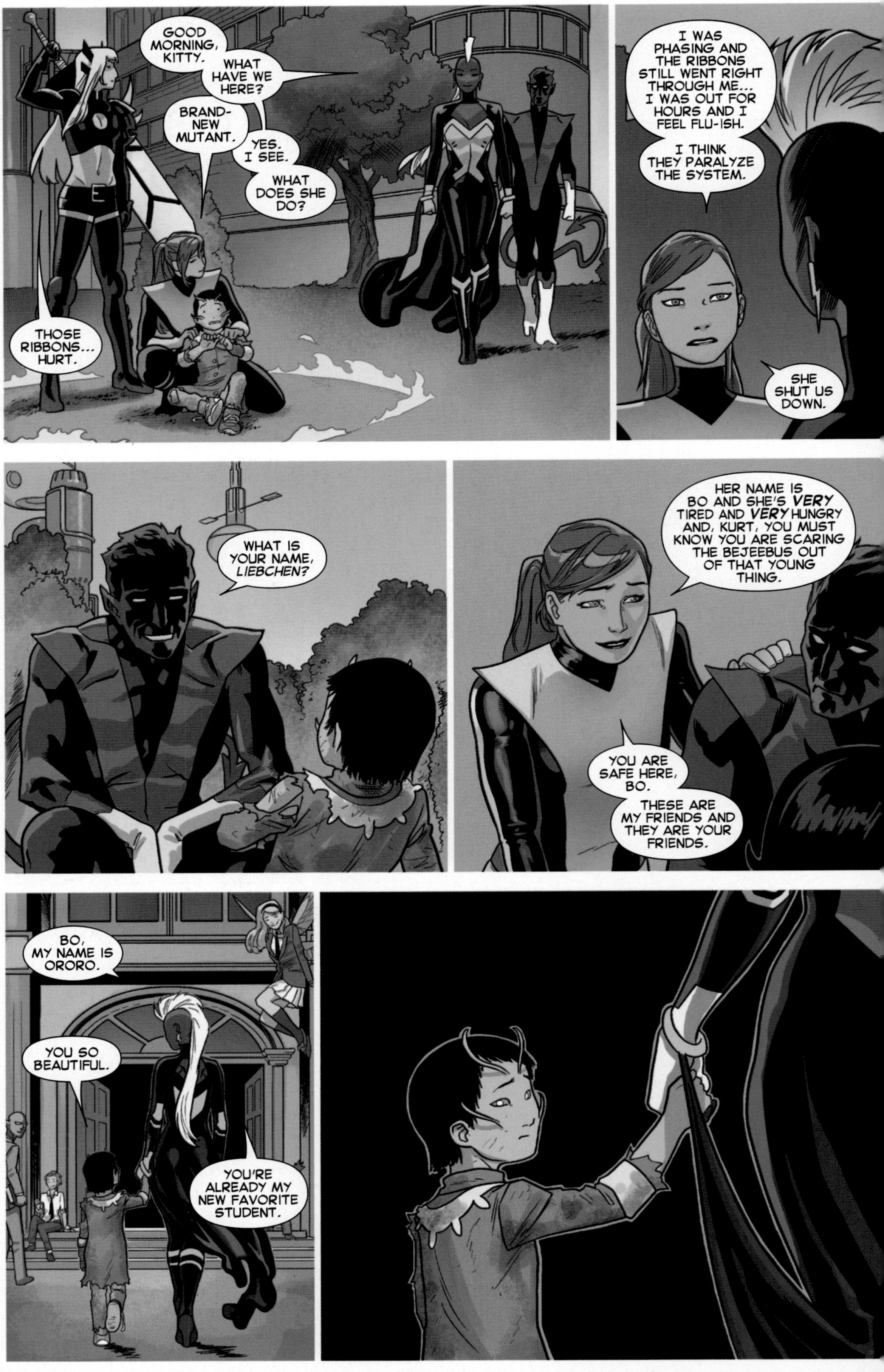
GOOD MORNING, KITTY.
WHAT HAVE WE HERE?
BRAND-NEW MUTANT.
YES. I SEE.
WHAT DOES SHE DO?
THOSE RIBBONS... HURT.
I WAS PHASING AND THE RIBBONS STILL WENT RIGHT THROUGH ME... I WAS OUT FOR HOURS AND I FEEL FLU-ISH.
I THINK THEY PARALYZE THE SYSTEM.
SHE SHUT US DOWN.
WHAT IS YOUR NAME, LIEBCHEN?
HER NAME IS BO AND SHE'S VERY TIRED AND VERY HUNGRY AND, KURT, YOU MUST KNOW YOU ARE SCARING THE BEJEEBUS OUT OF THAT YOUNG THING.
YOU ARE SAFE HERE, BO.
THESE ARE MY FRIENDS AND THEY ARE YOUR FRIENDS.
BO, MY NAME IS ORORO.
YOU SO BEAUTIFUL.
YOU'RE ALREADY MY NEW FAVORITE STUDENT.

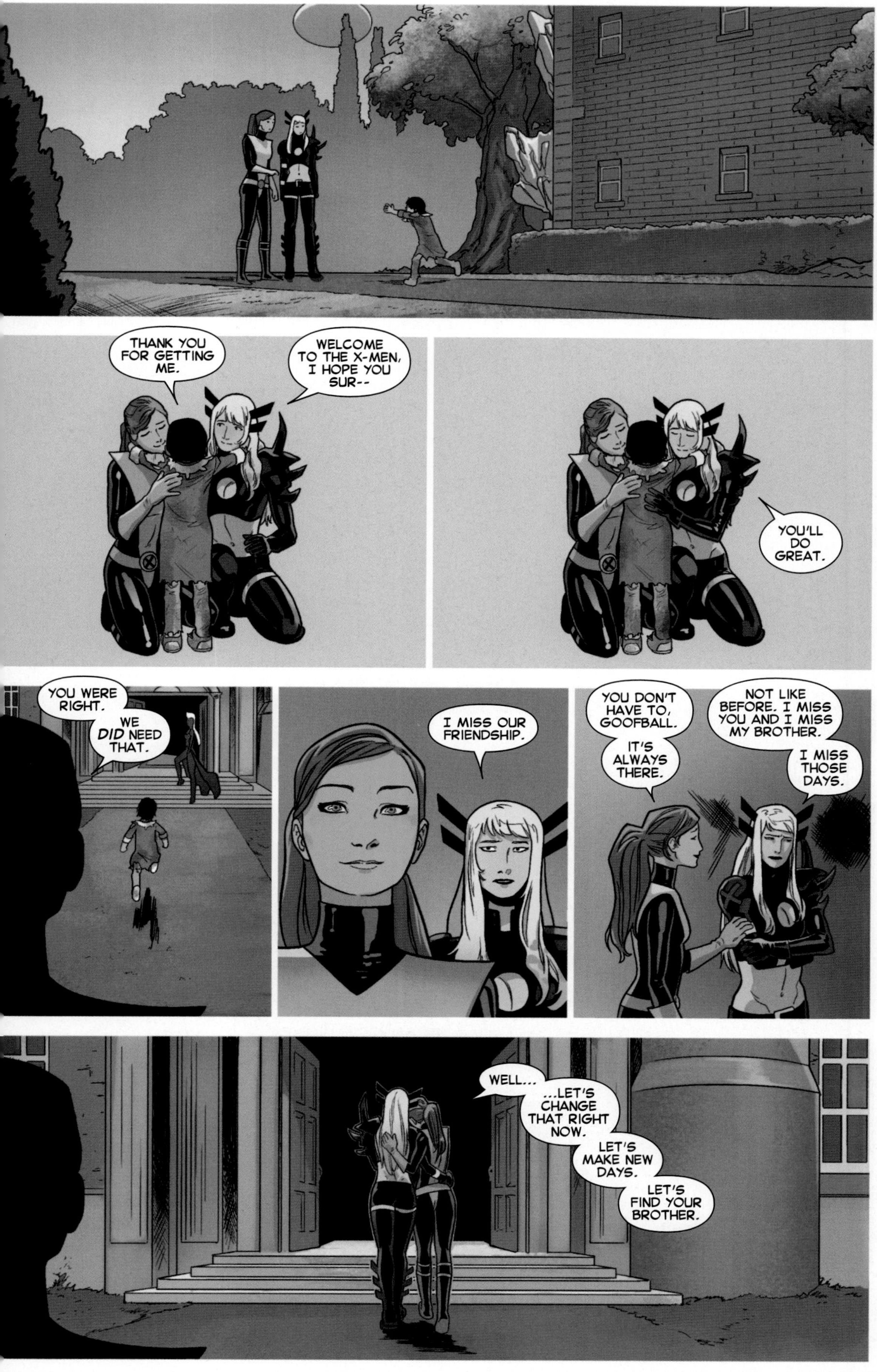
THANK YOU FOR GETTING ME.
WELCOME TO THE X-MEN, I HOPE YOU SUR--
YOU'LL DO GREAT.
YOU WERE RIGHT.
WE DID NEED THAT.
I MISS OUR FRIENDSHIP.
YOU DON'T HAVE TO, GOOFBALL.
IT'S ALWAYS THERE.
NOT LIKE BEFORE. I MISS YOU AND I MISS MY BROTHER.
I MISS THOSE DAYS.
WELL...
...LET'S CHANGE THAT RIGHT NOW.
LET'S MAKE NEW DAYS.
LET'S FIND YOUR BROTHER.

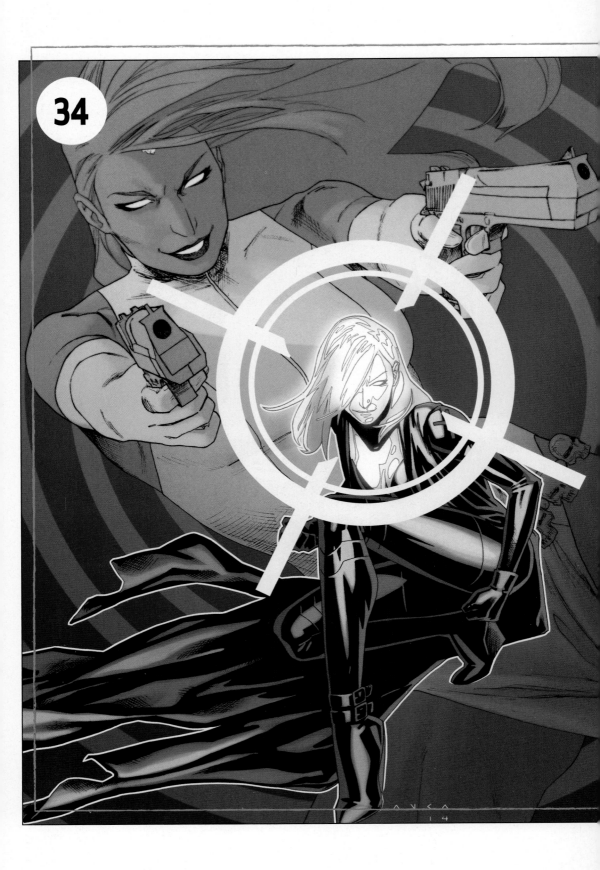

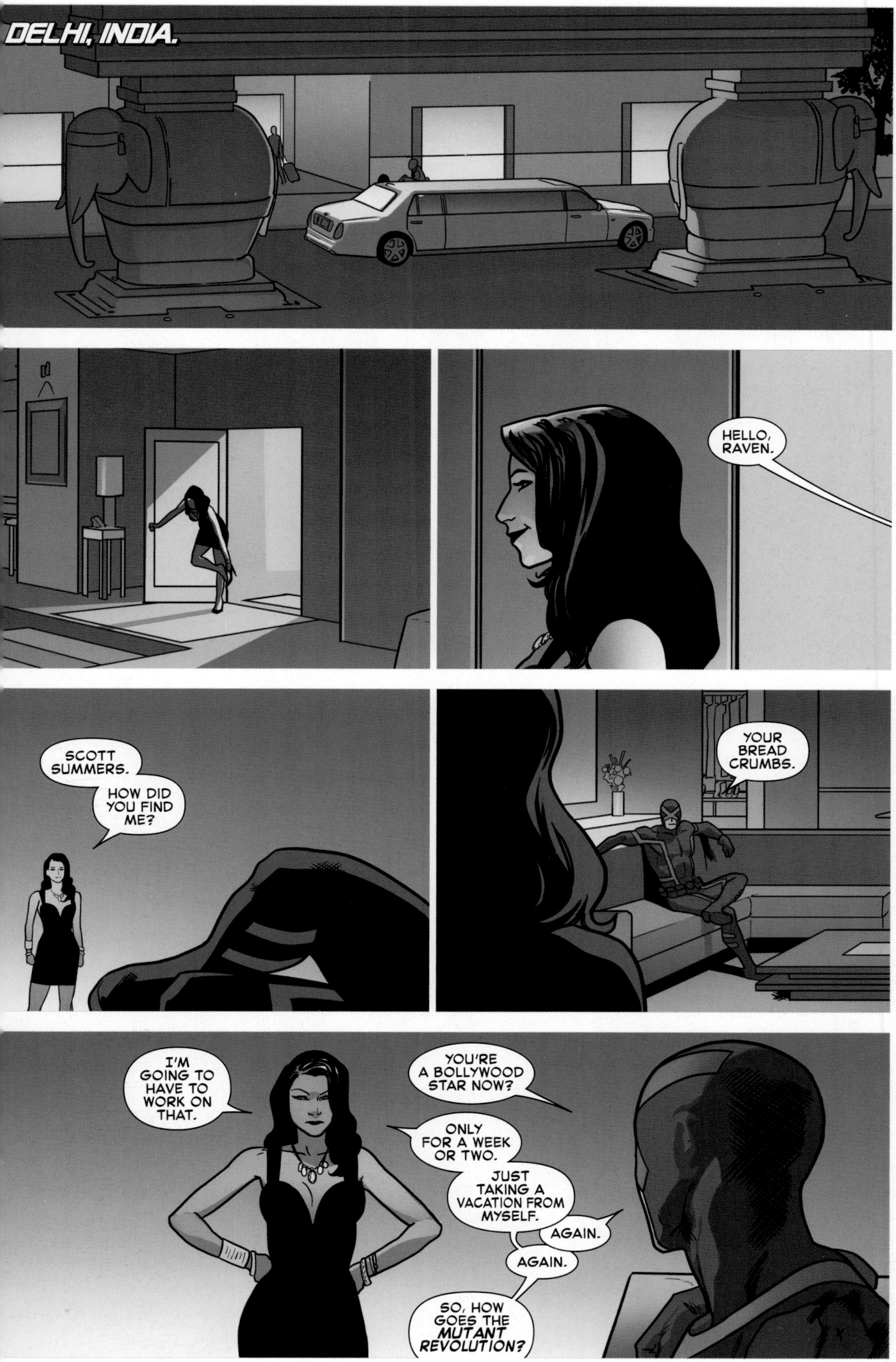
DELHI, INDIA.
HELLO, RAVEN.
SCOTT SUMMERS.
HOW DID YOU FIND ME?
YOUR BREAD CRUMBS.
YOU'RE A BOLLYWOOD STAR NOW?
I'M GOING TO HAVE TO WORK ON THAT.
ONLY FOR A WEEK OR TWO.
JUST TAKING A VACATION FROM MYSELF.
AGAIN.
AGAIN.
SO, HOW GOES THE *MUTANT REVOLUTION?*

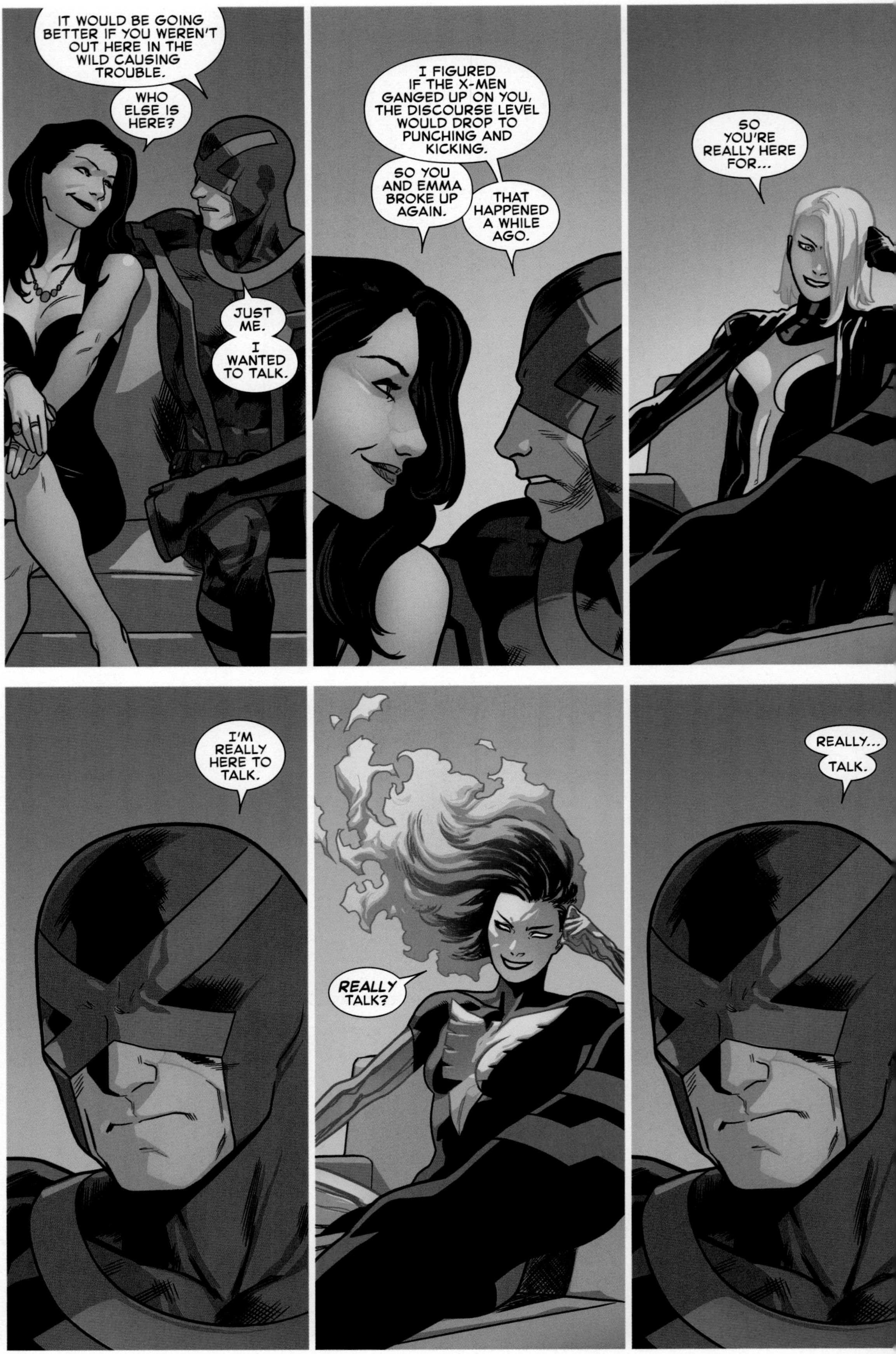
IT WOULD BE GOING BETTER IF YOU WEREN'T OUT HERE IN THE WILD CAUSING TROUBLE.
WHO ELSE IS HERE?
JUST ME.
I WANTED TO TALK.
I FIGURED IF THE X-MEN GANGED UP ON YOU, THE DISCOURSE LEVEL WOULD DROP TO PUNCHING AND KICKING.
SO YOU AND EMMA BROKE UP AGAIN.
THAT HAPPENED A WHILE AGO.
SO YOU'RE REALLY HERE FOR...
I'M REALLY HERE TO TALK.
REALLY TALK?
REALLY...
TALK.

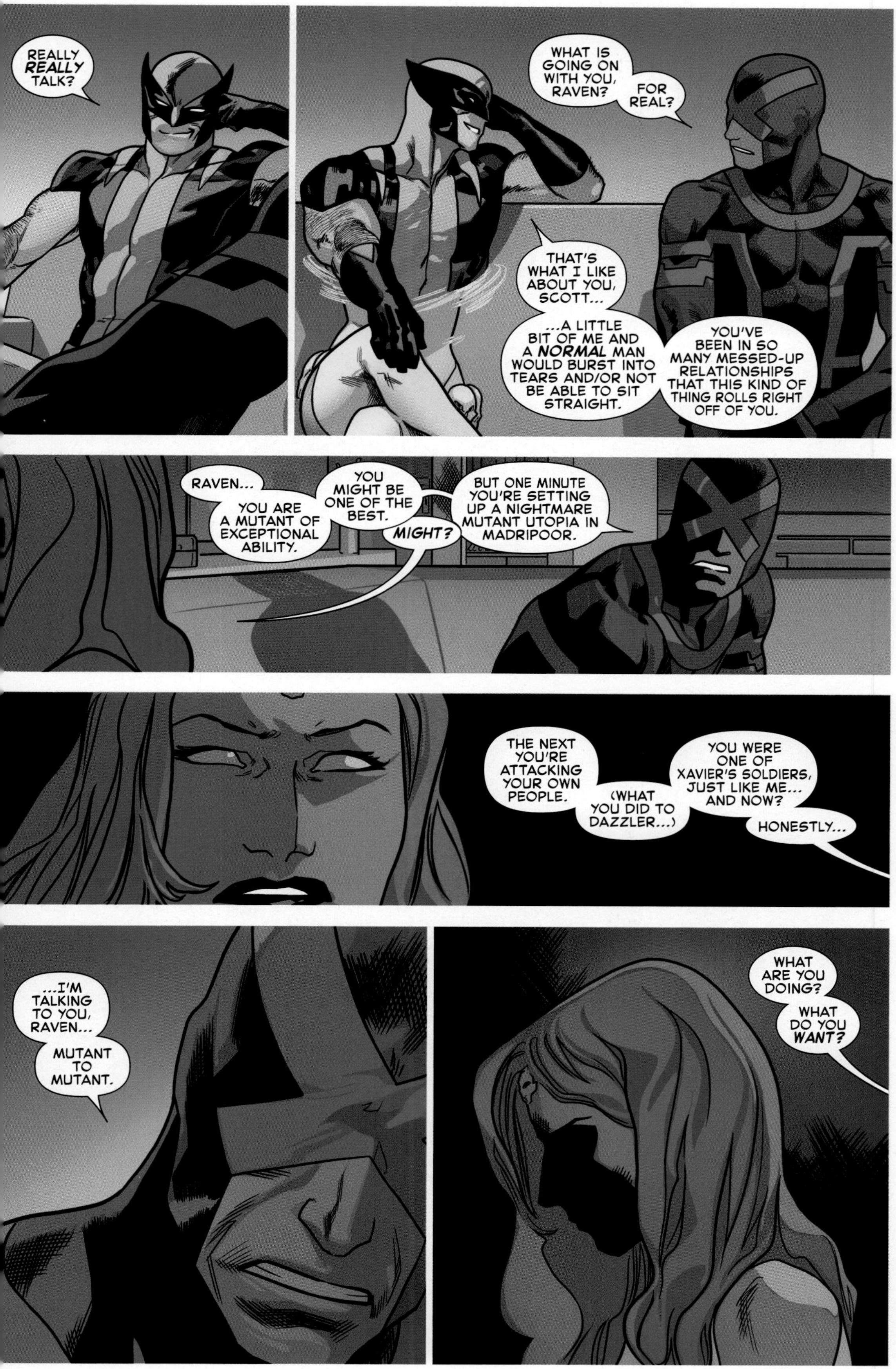

REALLY *REALLY* TALK?
WHAT IS GOING ON WITH YOU, RAVEN?
FOR REAL?
THAT'S WHAT I LIKE ABOUT YOU, SCOTT...
...A LITTLE BIT OF ME AND A *NORMAL* MAN WOULD BURST INTO TEARS AND/OR NOT BE ABLE TO SIT STRAIGHT.
YOU'VE BEEN IN SO MANY MESSED-UP RELATIONSHIPS THAT THIS KIND OF THING ROLLS RIGHT OFF OF YOU.
RAVEN...
YOU ARE A MUTANT OF EXCEPTIONAL ABILITY.
YOU MIGHT BE ONE OF THE BEST.
MIGHT?
BUT ONE MINUTE YOU'RE SETTING UP A NIGHTMARE MUTANT UTOPIA IN MADRIPOOR.
THE NEXT YOU'RE ATTACKING YOUR OWN PEOPLE.
(WHAT YOU DID TO DAZZLER...)
YOU WERE ONE OF XAVIER'S SOLDIERS, JUST LIKE ME... AND NOW?
HONESTLY...
...I'M TALKING TO YOU, RAVEN...
MUTANT TO MUTANT.
WHAT ARE YOU DOING?
WHAT DO YOU *WANT?*

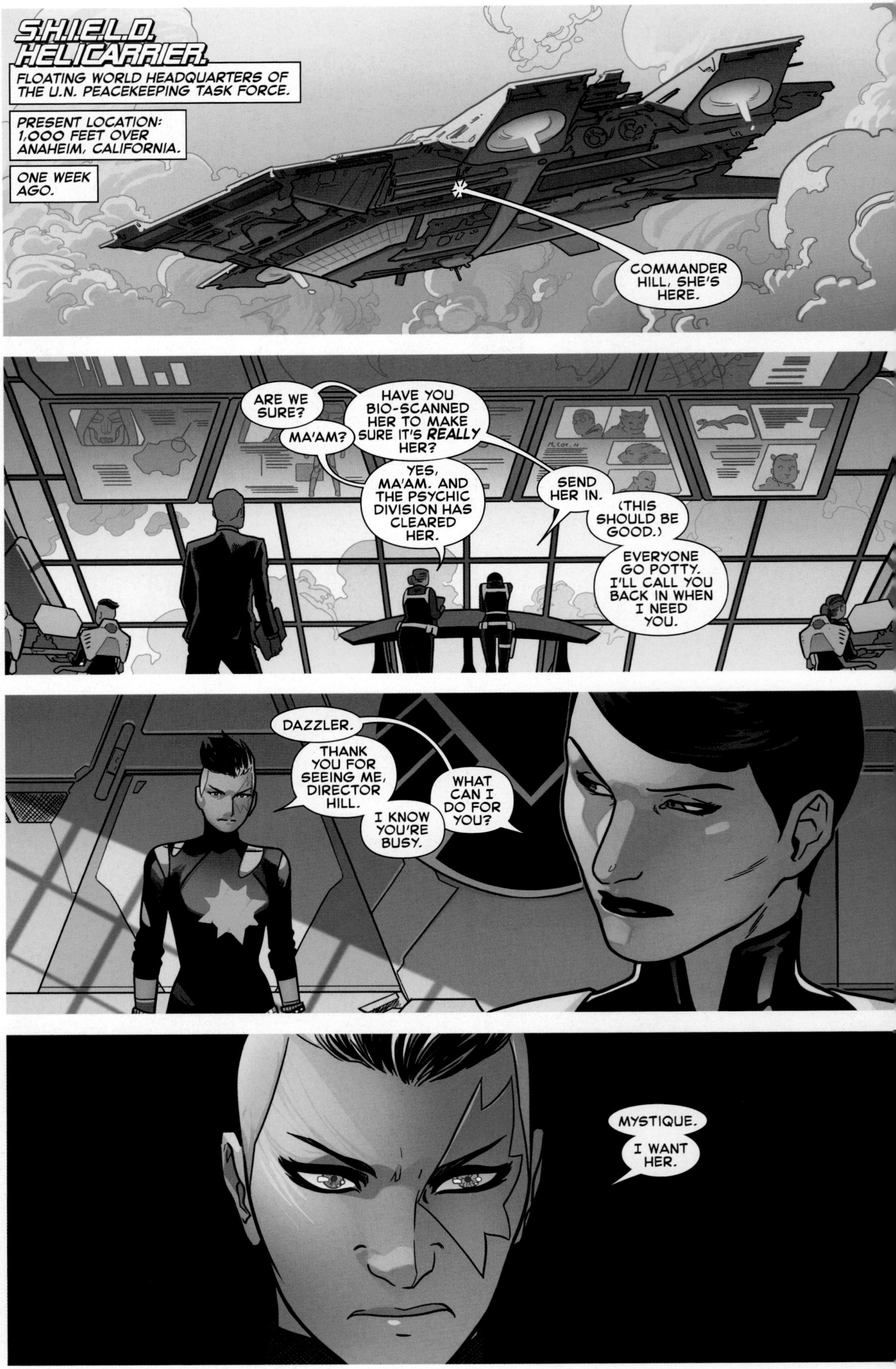
S.H.I.E.L.D. HELICARRIER.
FLOATING WORLD HEADQUARTERS OF THE U.N. PEACEKEEPING TASK FORCE.
PRESENT LOCATION: 1,000 FEET OVER ANAHEIM, CALIFORNIA.
ONE WEEK AGO.
COMMANDER HILL, SHE'S HERE.
ARE WE SURE?
HAVE YOU BIO-SCANNED HER TO MAKE SURE IT'S REALLY HER?
MA'AM?
YES, MA'AM. AND THE PSYCHIC DIVISION HAS CLEARED HER.
SEND HER IN.
(THIS SHOULD BE GOOD.)
EVERYONE GO POTTY. I'LL CALL YOU BACK IN WHEN I NEED YOU.
DAZZLER.
THANK YOU FOR SEEING ME, DIRECTOR HILL.
I KNOW YOU'RE BUSY.
WHAT CAN I DO FOR YOU?
MYSTIQUE.
I WANT HER.

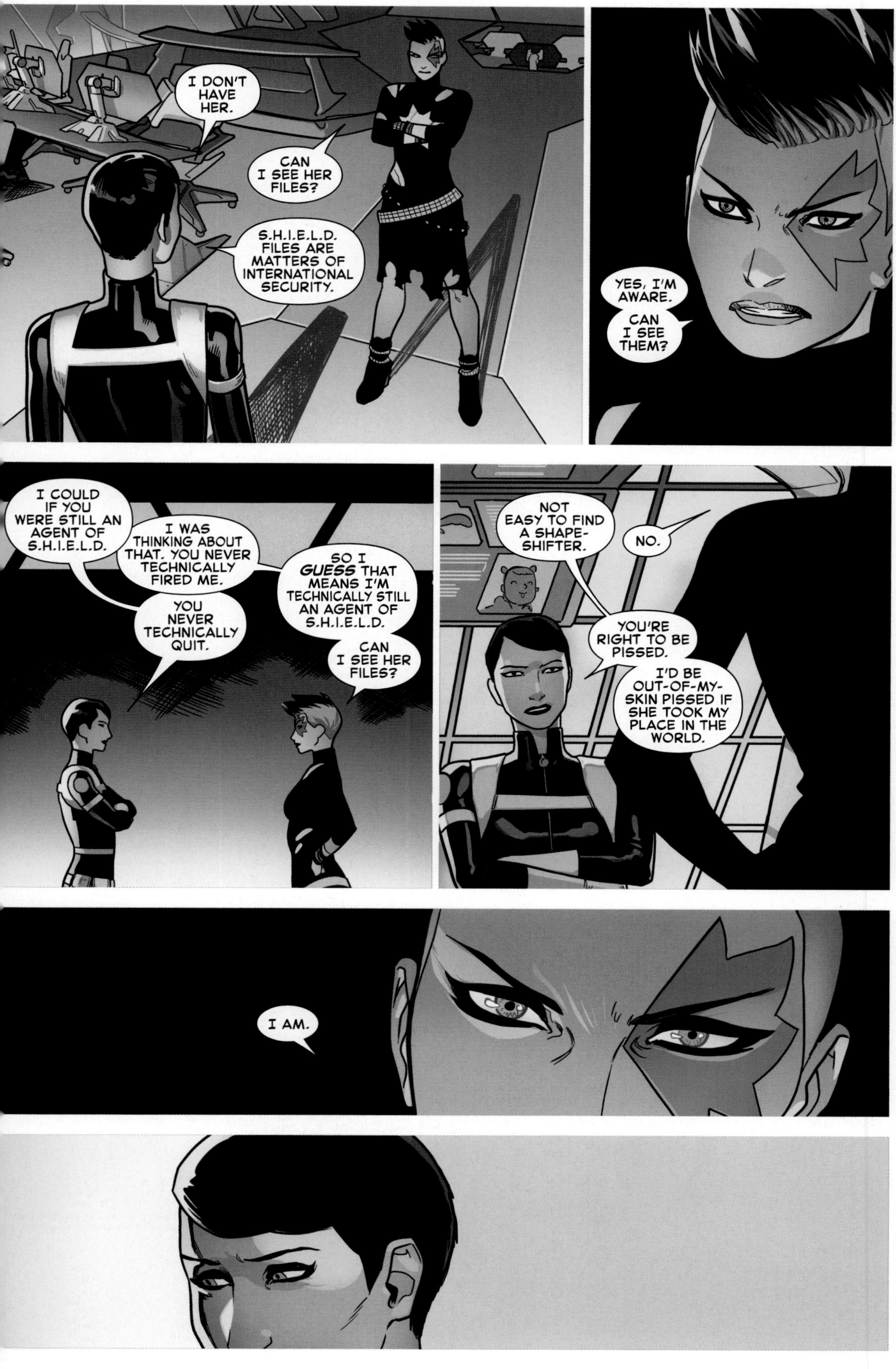
I DON'T HAVE HER.
CAN I SEE HER FILES?
S.H.I.E.L.D. FILES ARE MATTERS OF INTERNATIONAL SECURITY.
YES, I'M AWARE.
CAN I SEE THEM?
I COULD IF YOU WERE STILL AN AGENT OF S.H.I.E.L.D.
I WAS THINKING ABOUT THAT. YOU NEVER TECHNICALLY FIRED ME.
YOU NEVER TECHNICALLY QUIT.
SO I *GUESS* THAT MEANS I'M TECHNICALLY STILL AN AGENT OF S.H.I.E.L.D.
CAN I SEE HER FILES?
NOT EASY TO FIND A SHAPE-SHIFTER.
NO.
YOU'RE RIGHT TO BE PISSED.
I'D BE OUT-OF-MY-SKIN PISSED IF SHE TOOK MY PLACE IN THE WORLD.
I AM.

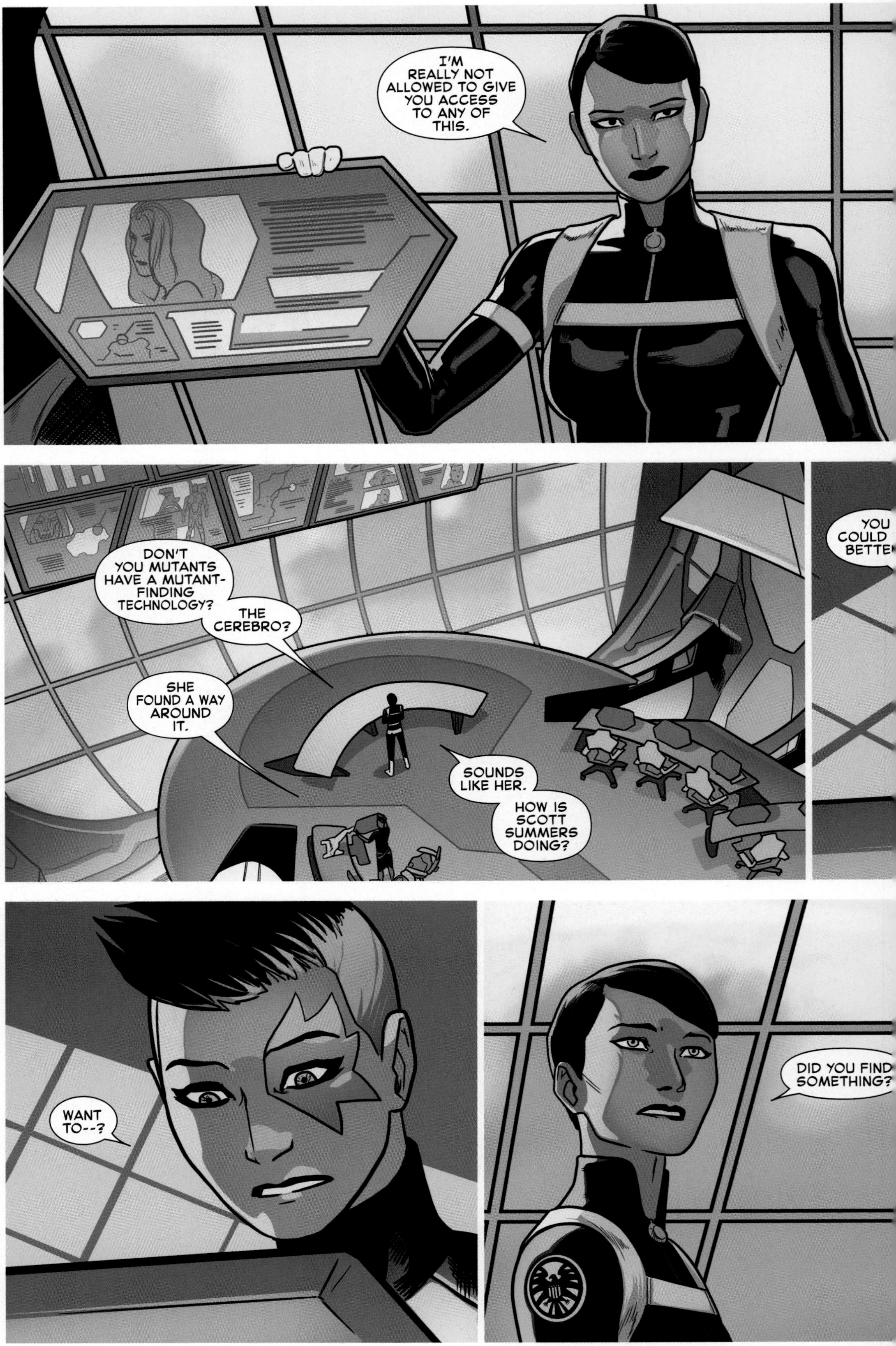
I'M REALLY NOT ALLOWED TO GIVE YOU ACCESS TO ANY OF THIS.
DON'T YOU MUTANTS HAVE A MUTANT-FINDING TECHNOLOGY?
THE CEREBRO?
SHE FOUND A WAY AROUND IT.
SOUNDS LIKE HER.
HOW IS SCOTT SUMMERS DOING?
WANT TO--?
DID YOU FIND SOMETHING?

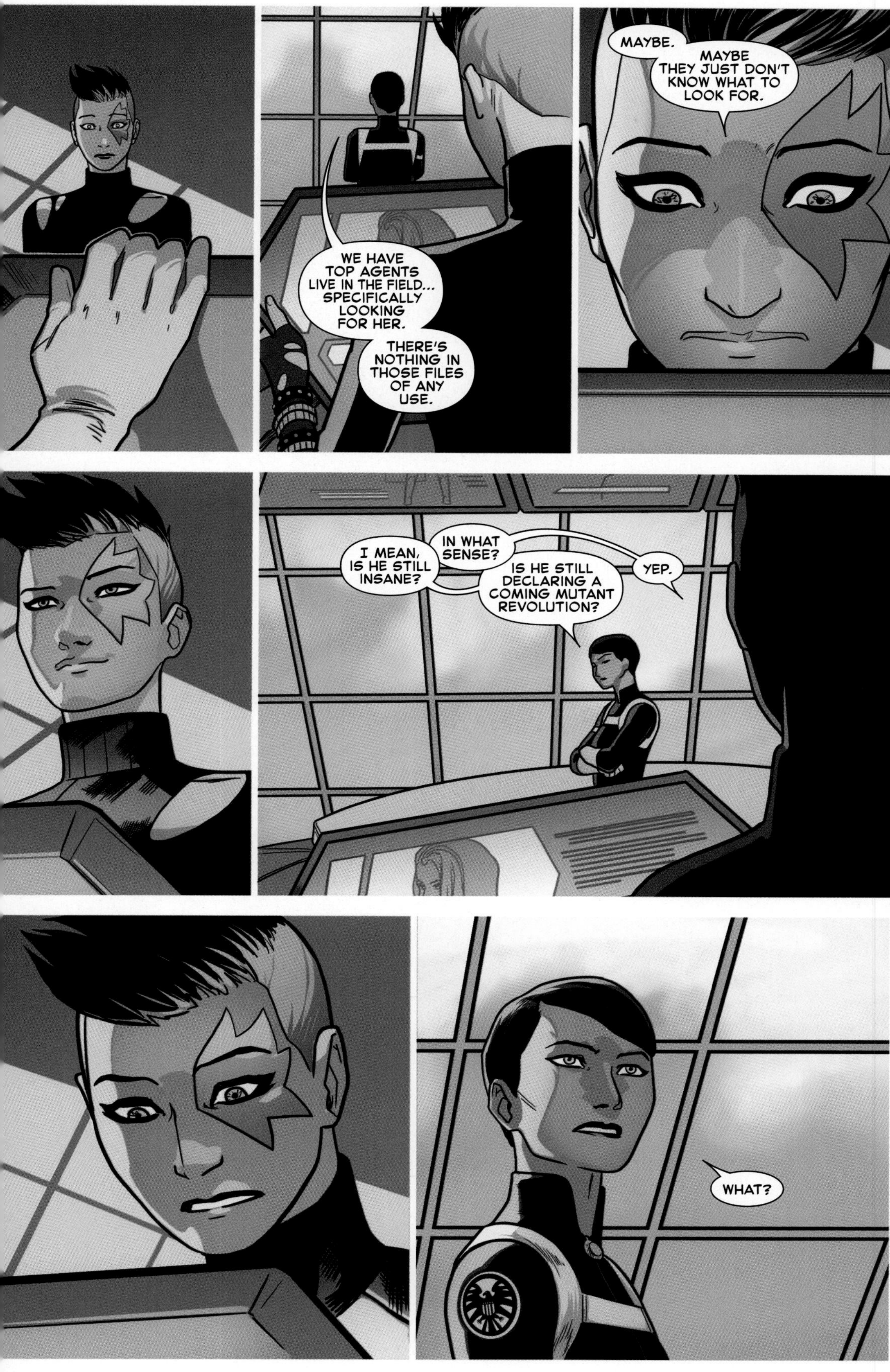
WE HAVE TOP AGENTS LIVE IN THE FIELD... SPECIFICALLY LOOKING FOR HER.
THERE'S NOTHING IN THOSE FILES OF ANY USE.
MAYBE.
MAYBE THEY JUST DON'T KNOW WHAT TO LOOK FOR.
I MEAN, IS HE STILL INSANE?
IN WHAT SENSE?
IS HE STILL DECLARING A COMING MUTANT REVOLUTION?
YEP.
WHAT?

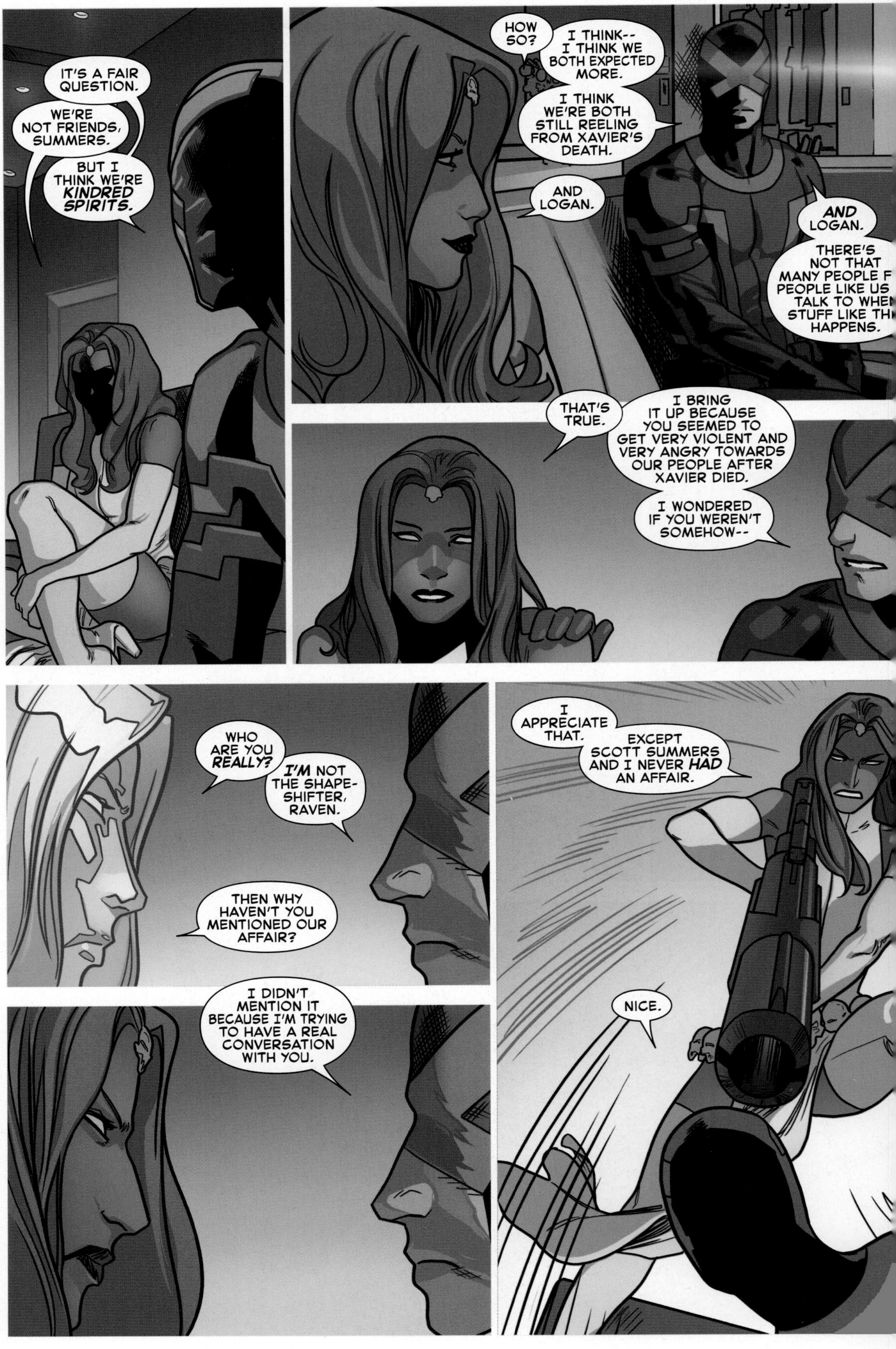

IT'S A FAIR QUESTION.
WE'RE NOT FRIENDS, SUMMERS.
BUT I THINK WE'RE *KINDRED SPIRITS.*
HOW SO?
I THINK-- I THINK WE BOTH EXPECTED MORE.
I THINK WE'RE BOTH STILL REELING FROM XAVIER'S DEATH.
AND LOGAN.
AND LOGAN.
THERE'S NOT THAT MANY PEOPLE F PEOPLE LIKE US TALK TO WHEN STUFF LIKE TH HAPPENS.
THAT'S TRUE.
I BRING IT UP BECAUSE YOU SEEMED TO GET VERY VIOLENT AND VERY ANGRY TOWARDS OUR PEOPLE AFTER XAVIER DIED.
I WONDERED IF YOU WEREN'T SOMEHOW--
WHO ARE YOU *REALLY?*
I'M NOT THE SHAPE-SHIFTER, RAVEN.
THEN WHY HAVEN'T YOU MENTIONED OUR AFFAIR?
I DIDN'T MENTION IT BECAUSE I'M TRYING TO HAVE A REAL CONVERSATION WITH YOU.
I APPRECIATE THAT.
EXCEPT SCOTT SUMMERS AND I NEVER *HAD* AN AFFAIR.
NICE.

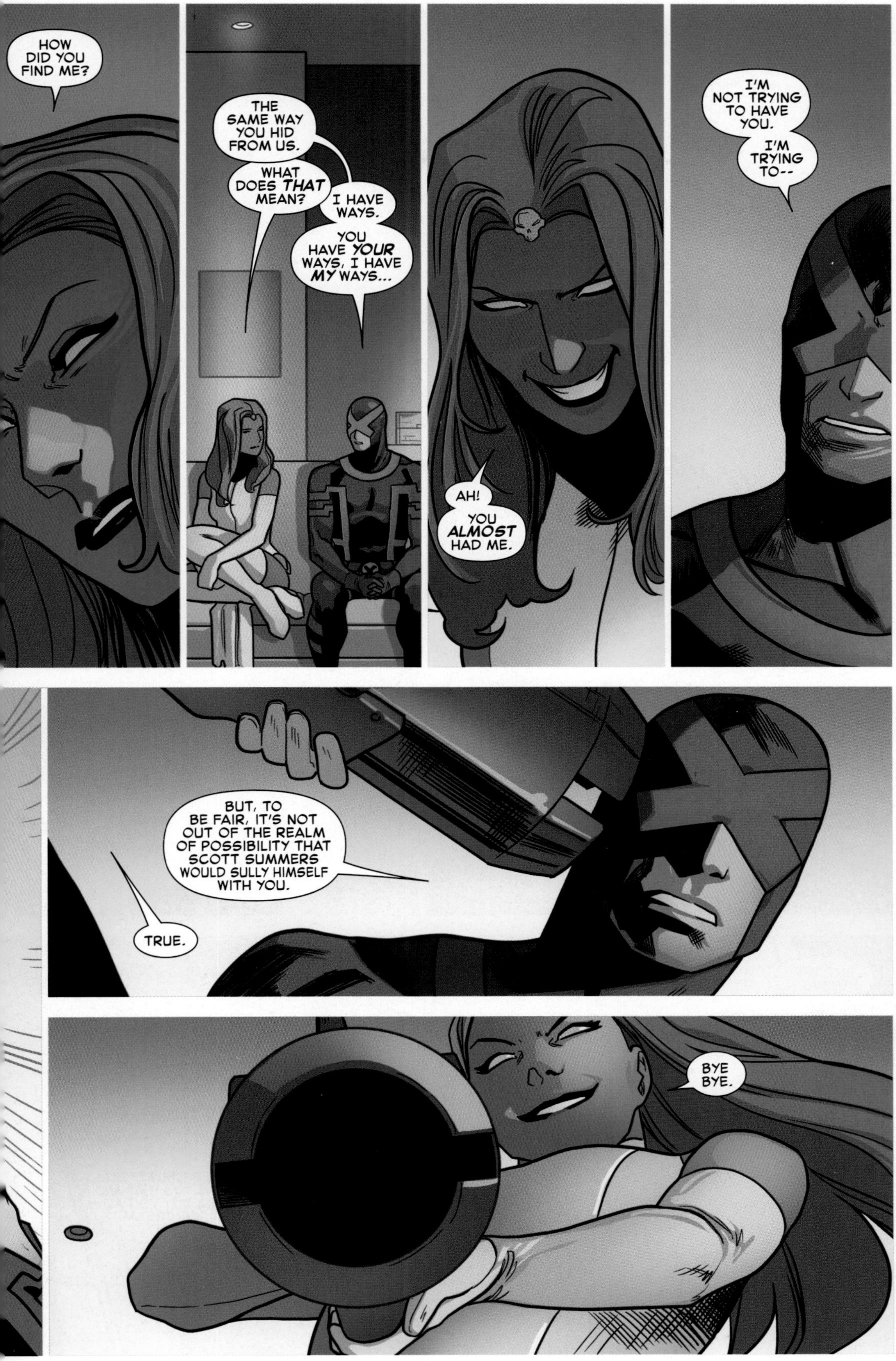
HOW DID YOU FIND ME?
THE SAME WAY YOU HID FROM US.
WHAT DOES THAT MEAN?
I HAVE WAYS.
YOU HAVE YOUR WAYS, I HAVE MY WAYS...
AH!
YOU ALMOST HAD ME.
I'M NOT TRYING TO HAVE YOU.
I'M TRYING TO--
BUT, TO BE FAIR, IT'S NOT OUT OF THE REALM OF POSSIBILITY THAT SCOTT SUMMERS WOULD SULLY HIMSELF WITH YOU.
TRUE.
BYE BYE.

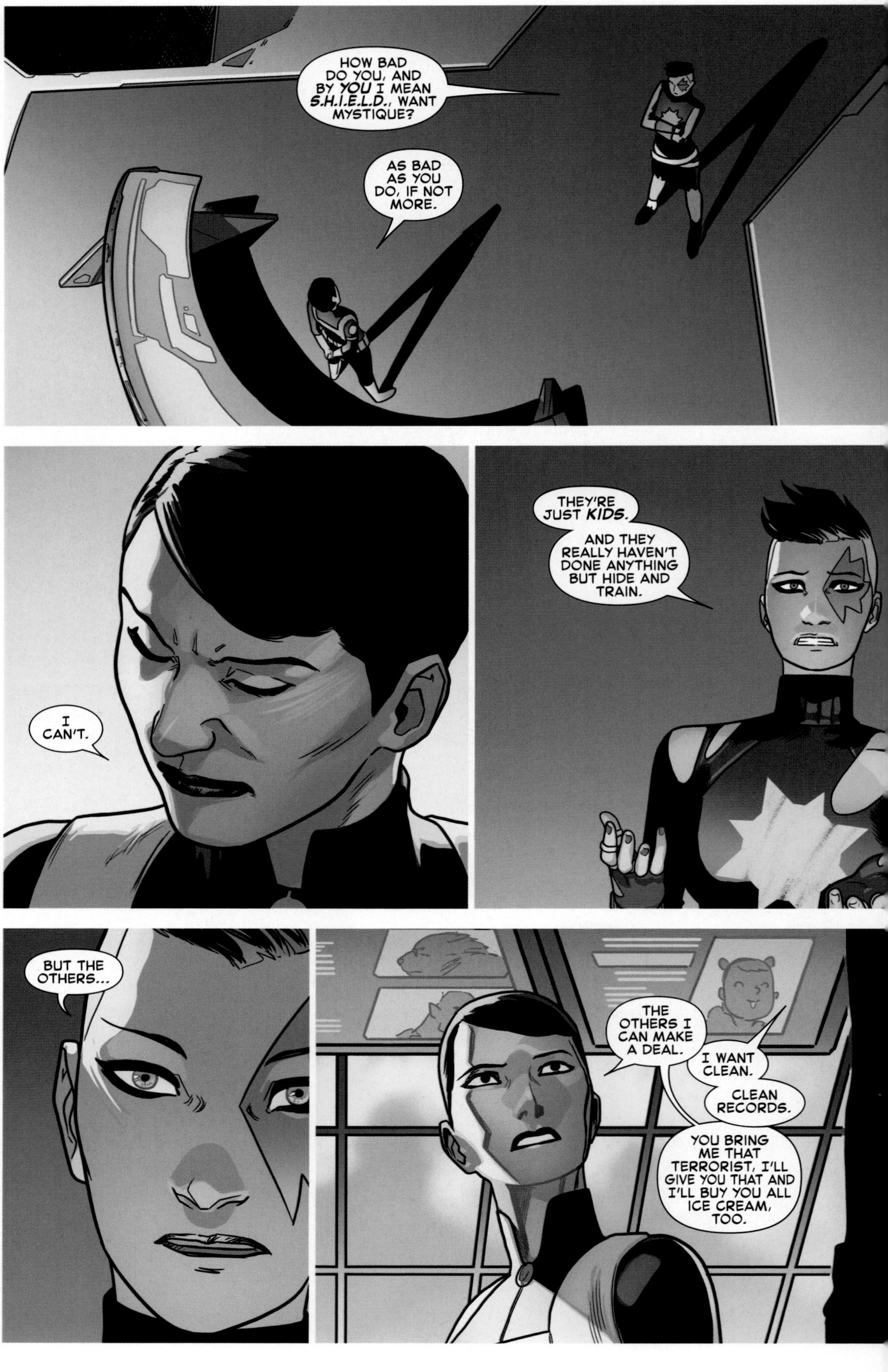
HOW BAD DO YOU, AND BY *YOU* I MEAN *S.H.I.E.L.D.*, WANT MYSTIQUE?
AS BAD AS YOU DO, IF NOT MORE.
I CAN'T.
THEY'RE JUST *KIDS.*
AND THEY REALLY HAVEN'T DONE ANYTHING BUT HIDE AND TRAIN.
BUT THE OTHERS...
THE OTHERS I CAN MAKE A DEAL.
I WANT CLEAN.
CLEAN RECORDS.
YOU BRING ME THAT TERRORIST, I'LL GIVE YOU THAT AND I'LL BUY YOU ALL ICE CREAM, TOO.

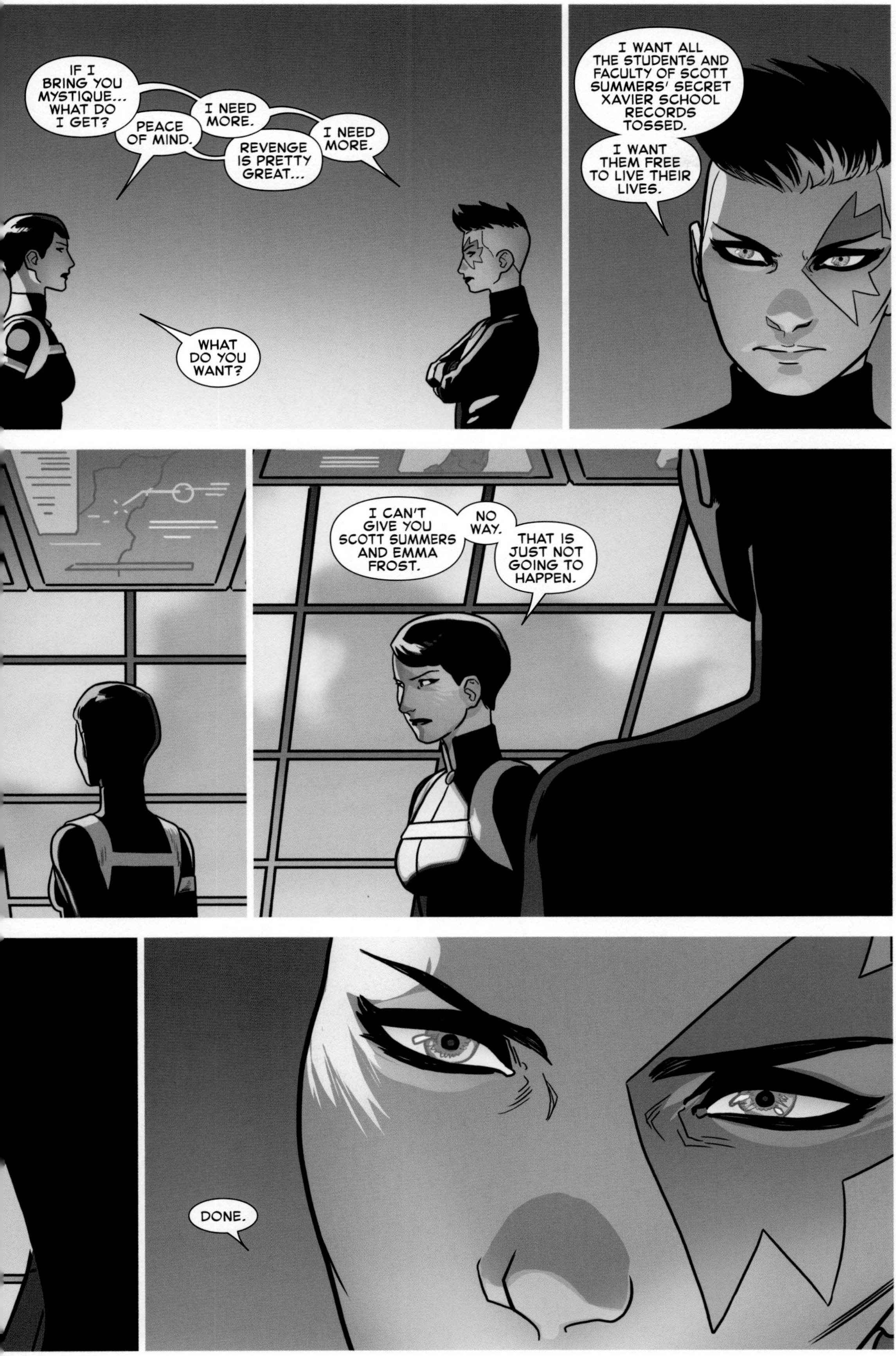
IF I BRING YOU MYSTIQUE... WHAT DO I GET?
PEACE OF MIND.
I NEED MORE.
REVENGE IS PRETTY GREAT...
I NEED MORE.
WHAT DO YOU WANT?
I WANT ALL THE STUDENTS AND FACULTY OF SCOTT SUMMERS' SECRET XAVIER SCHOOL RECORDS TOSSED.
I WANT THEM FREE TO LIVE THEIR LIVES.
I CAN'T GIVE YOU SCOTT SUMMERS AND EMMA FROST.
NO WAY.
THAT IS JUST NOT GOING TO HAPPEN.
DONE.

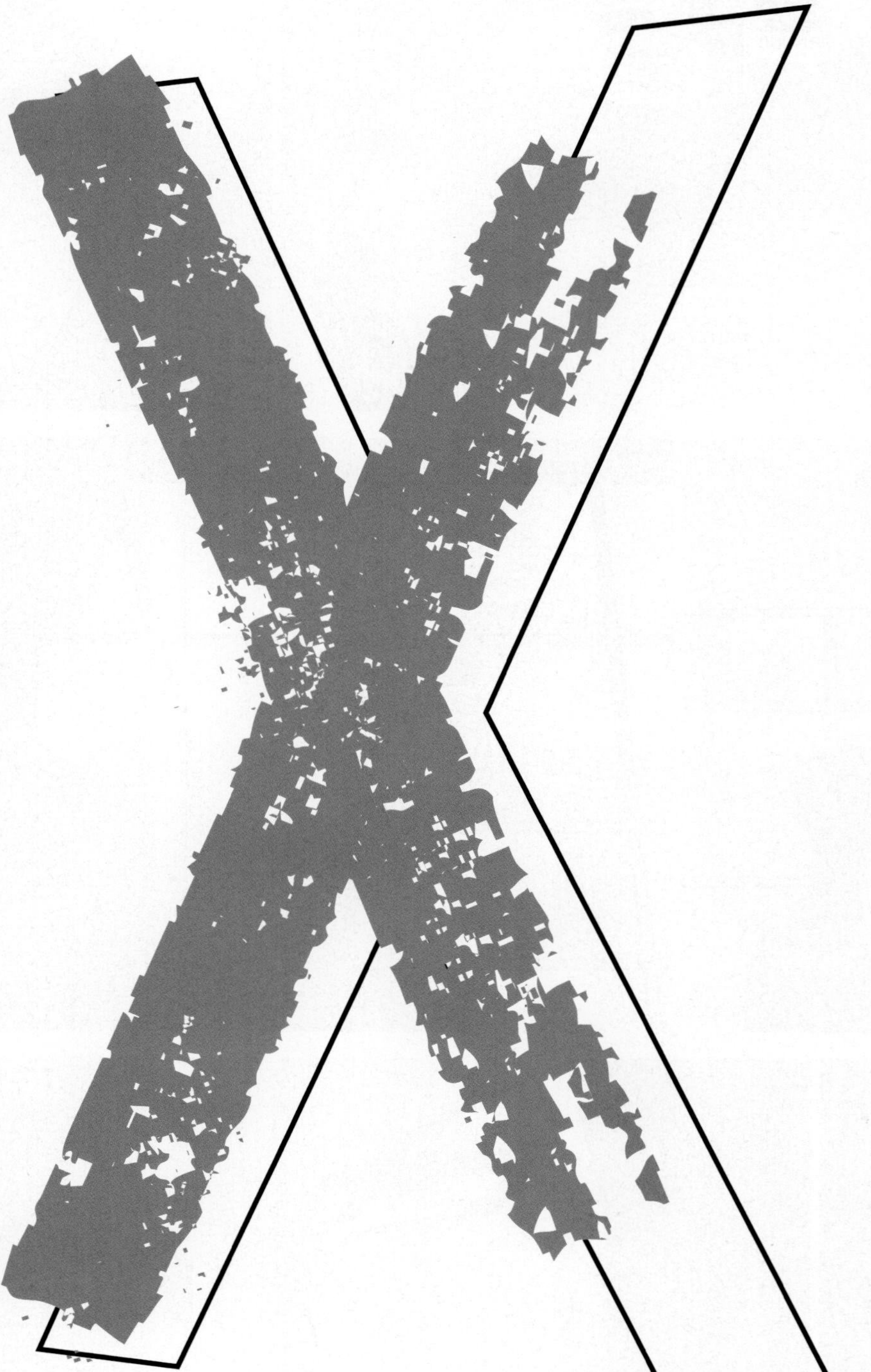

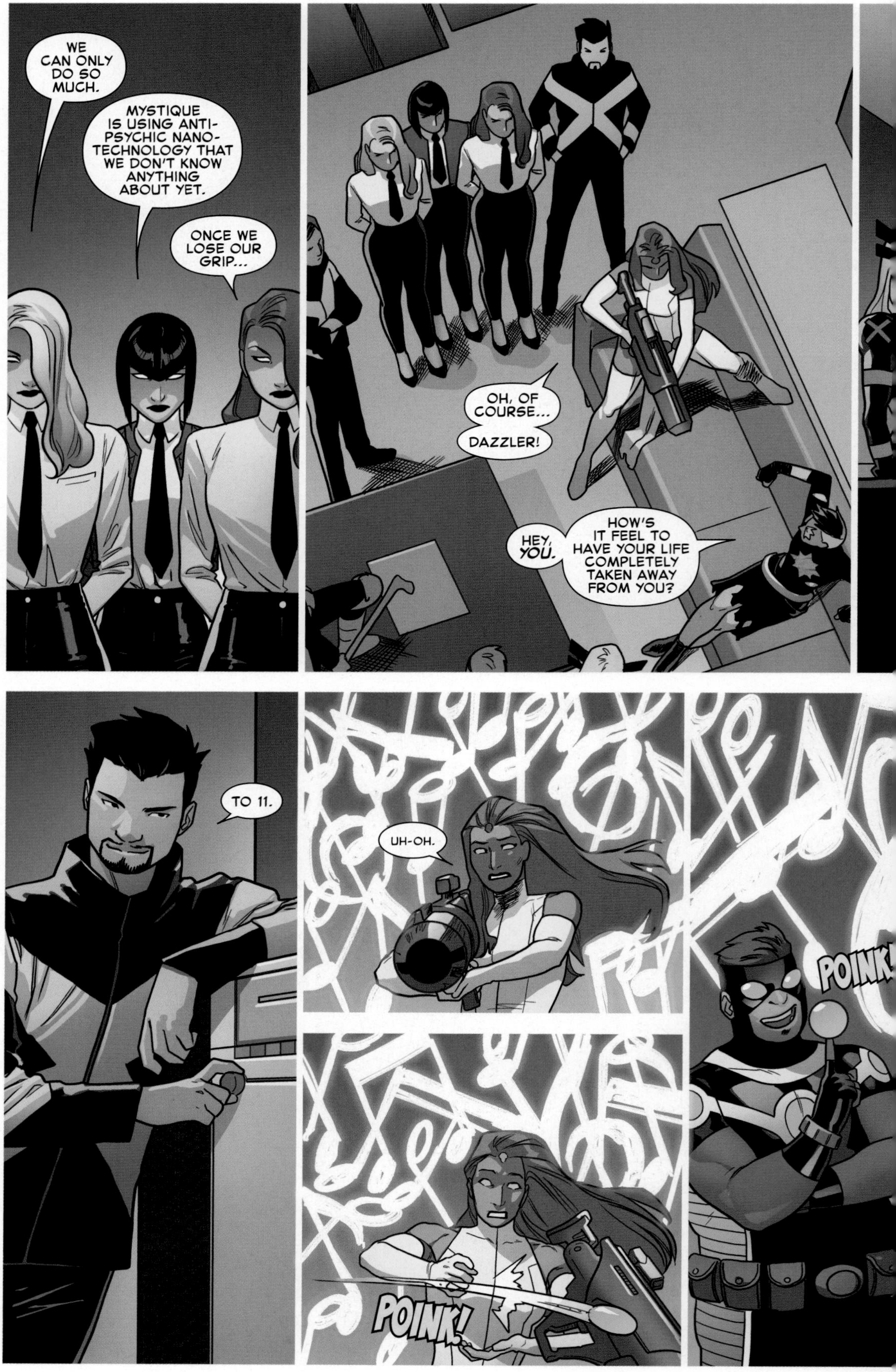
WE CAN ONLY DO SO MUCH.
MYSTIQUE IS USING ANTI-PSYCHIC NANO-TECHNOLOGY THAT WE DON'T KNOW ANYTHING ABOUT YET.
ONCE WE LOSE OUR GRIP...
OH, OF COURSE...
DAZZLER!
HEY, YOU.
HOW'S IT FEEL TO HAVE YOUR LIFE COMPLETELY TAKEN AWAY FROM YOU?
TO 11.
UH-OH.
POINK!
POINK!

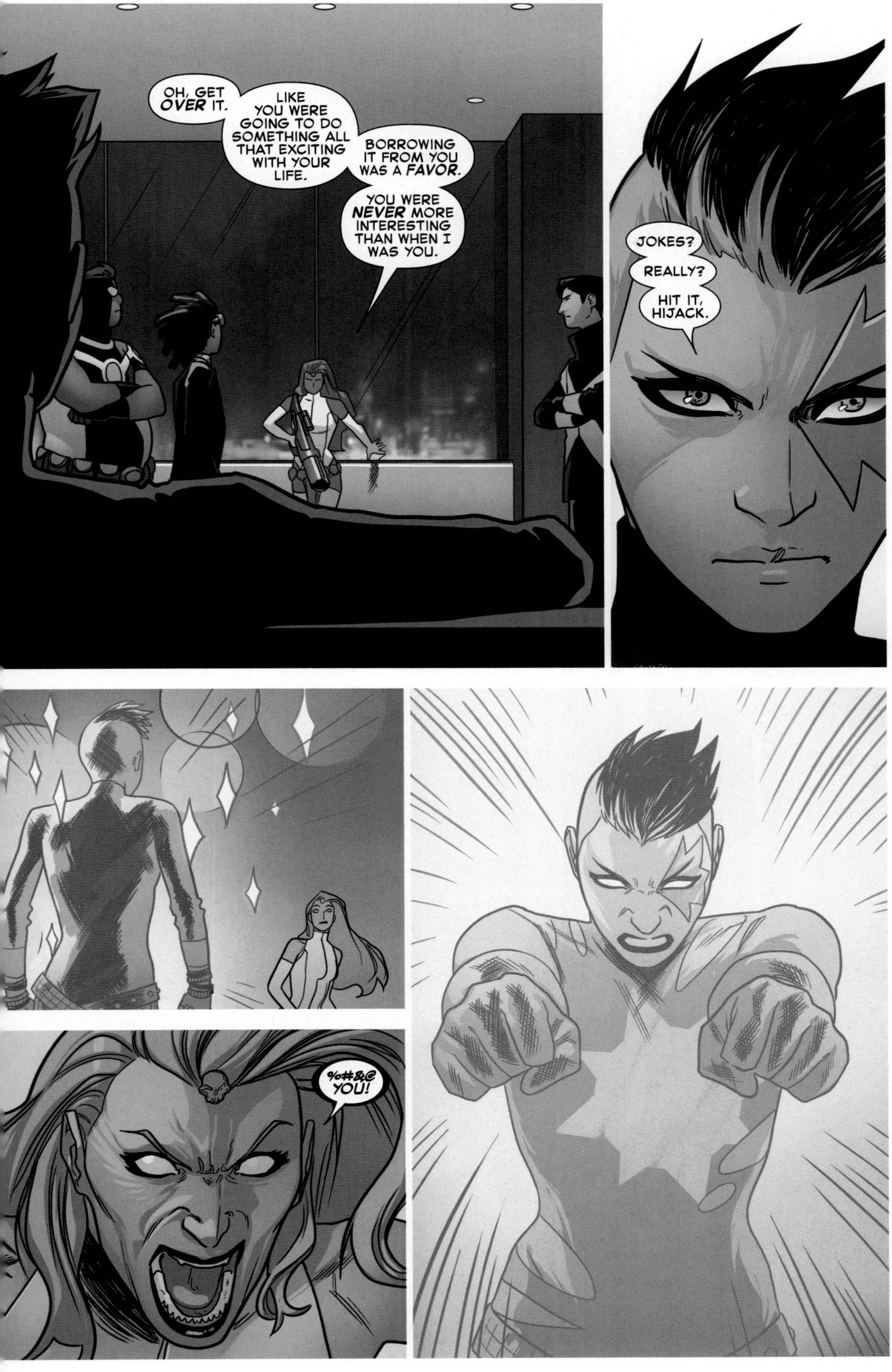
OH, GET OVER IT.
LIKE YOU WERE GOING TO DO SOMETHING ALL THAT EXCITING WITH YOUR LIFE.
BORROWING IT FROM YOU WAS A FAVOR.
YOU WERE NEVER MORE INTERESTING THAN WHEN I WAS YOU.
JOKES?
REALLY?
HIT IT, HIJACK.
%#&@ YOU!

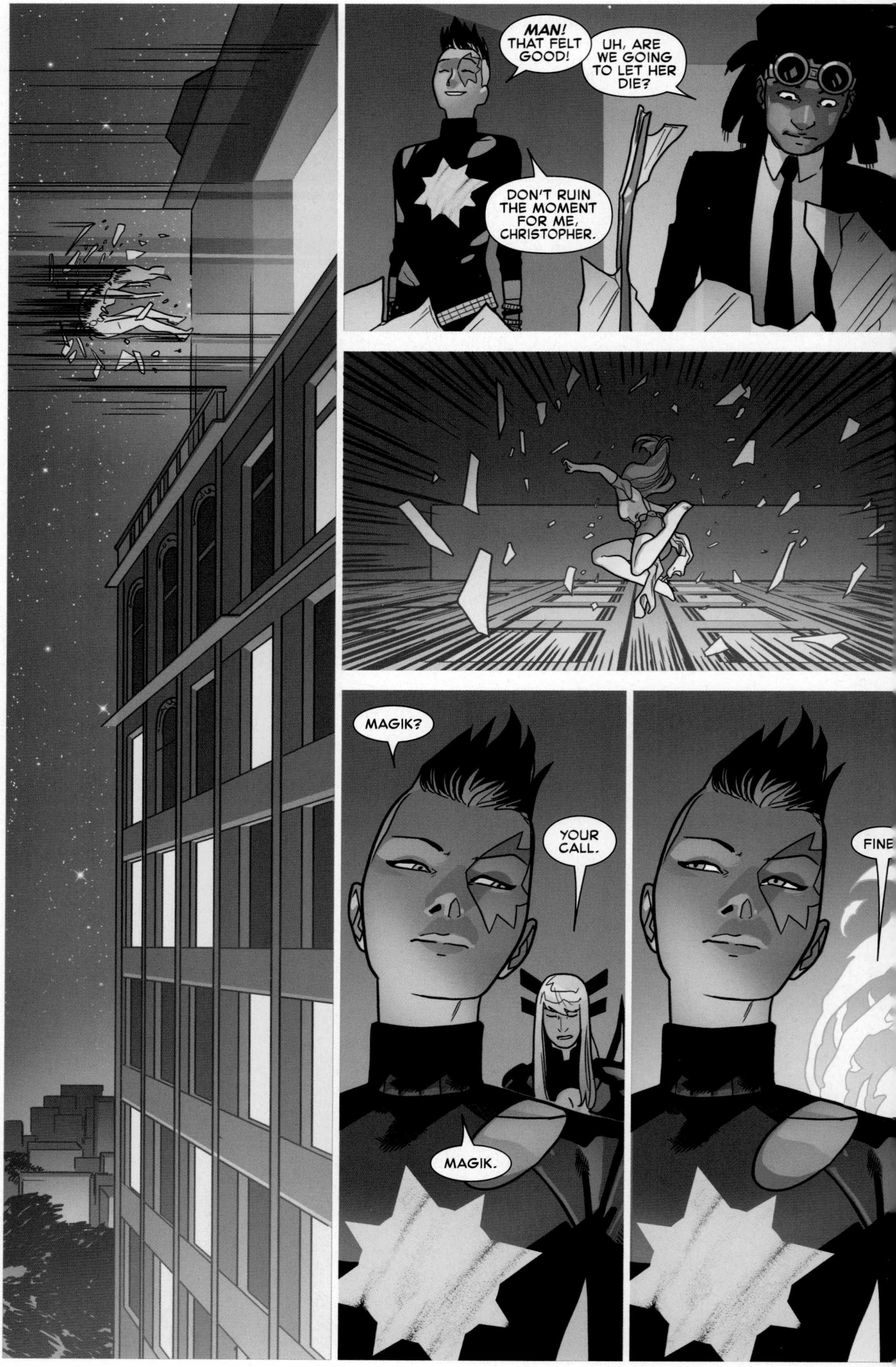
MAN! THAT FELT GOOD!
UH, ARE WE GOING TO LET HER DIE?
DON'T RUIN THE MOMENT FOR ME, CHRISTOPHER.
MAGIK?
YOUR CALL.
MAGIK.
FINE

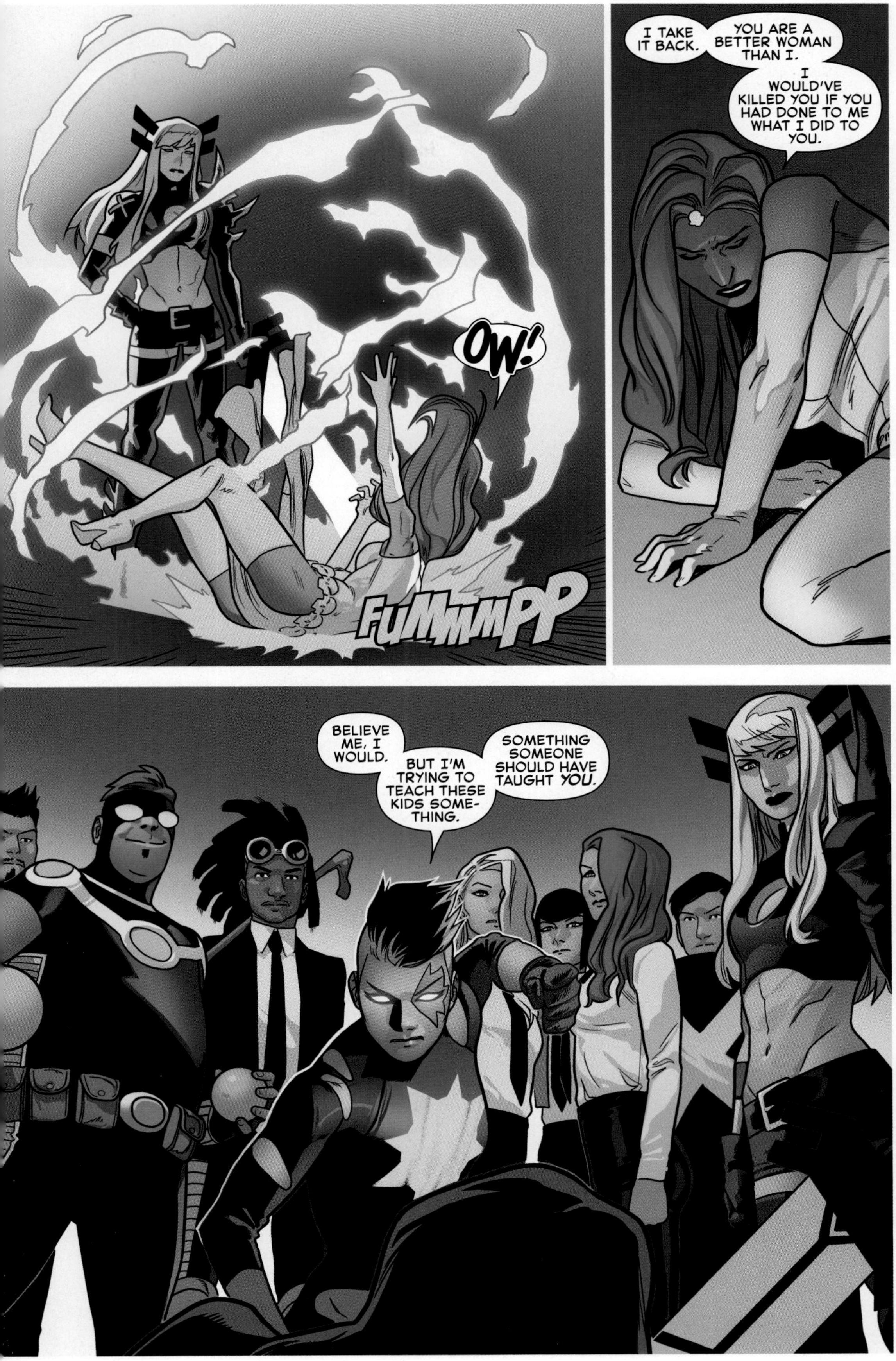
OW!
FUMMMMPP
I TAKE IT BACK.
YOU ARE A BETTER WOMAN THAN I.
I WOULD'VE KILLED YOU IF YOU HAD DONE TO ME WHAT I DID TO YOU.
BELIEVE ME, I WOULD.
BUT I'M TRYING TO TEACH THESE KIDS SOME-THING.
SOMETHING SOMEONE SHOULD HAVE TAUGHT YOU.

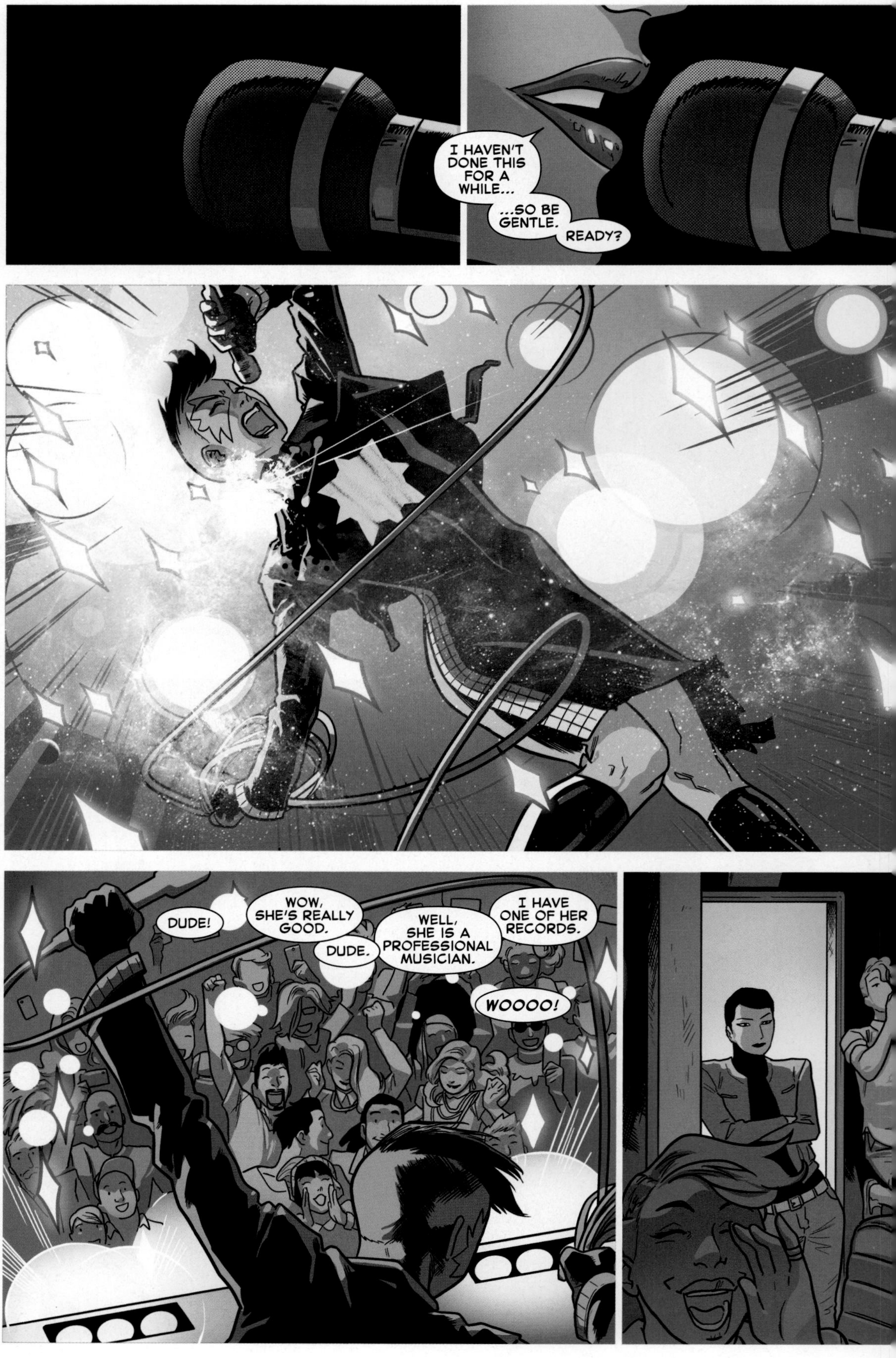

I HAVEN'T DONE THIS FOR A WHILE...
...SO BE GENTLE.
READY?
DUDE!
WOW, SHE'S REALLY GOOD.
DUDE.
WELL, SHE IS A PROFESSIONAL MUSICIAN.
I HAVE ONE OF HER RECORDS.
WOOOO!

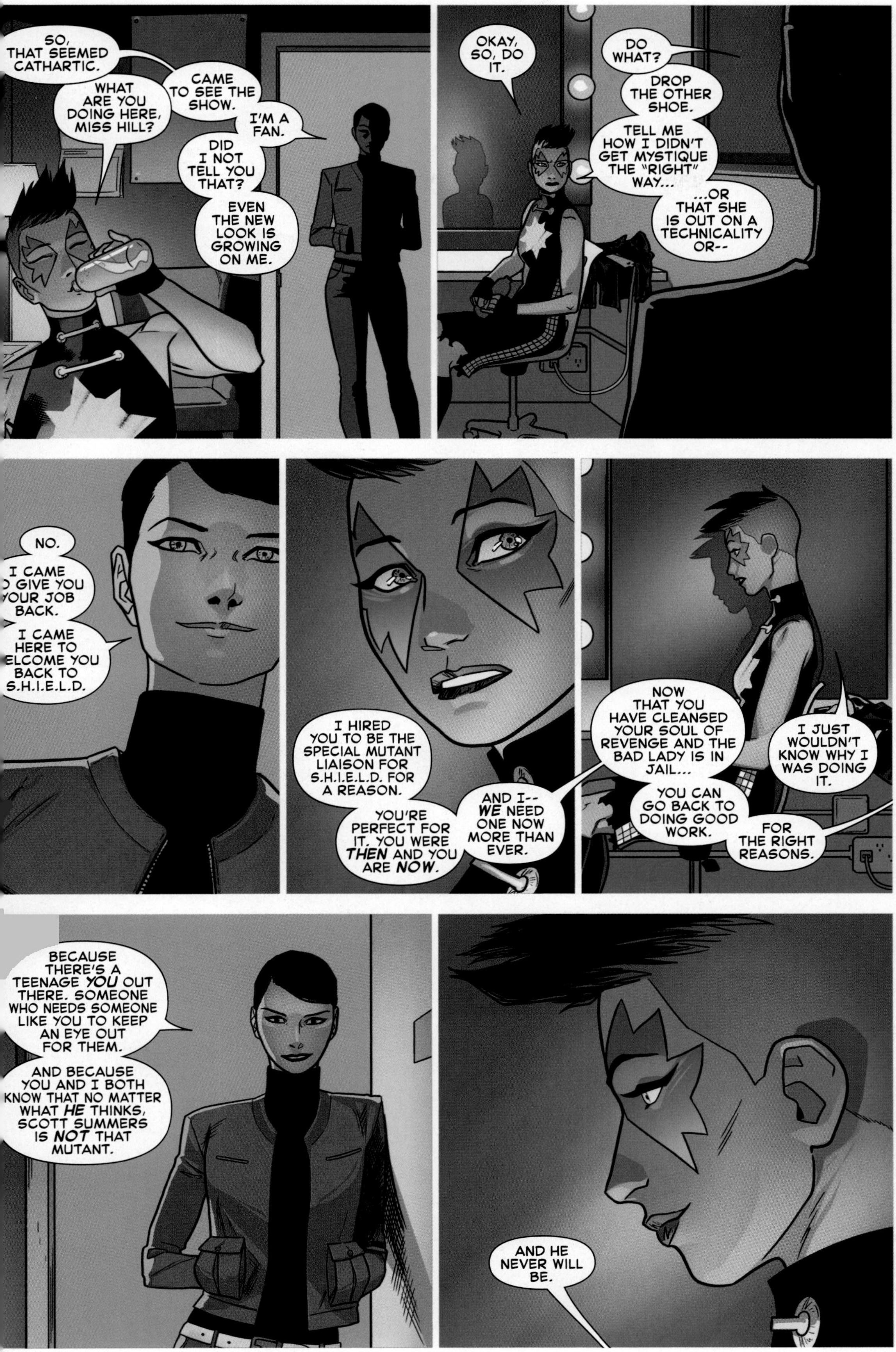

SO, THAT SEEMED CATHARTIC.
WHAT ARE YOU DOING HERE, MISS HILL?
CAME TO SEE THE SHOW.
I'M A FAN.
DID I NOT TELL YOU THAT?
EVEN THE NEW LOOK IS GROWING ON ME.
OKAY, SO, DO IT.
DO WHAT?
DROP THE OTHER SHOE.
TELL ME HOW I DIDN'T GET MYSTIQUE THE "RIGHT" WAY...
...OR THAT SHE IS OUT ON A TECHNICALITY OR--
NO.
I CAME O GIVE YOU YOUR JOB BACK.
I CAME HERE TO ELCOME YOU BACK TO S.H.I.E.L.D.
I HIRED YOU TO BE THE SPECIAL MUTANT LIAISON FOR S.H.I.E.L.D. FOR A REASON.
YOU'RE PERFECT FOR IT. YOU WERE THEN AND YOU ARE NOW.
AND I-- WE NEED ONE NOW MORE THAN EVER.
NOW THAT YOU HAVE CLEANSED YOUR SOUL OF REVENGE AND THE BAD LADY IS IN JAIL...
YOU CAN GO BACK TO DOING GOOD WORK.
I JUST WOULDN'T KNOW WHY I WAS DOING IT.
FOR THE RIGHT REASONS.
BECAUSE THERE'S A TEENAGE YOU OUT THERE. SOMEONE WHO NEEDS SOMEONE LIKE YOU TO KEEP AN EYE OUT FOR THEM.
AND BECAUSE YOU AND I BOTH KNOW THAT NO MATTER WHAT HE THINKS, SCOTT SUMMERS IS NOT THAT MUTANT.
AND HE NEVER WILL BE.

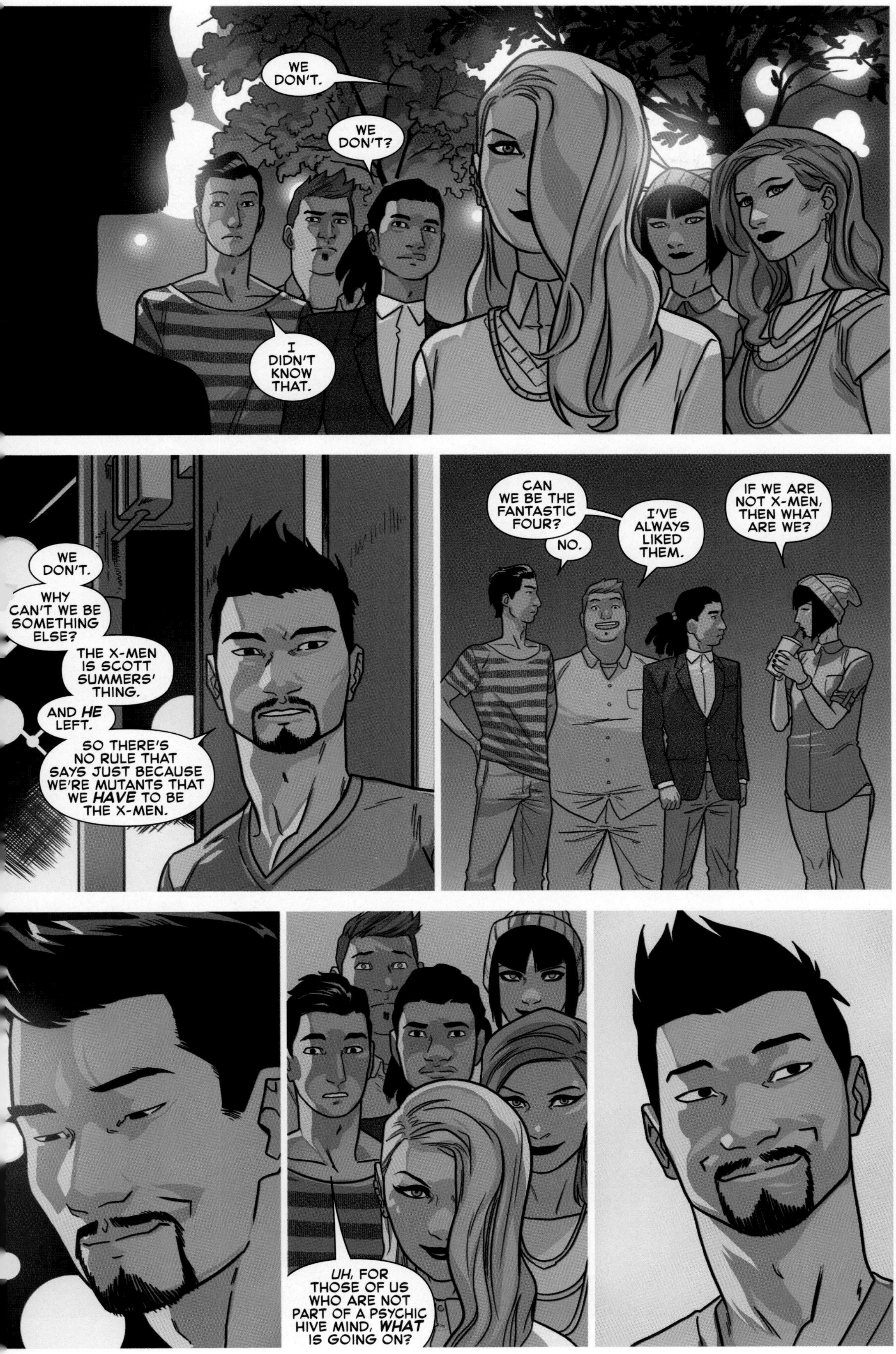
WE DON'T.
WE DON'T?
I DIDN'T KNOW THAT.
WE DON'T.
WHY CAN'T WE BE SOMETHING ELSE?
THE X-MEN IS SCOTT SUMMERS' THING.
AND *HE* LEFT.
SO THERE'S NO RULE THAT SAYS JUST BECAUSE WE'RE MUTANTS THAT WE *HAVE* TO BE THE X-MEN.
CAN WE BE THE FANTASTIC FOUR?
NO.
I'VE ALWAYS LIKED THEM.
IF WE ARE NOT X-MEN, THEN WHAT ARE WE?
UH, FOR THOSE OF US WHO ARE NOT PART OF A PSYCHIC HIVE MIND, *WHAT* IS GOING ON?

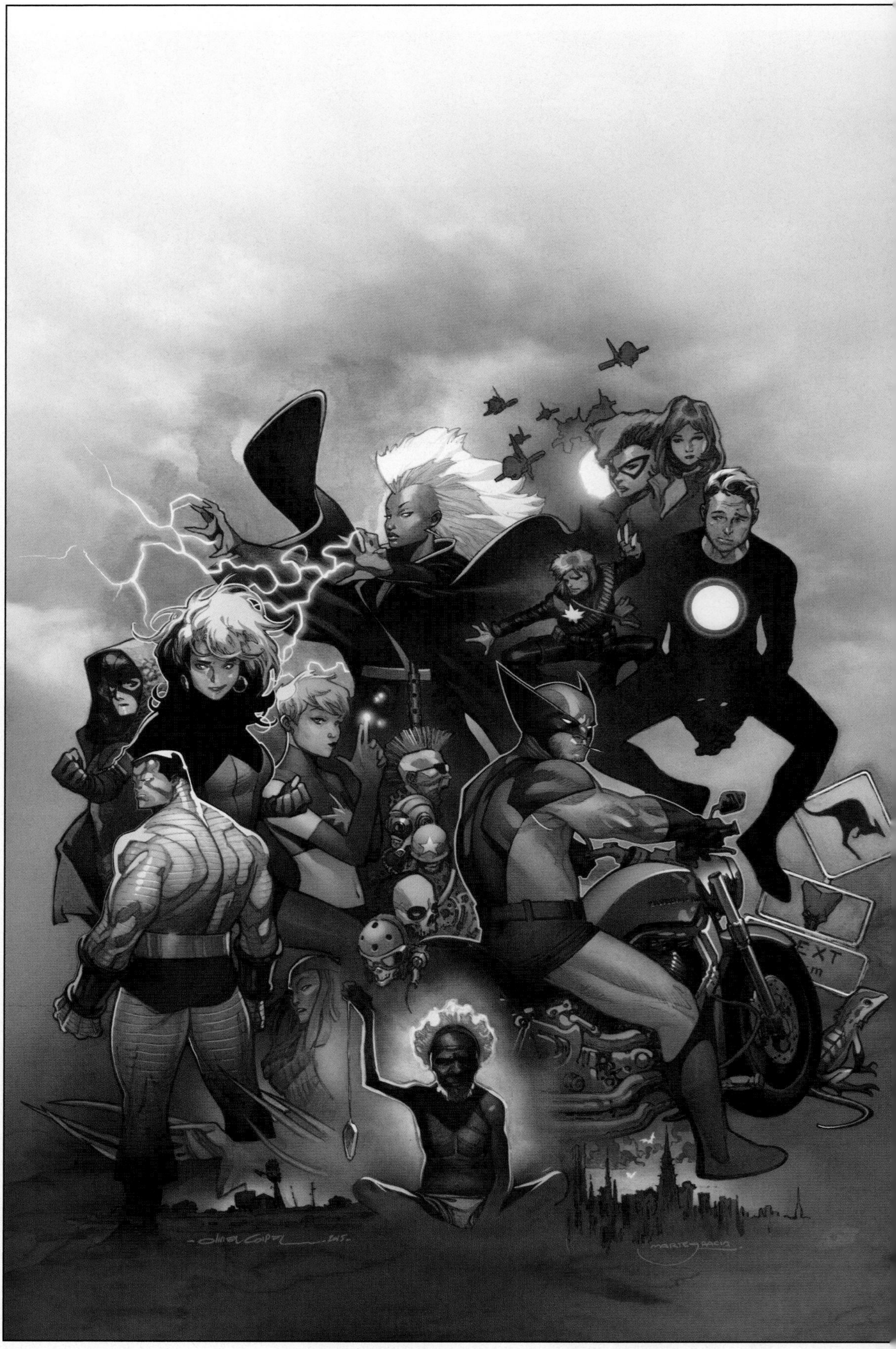

UNCANNY X-MEN #600 VARIANT
BY OLIVIER COIPEL & MARTE GRACIA

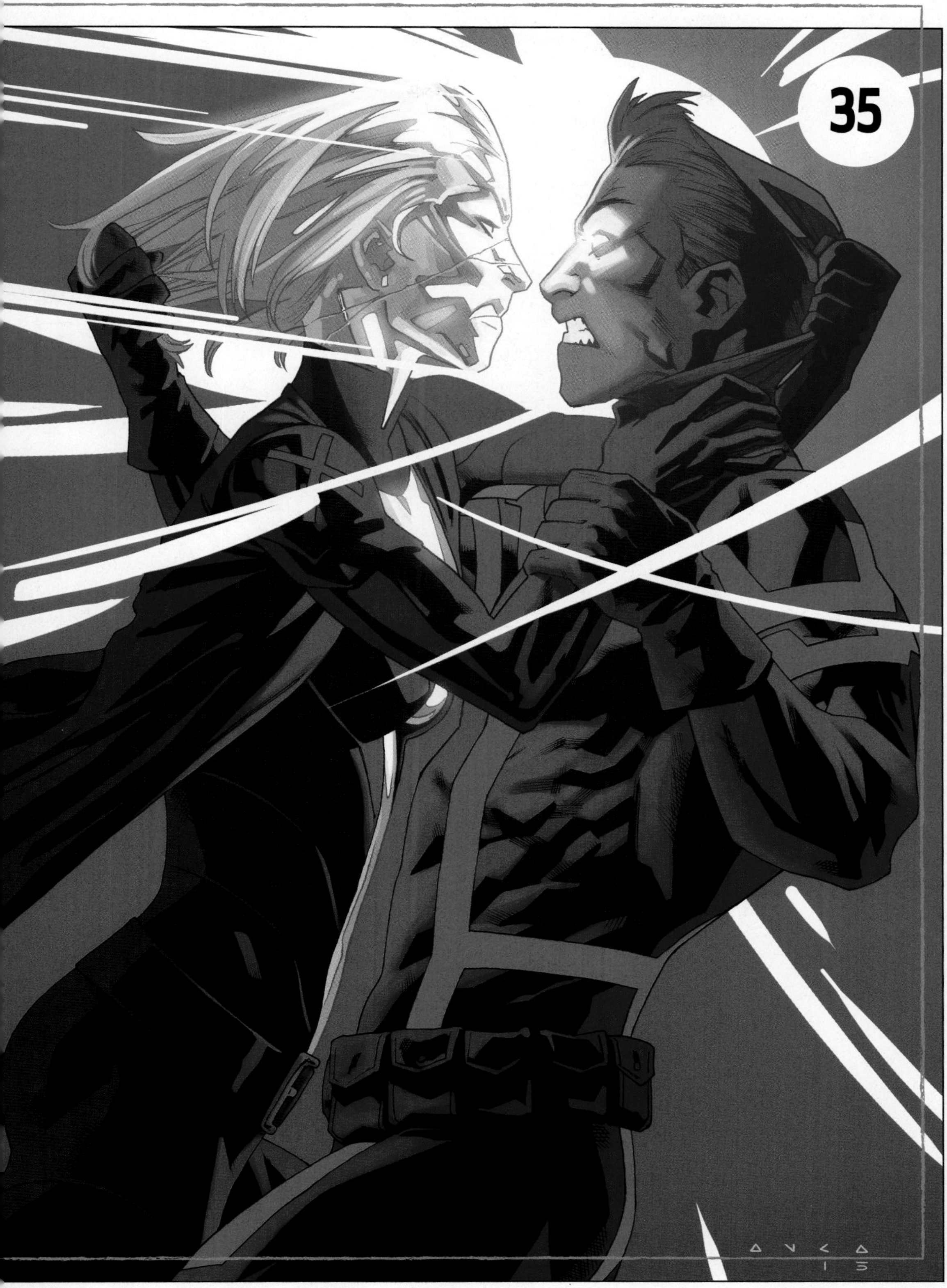
35

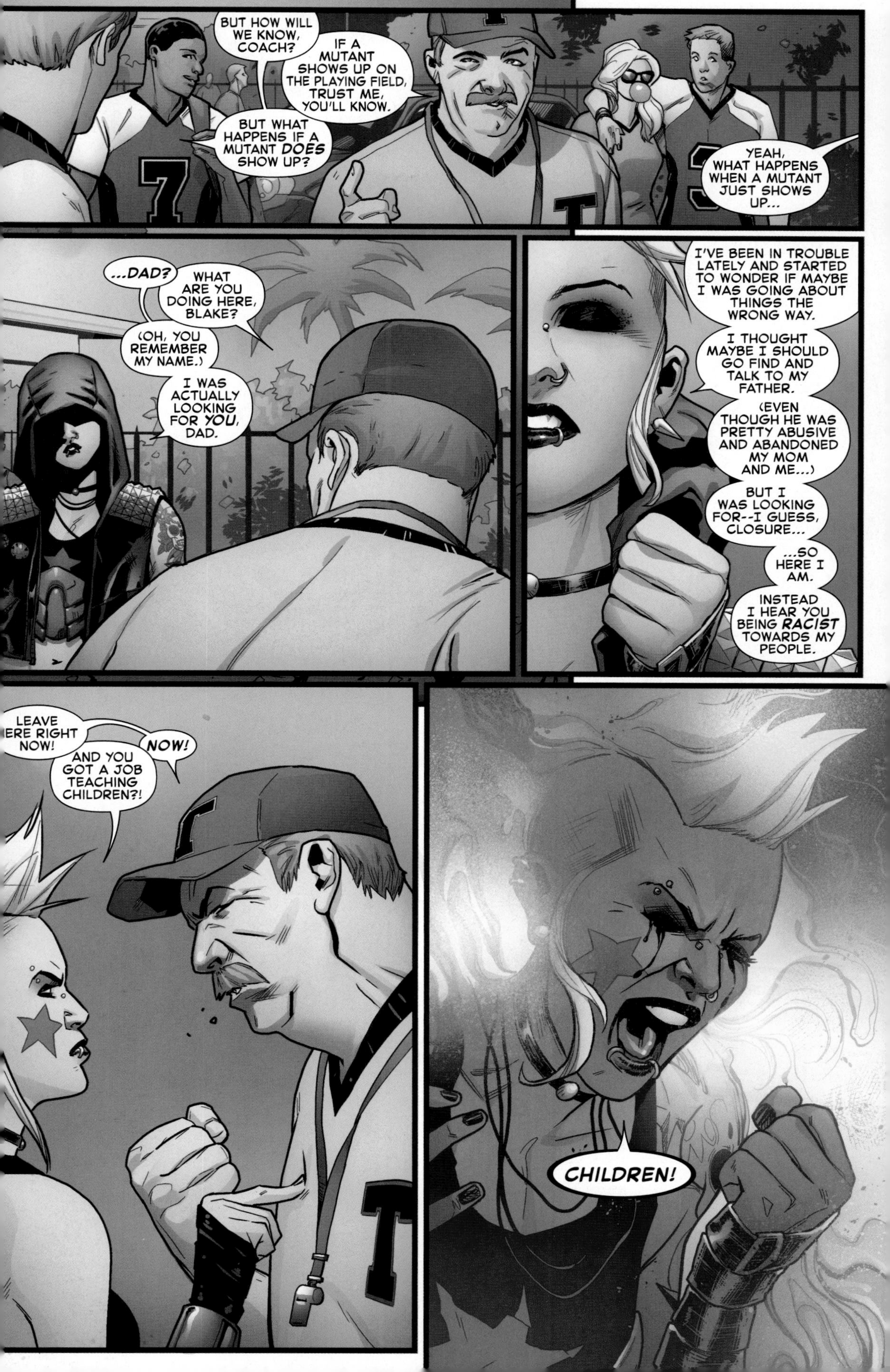

BUT HOW WILL WE KNOW, COACH?
IF A MUTANT SHOWS UP ON THE PLAYING FIELD, TRUST ME, YOU'LL KNOW.
BUT WHAT HAPPENS IF A MUTANT DOES SHOW UP?
YEAH, WHAT HAPPENS WHEN A MUTANT JUST SHOWS UP...
...DAD?
WHAT ARE YOU DOING HERE, BLAKE?
(OH, YOU REMEMBER MY NAME.)
I WAS ACTUALLY LOOKING FOR YOU, DAD.
I'VE BEEN IN TROUBLE LATELY AND STARTED TO WONDER IF MAYBE I WAS GOING ABOUT THINGS THE WRONG WAY.
I THOUGHT MAYBE I SHOULD GO FIND AND TALK TO MY FATHER.
(EVEN THOUGH HE WAS PRETTY ABUSIVE AND ABANDONED MY MOM AND ME...)
BUT I WAS LOOKING FOR--I GUESS, CLOSURE...
...SO HERE I AM.
INSTEAD I HEAR YOU BEING RACIST TOWARDS MY PEOPLE.
LEAVE ERE RIGHT NOW!
NOW!
AND YOU GOT A JOB TEACHING CHILDREN?!
CHILDREN!

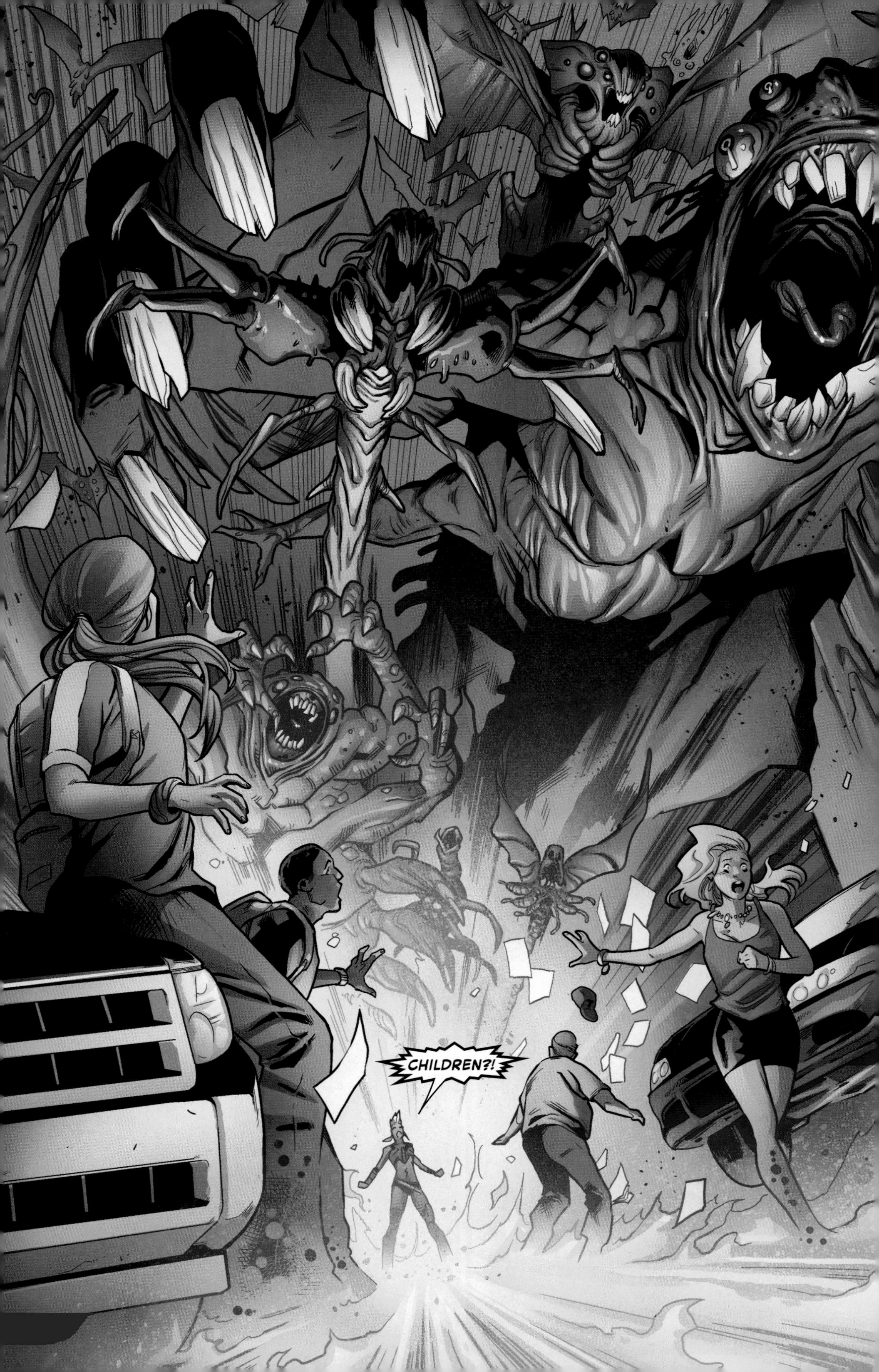
CHILDREN?!

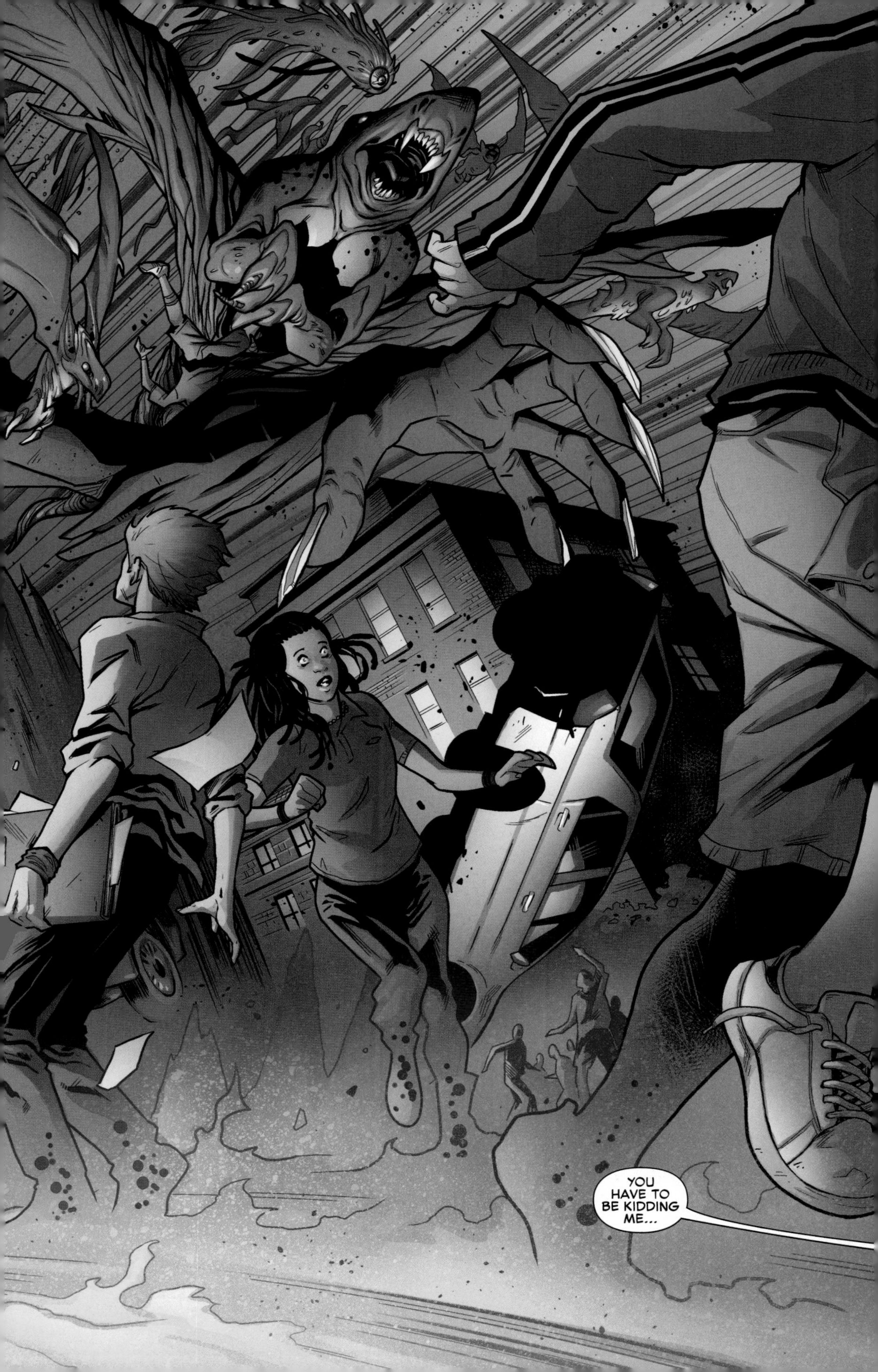
YOU HAVE TO BE KIDDING ME...

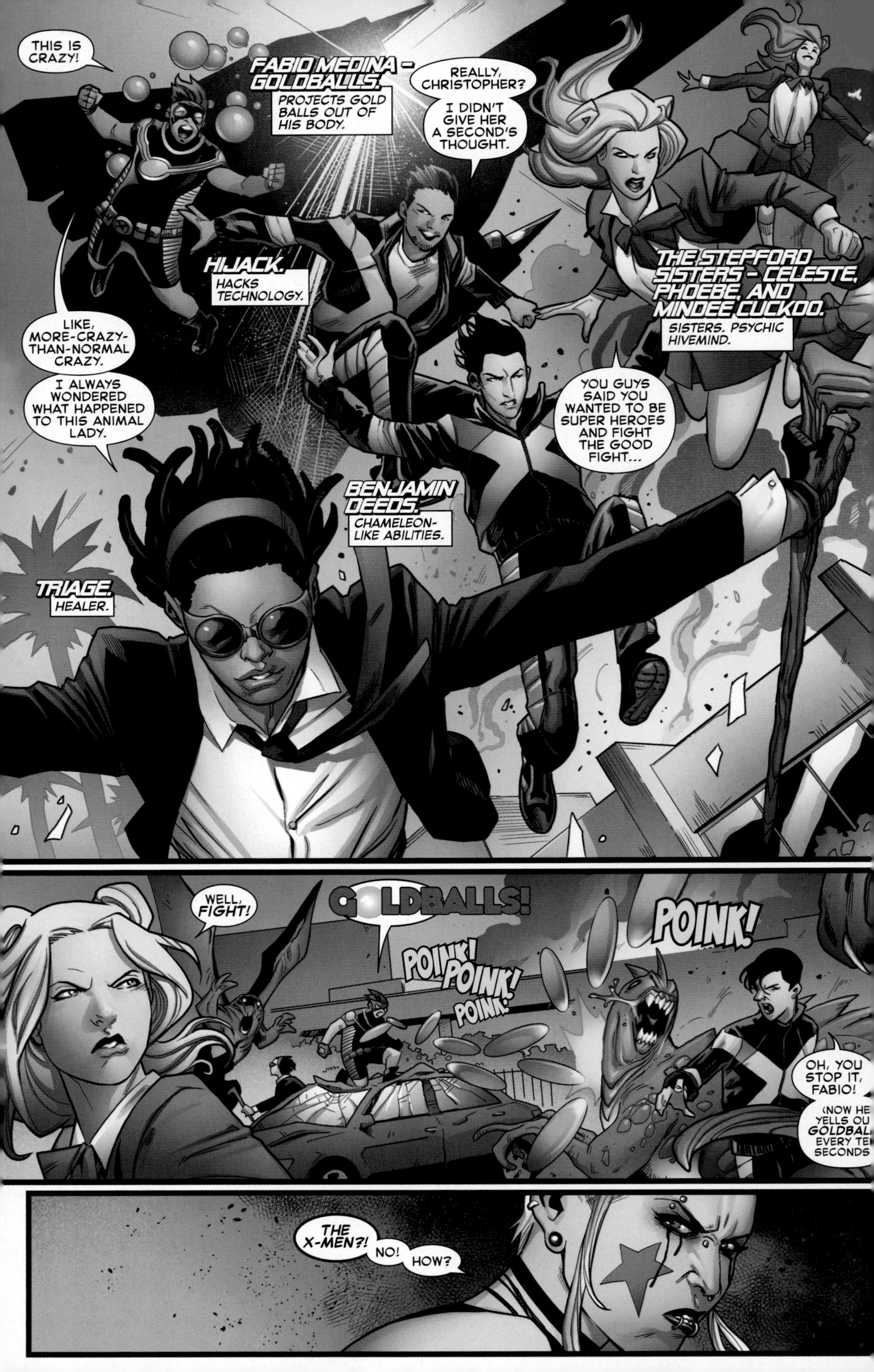
THIS IS CRAZY!
FABIO MEDINA - GOLDBALLS.
PROJECTS GOLD BALLS OUT OF HIS BODY.
REALLY, CHRISTOPHER?
I DIDN'T GIVE HER A SECOND'S THOUGHT.
HIJACK.
HACKS TECHNOLOGY.
THE STEPFORD SISTERS - CELESTE, PHOEBE, AND MINDEE CUCKOO.
SISTERS. PSYCHIC HIVEMIND.
LIKE, MORE-CRAZY-THAN-NORMAL CRAZY.
I ALWAYS WONDERED WHAT HAPPENED TO THIS ANIMAL LADY.
YOU GUYS SAID YOU WANTED TO BE SUPER HEROES AND FIGHT THE GOOD FIGHT...
BENJAMIN DEEDS.
CHAMELEON-LIKE ABILITIES.
TRIAGE.
HEALER.
WELL, FIGHT!
GOLDBALLS!
POINK!
POINK!
POINK!
POINK!
OH, YOU STOP IT, FABIO!
THE X-MEN?!
NO!
HOW?

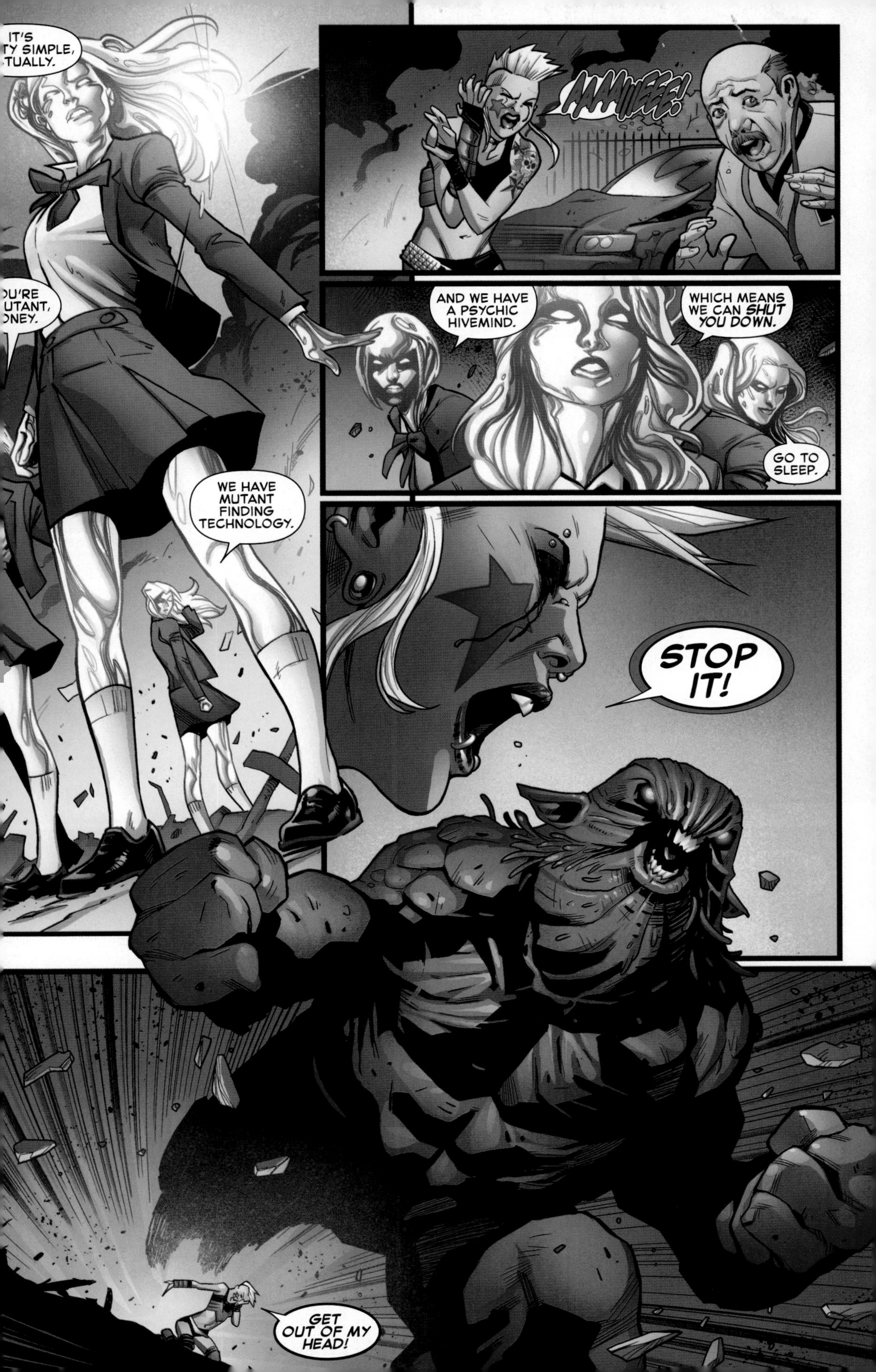
IT'S
TY SIMPLE,
TUALLY.
OU'RE
UTANT,
ONEY.
WE HAVE MUTANT FINDING TECHNOLOGY.
AAAAIIIEEE!
AND WE HAVE A PSYCHIC HIVEMIND.
WHICH MEANS WE CAN SHUT YOU DOWN.
GO TO SLEEP.
STOP IT!
GET OUT OF MY HEAD!

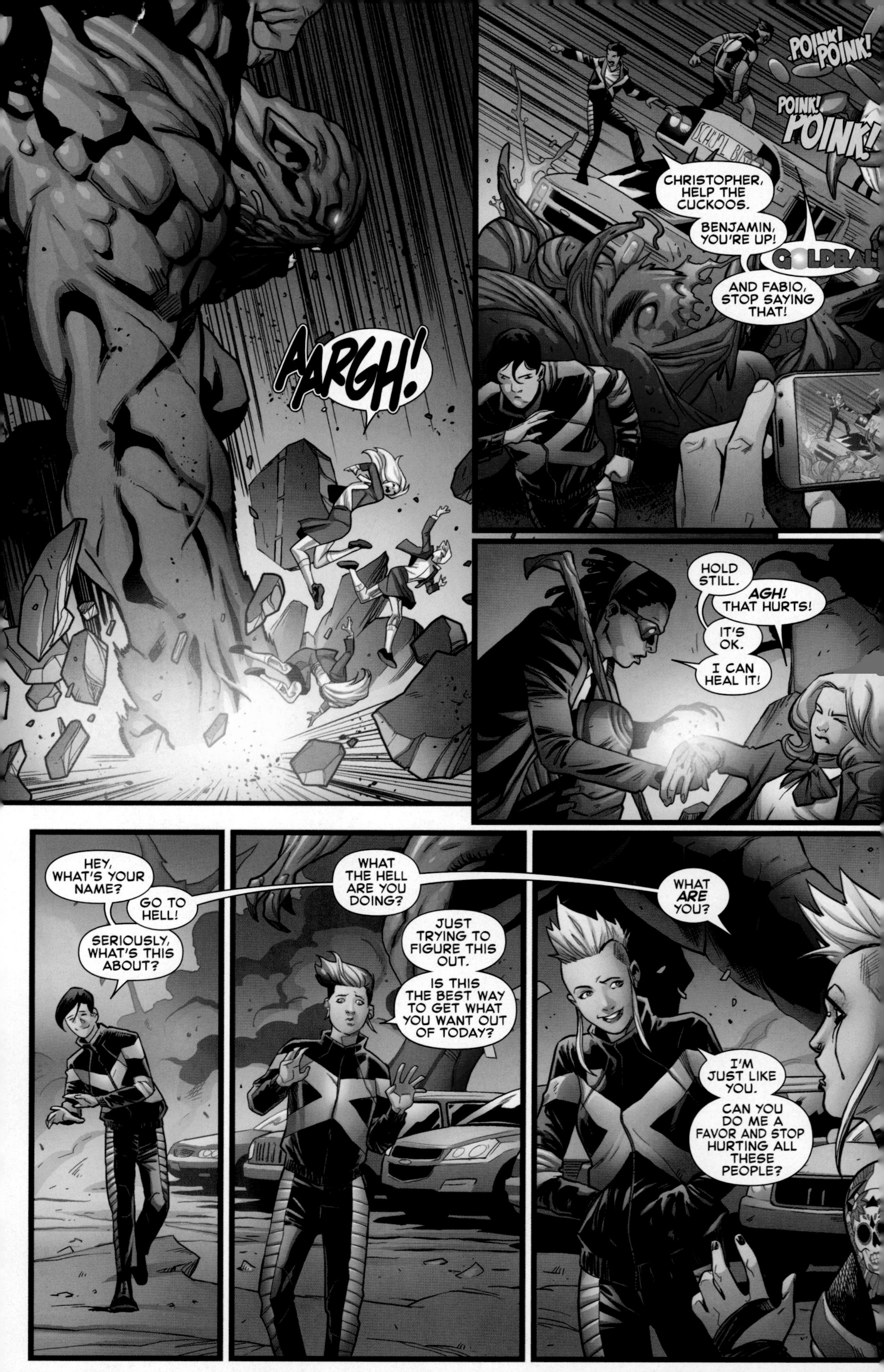
AARGH!
POINK! POINK!
POINK! POINK!
CHRISTOPHER, HELP THE CUCKOOS.
BENJAMIN, YOU'RE UP!
AND FABIO, STOP SAYING THAT!
HOLD STILL.
AGH! THAT HURTS!
IT'S OK.
I CAN HEAL IT!
HEY, WHAT'S YOUR NAME?
GO TO HELL!
SERIOUSLY, WHAT'S THIS ABOUT?
WHAT THE HELL ARE YOU DOING?
WHAT ARE YOU?
JUST TRYING TO FIGURE THIS OUT.
IS THIS THE BEST WAY TO GET WHAT YOU WANT OUT OF TODAY?
I'M JUST LIKE YOU.
CAN YOU DO ME A FAVOR AND STOP HURTING ALL THESE PEOPLE?

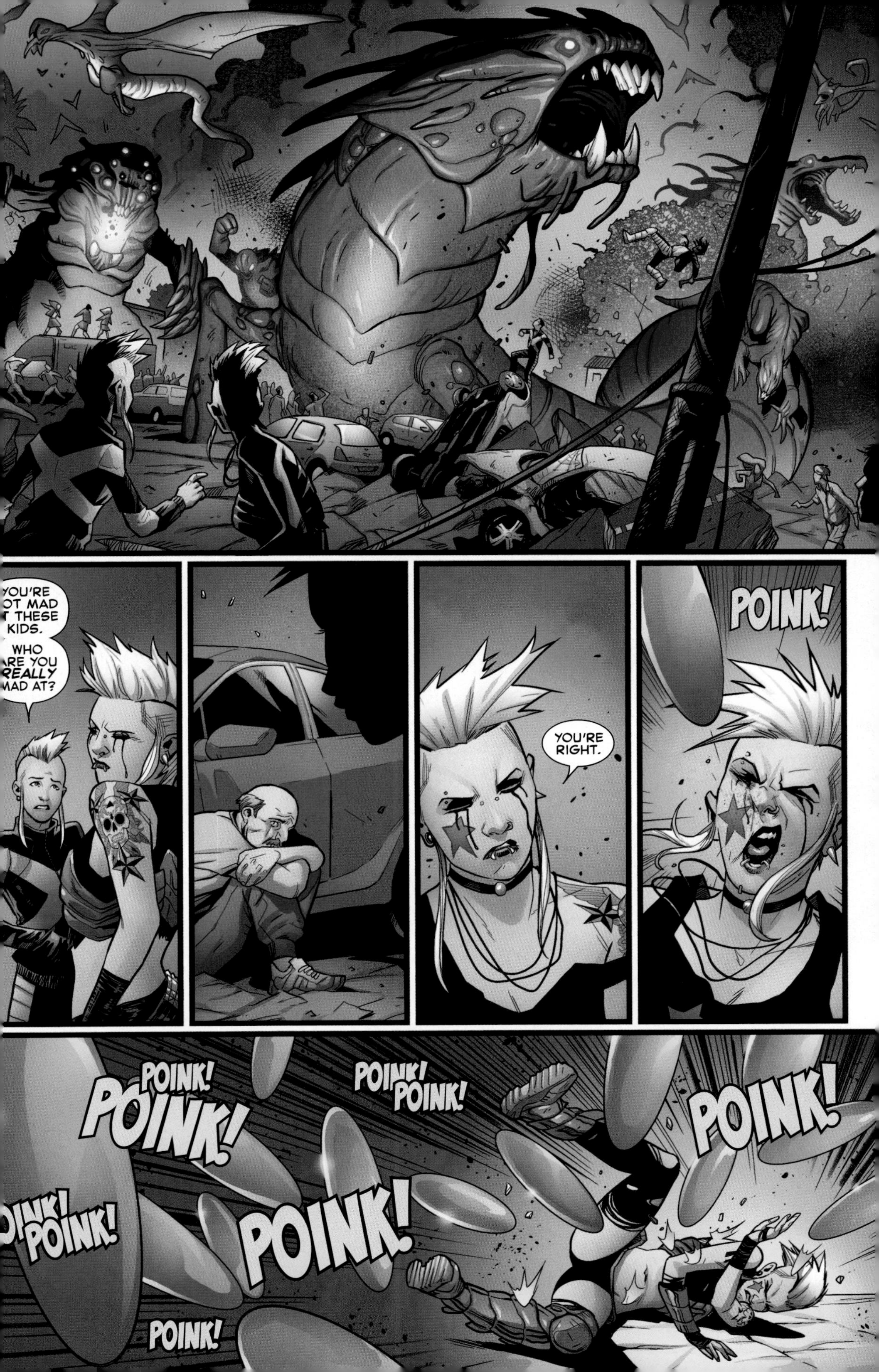
YOU'RE
OT MAD
T THESE
KIDS.
WHO
ARE YOU
REALLY
MAD AT?
YOU'RE RIGHT.
POINK!
POINK!
POINK!
POINK!
POINK!
POINK!
POINK!
POINK!
POINK!
POINK!

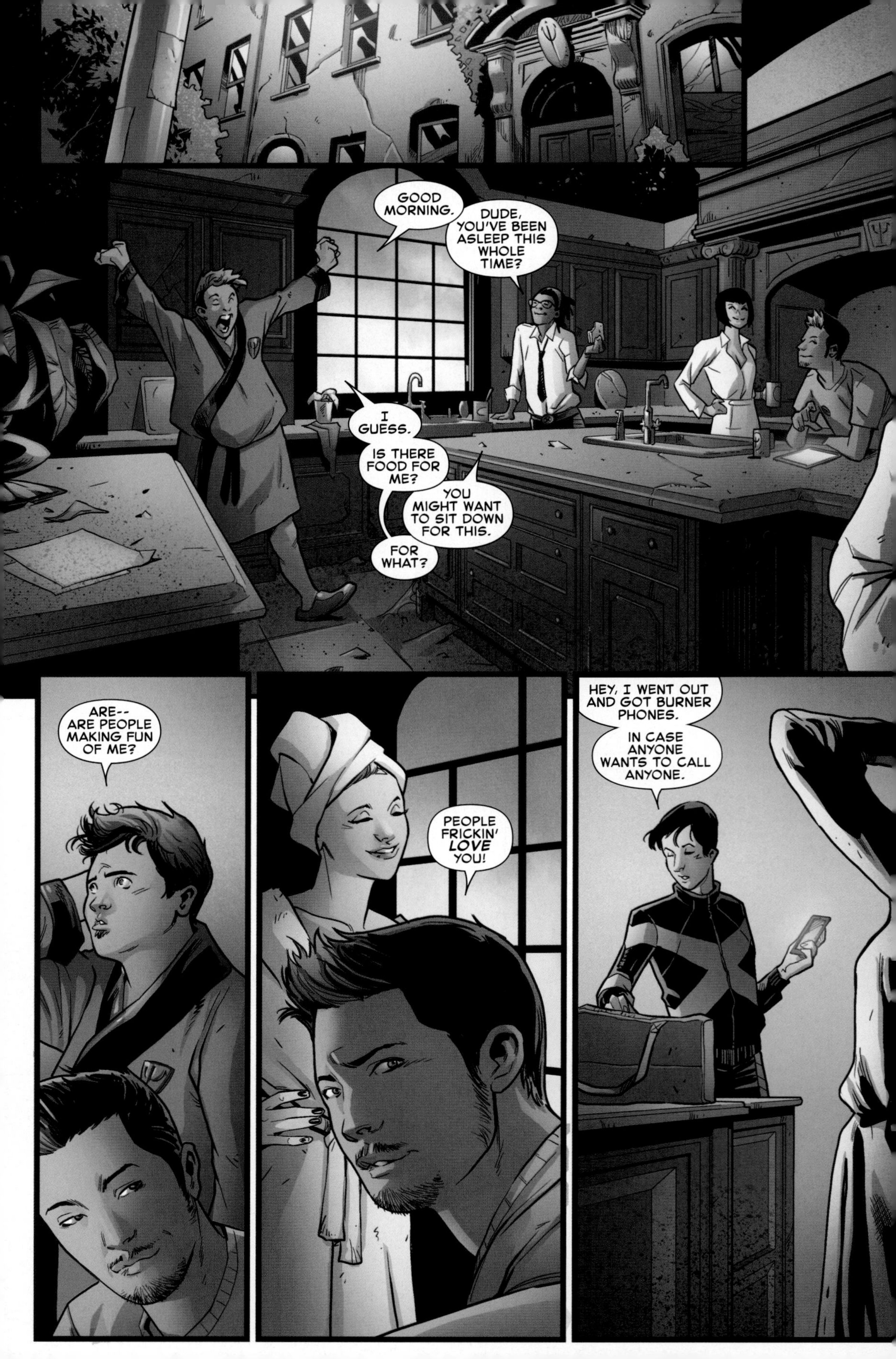
GOOD MORNING.
DUDE, YOU'VE BEEN ASLEEP THIS WHOLE TIME?
I GUESS.
IS THERE FOOD FOR ME?
YOU MIGHT WANT TO SIT DOWN FOR THIS.
FOR WHAT?
ARE-- ARE PEOPLE MAKING FUN OF ME?
PEOPLE FRICKIN' LOVE YOU!
HEY, I WENT OUT AND GOT BURNER PHONES.
IN CASE ANYONE WANTS TO CALL ANYONE.

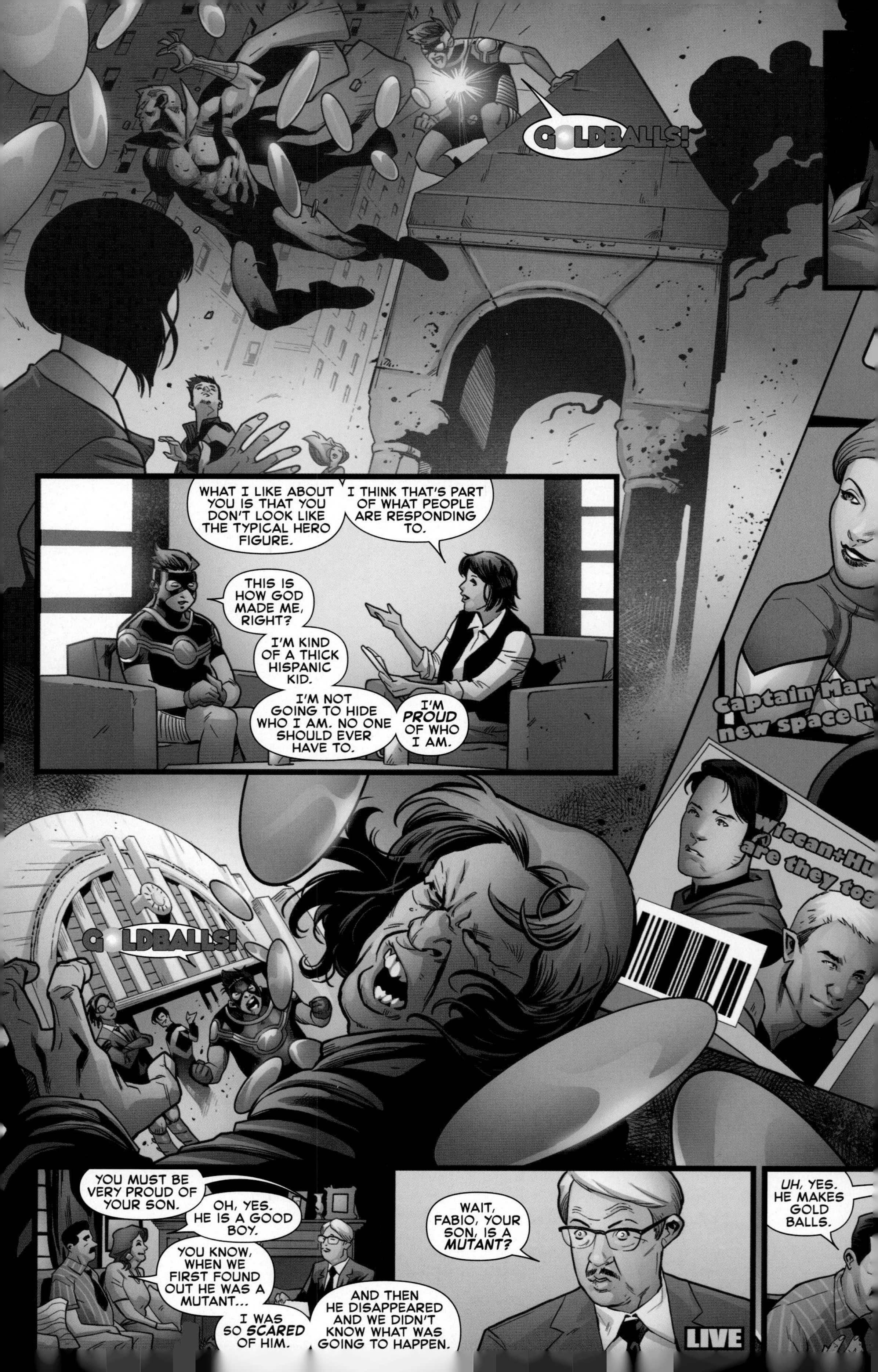

GOLDBALLS!
WHAT I LIKE ABOUT YOU IS THAT YOU DON'T LOOK LIKE THE TYPICAL HERO FIGURE.
I THINK THAT'S PART OF WHAT PEOPLE ARE RESPONDING TO.
THIS IS HOW GOD MADE ME, RIGHT?
I'M KIND OF A THICK HISPANIC KID.
I'M NOT GOING TO HIDE WHO I AM. NO ONE SHOULD EVER HAVE TO.
I'M *PROUD* OF WHO I AM.
Captain Mar
new space h
Wiccan+Hu
are they tog
GOLDBALLS!
YOU MUST BE VERY PROUD OF YOUR SON.
OH, YES. HE IS A GOOD BOY.
YOU KNOW, WHEN WE FIRST FOUND OUT HE WAS A MUTANT...
I WAS SO *SCARED* OF HIM.
AND THEN HE DISAPPEARED AND WE DIDN'T KNOW WHAT WAS GOING TO HAPPEN.
WAIT, FABIO, YOUR SON, IS A *MUTANT?*
LIVE
UH, YES. HE MAKES GOLD BALLS.

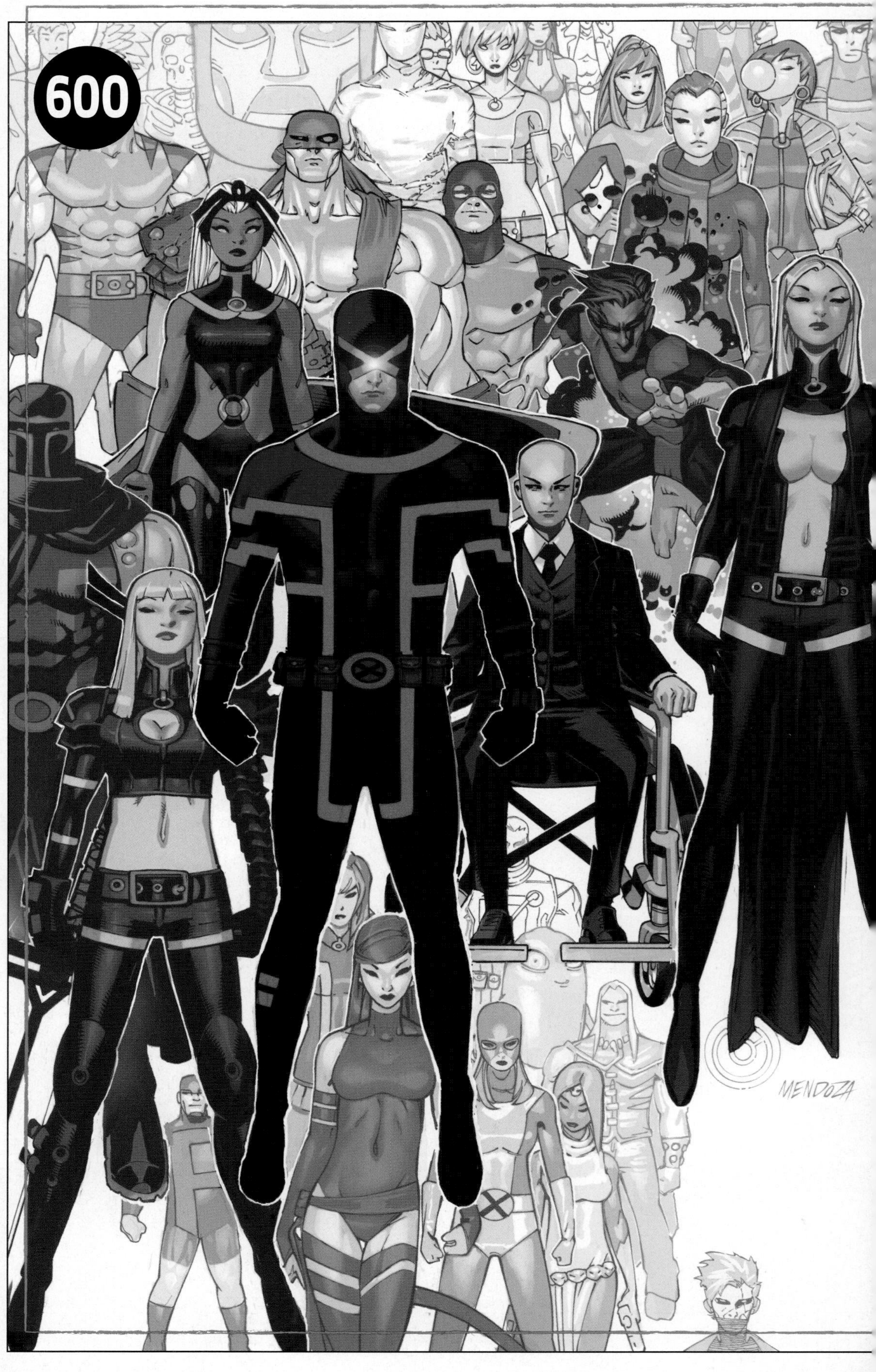
600
MENDOZA

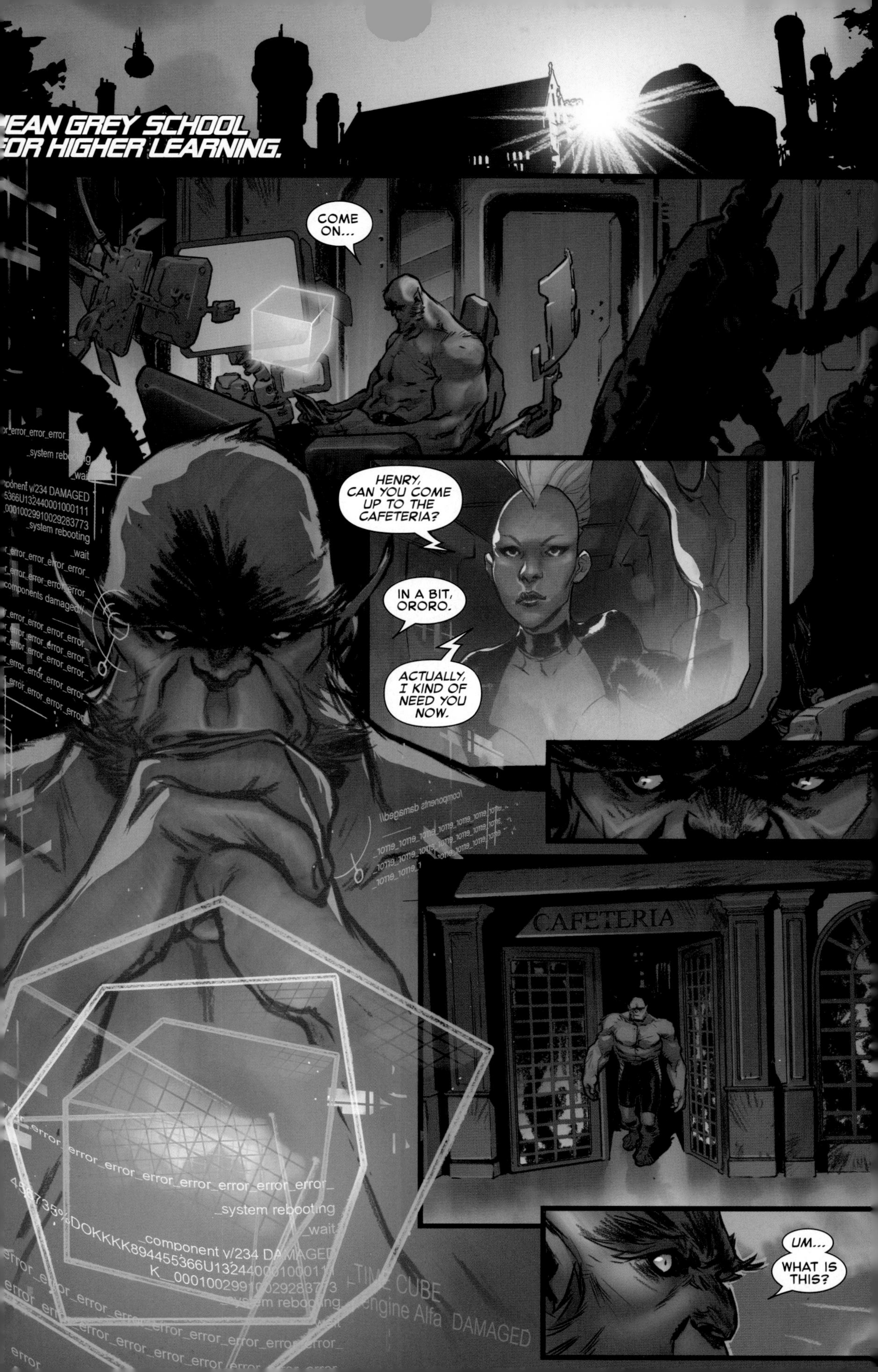
EAN GREY SCHOOL
OR HIGHER LEARNING.
COME ON...
HENRY, CAN YOU COME UP TO THE CAFETERIA?
IN A BIT, ORORO.
ACTUALLY, I KIND OF NEED YOU NOW.
CAFETERIA
_system rebooting
_wait
_component v/234 DAMAGED
TIME CUBE
engine Alfa DAMAGED
UM... WHAT IS THIS?

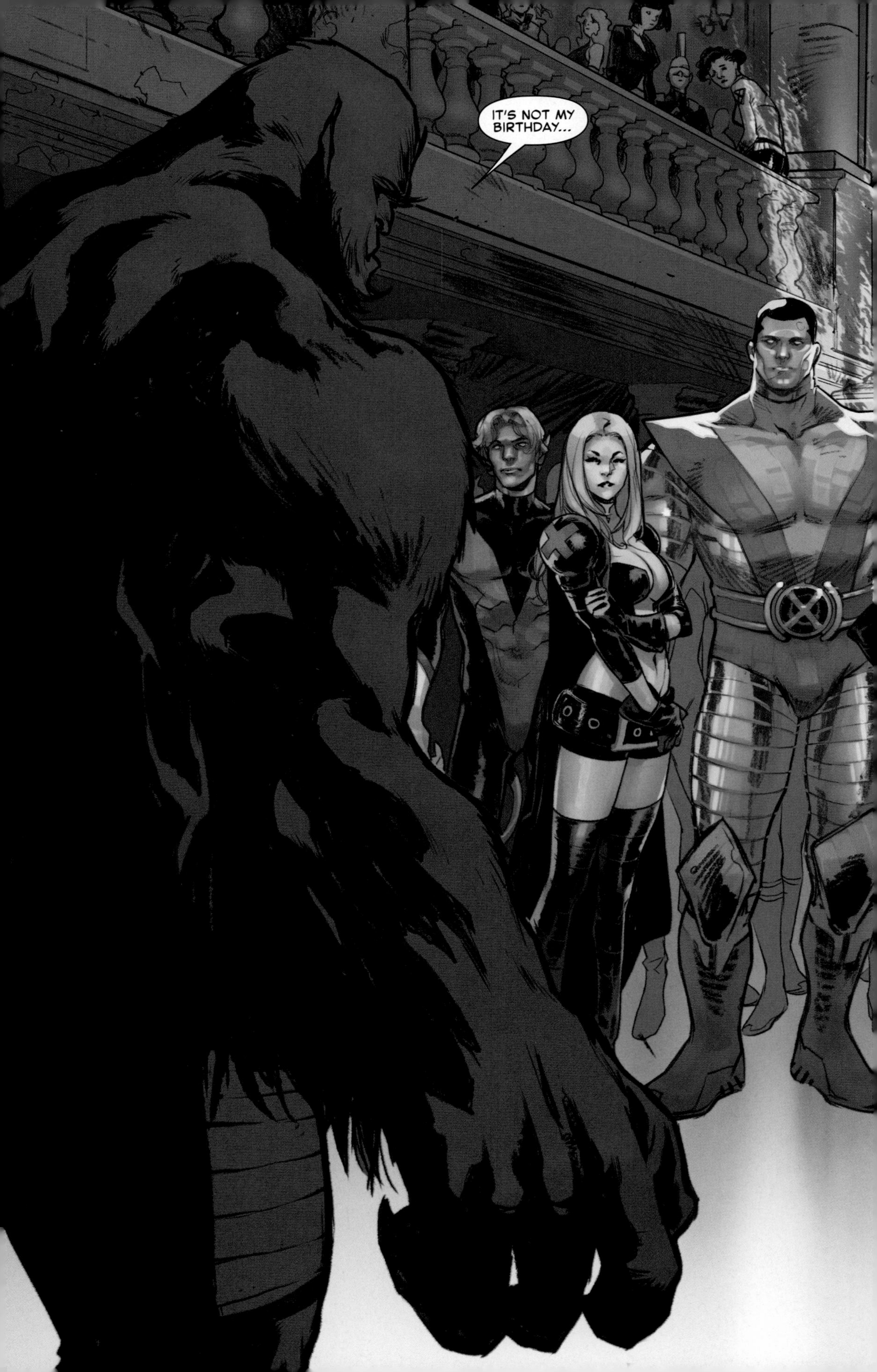
IT'S NOT MY BIRTHDAY...

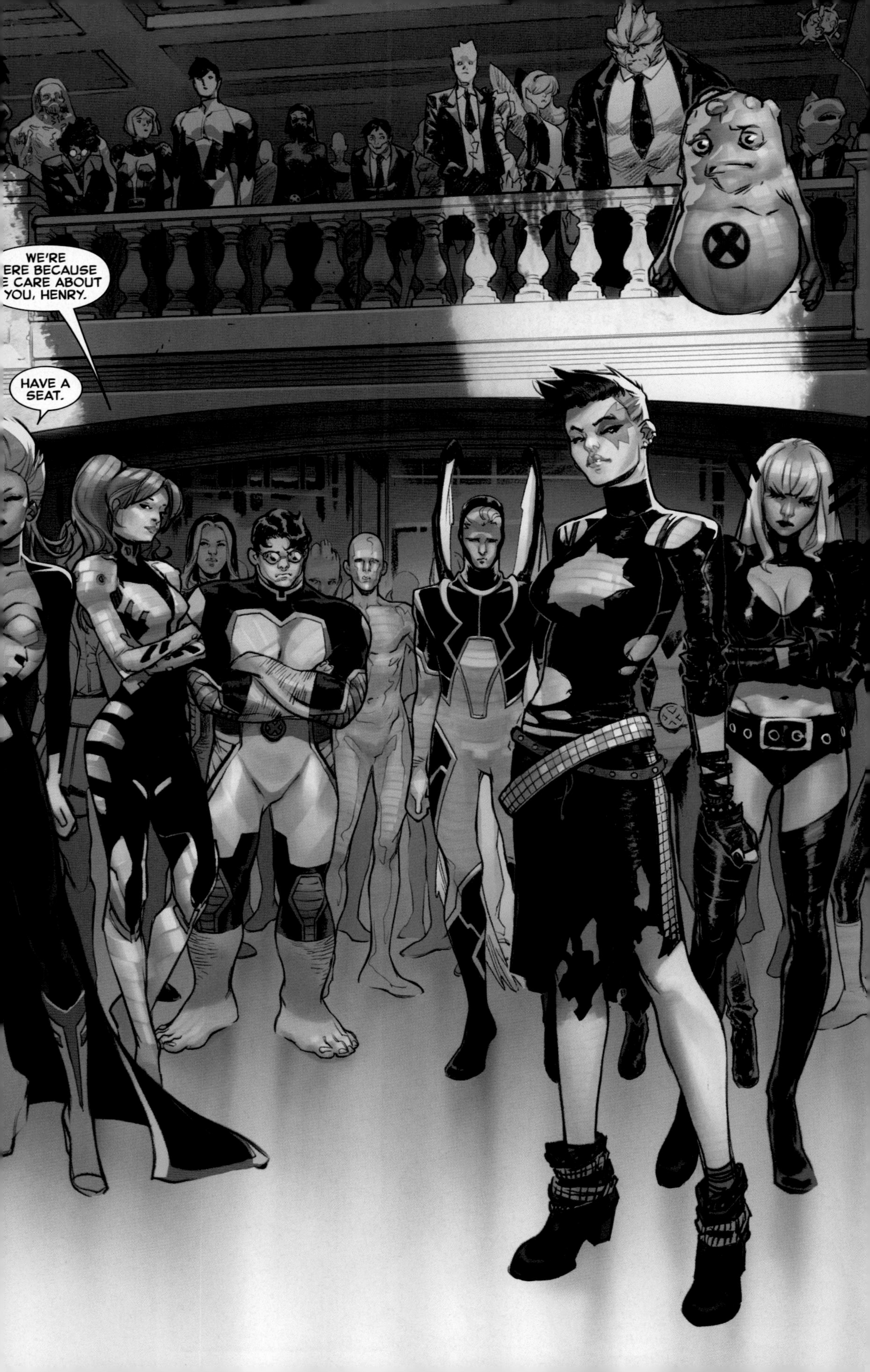

WE'RE
ERE BECAUSE
E CARE ABOUT
YOU, HENRY.
HAVE A SEAT.

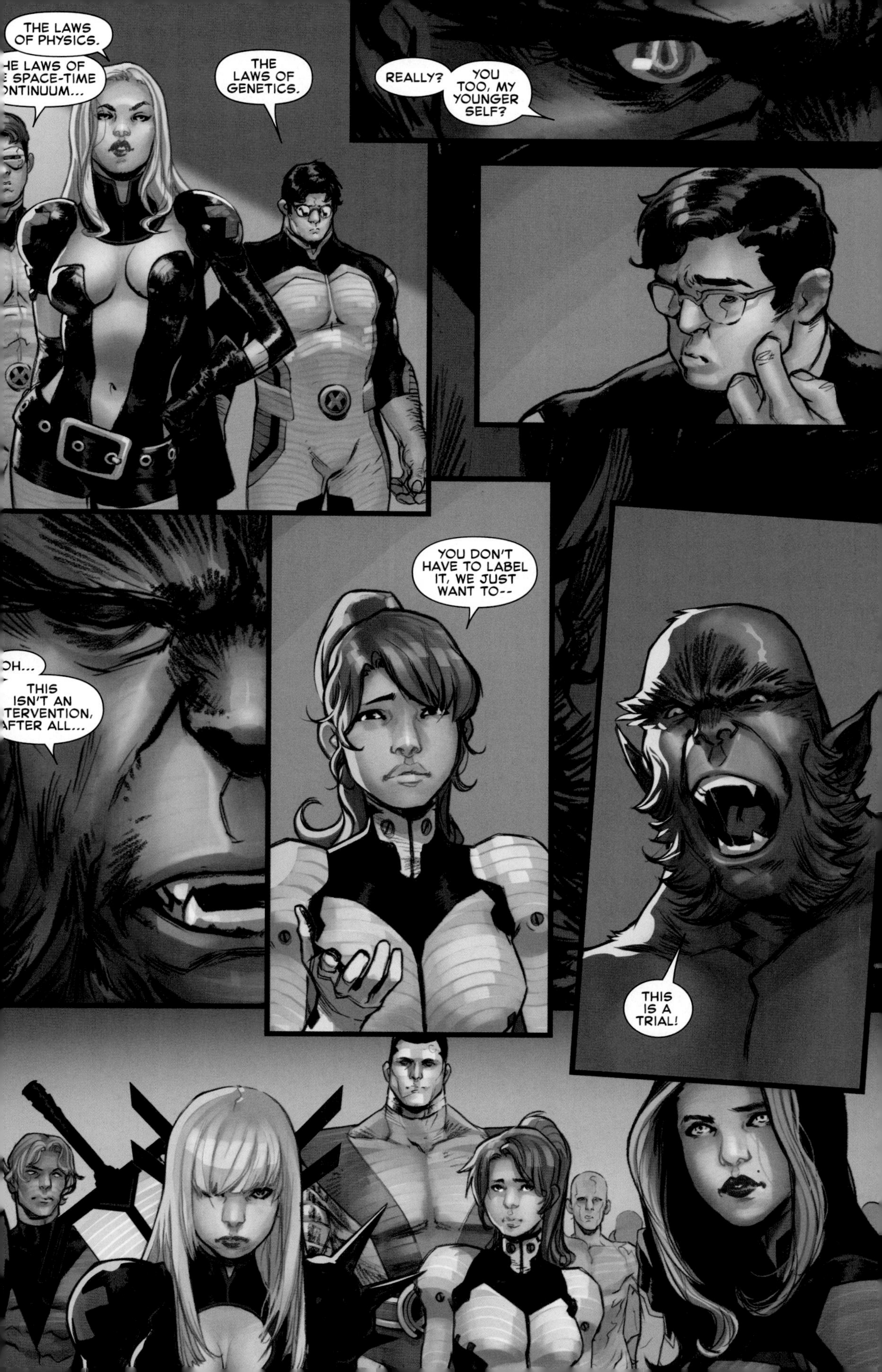
THE LAWS OF PHYSICS.
HE LAWS OF E SPACE-TIME ONTINUUM...
THE LAWS OF GENETICS.
REALLY?
YOU TOO, MY YOUNGER SELF?
OH...
THIS ISN'T AN TERVENTION, AFTER ALL...
YOU DON'T HAVE TO LABEL IT, WE JUST WANT TO--
THIS IS A TRIAL!

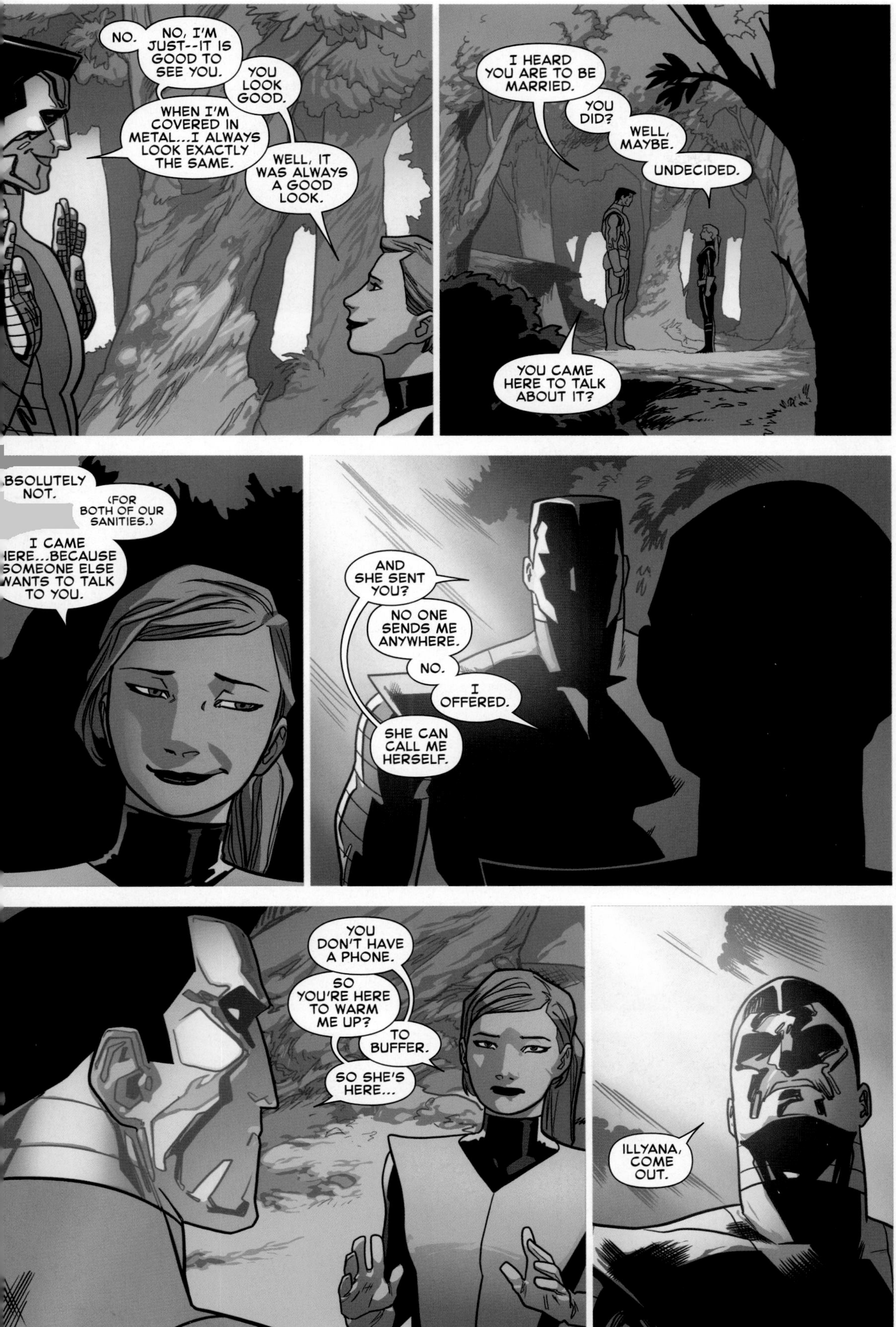

NO.
NO, I'M JUST--IT IS GOOD TO SEE YOU.
YOU LOOK GOOD.
WHEN I'M COVERED IN METAL...I ALWAYS LOOK EXACTLY THE SAME.
WELL, IT WAS ALWAYS A GOOD LOOK.
I HEARD YOU ARE TO BE MARRIED.
YOU DID?
WELL, MAYBE.
UNDECIDED.
YOU CAME HERE TO TALK ABOUT IT?
BSOLUTELY NOT.
(FOR BOTH OF OUR SANITIES.)
I CAME HERE...BECAUSE SOMEONE ELSE WANTS TO TALK TO YOU.
AND SHE SENT YOU?
NO ONE SENDS ME ANYWHERE.
NO.
I OFFERED.
SHE CAN CALL ME HERSELF.
YOU DON'T HAVE A PHONE.
SO YOU'RE HERE TO WARM ME UP?
TO BUFFER.
SO SHE'S HERE...
ILLYANA, COME OUT.

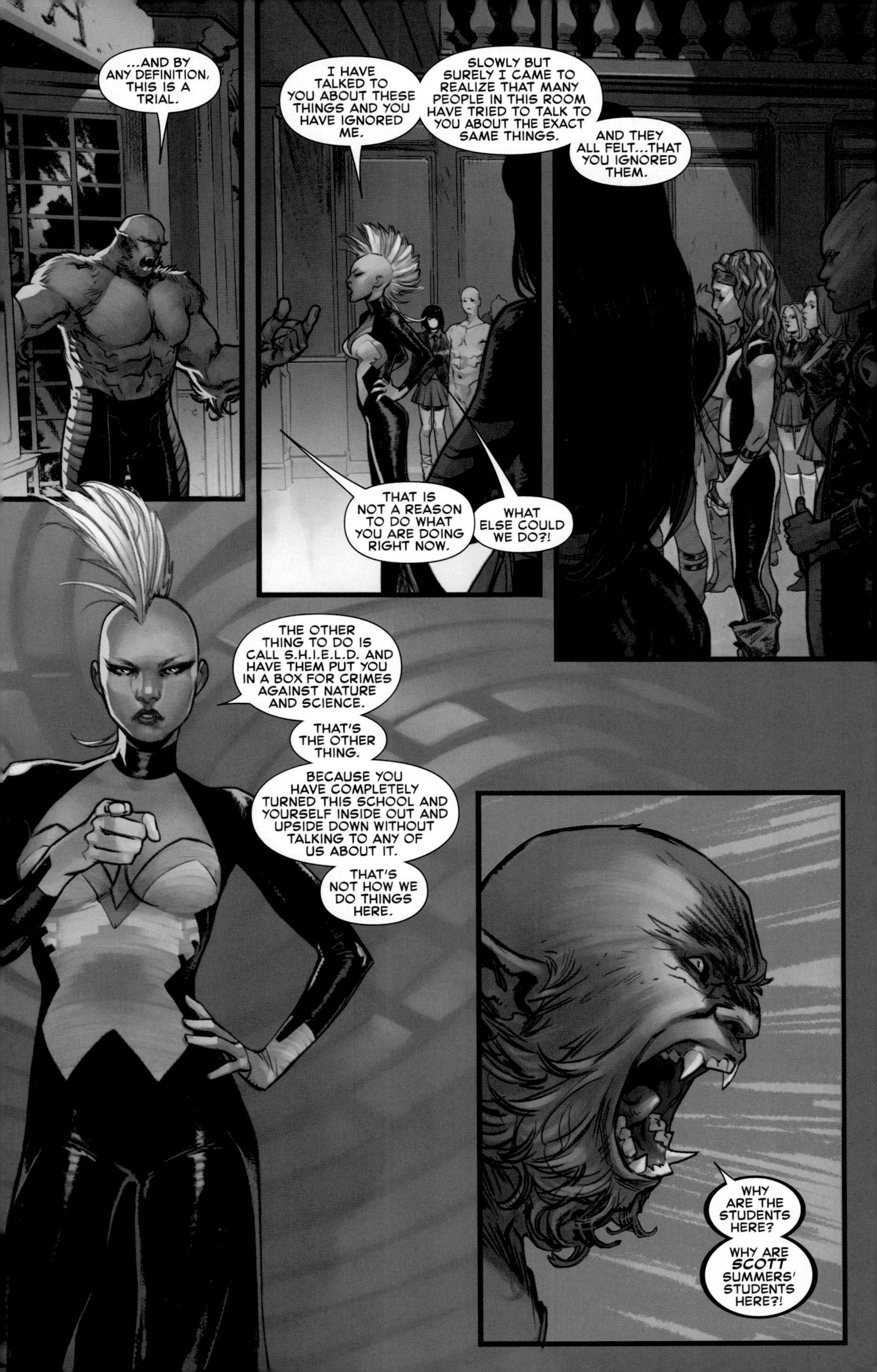
...AND BY ANY DEFINITION, THIS IS A TRIAL.
I HAVE TALKED TO YOU ABOUT THESE THINGS AND YOU HAVE IGNORED ME.
SLOWLY BUT SURELY I CAME TO REALIZE THAT MANY PEOPLE IN THIS ROOM HAVE TRIED TO TALK TO YOU ABOUT THE EXACT SAME THINGS.
AND THEY ALL FELT...THAT YOU IGNORED THEM.
THAT IS NOT A REASON TO DO WHAT YOU ARE DOING RIGHT NOW.
WHAT ELSE COULD WE DO?!
THE OTHER THING TO DO IS CALL S.H.I.E.L.D. AND HAVE THEM PUT YOU IN A BOX FOR CRIMES AGAINST NATURE AND SCIENCE.
THAT'S THE OTHER THING.
BECAUSE YOU HAVE COMPLETELY TURNED THIS SCHOOL AND YOURSELF INSIDE OUT AND UPSIDE DOWN WITHOUT TALKING TO ANY OF US ABOUT IT.
THAT'S NOT HOW WE DO THINGS HERE.
WHY ARE THE STUDENTS HERE?
WHY ARE *SCOTT* SUMMERS' STUDENTS HERE?!

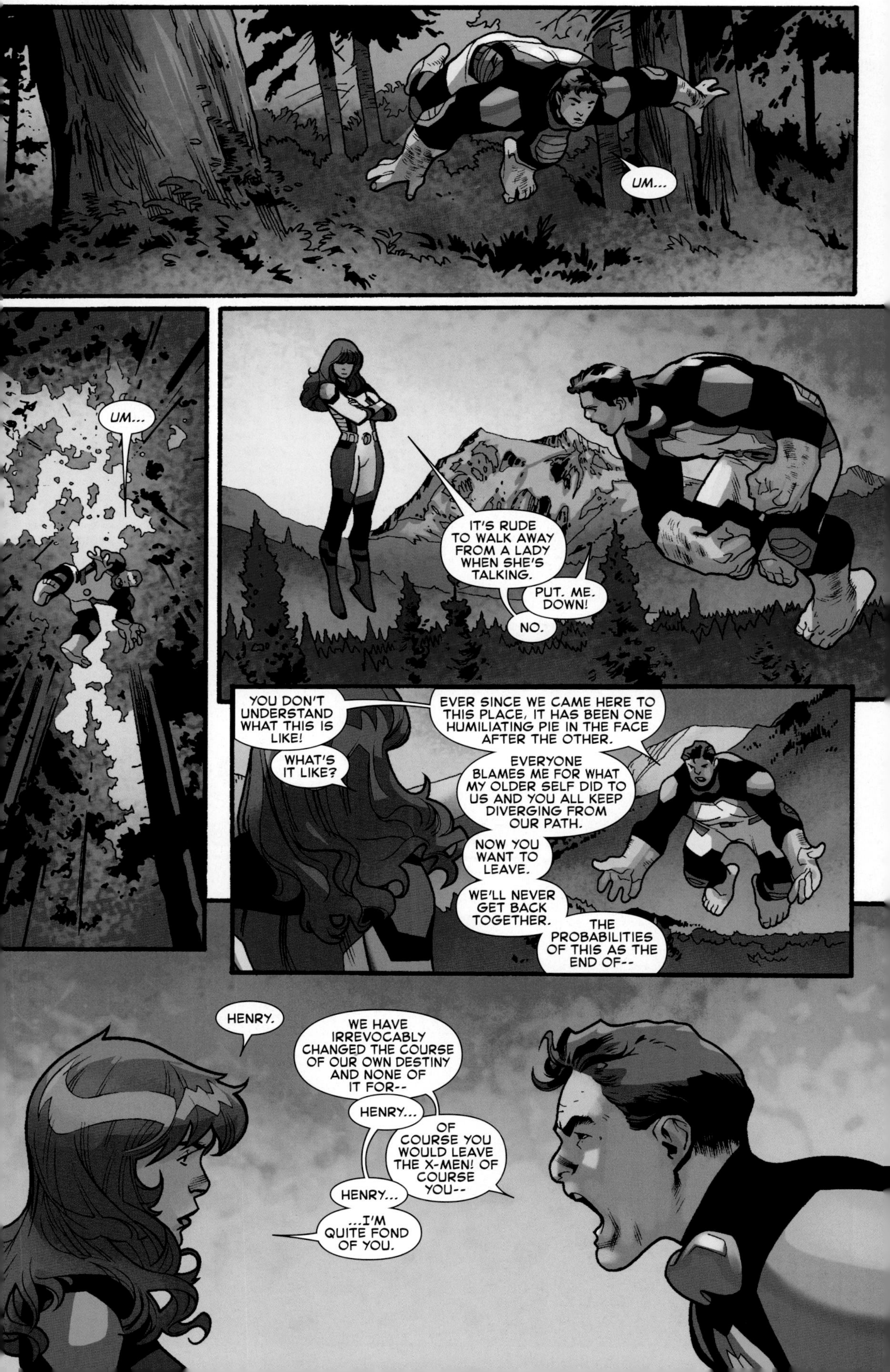
UM...
UM...
IT'S RUDE TO WALK AWAY FROM A LADY WHEN SHE'S TALKING.
PUT. ME. DOWN!
NO.
YOU DON'T UNDERSTAND WHAT THIS IS LIKE!
WHAT'S IT LIKE?
EVER SINCE WE CAME HERE TO THIS PLACE, IT HAS BEEN ONE HUMILIATING PIE IN THE FACE AFTER THE OTHER.
EVERYONE BLAMES ME FOR WHAT MY OLDER SELF DID TO US AND YOU ALL KEEP DIVERGING FROM OUR PATH.
NOW YOU WANT TO LEAVE.
WE'LL NEVER GET BACK TOGETHER.
THE PROBABILITIES OF THIS AS THE END OF--
HENRY.
WE HAVE IRREVOCABLY CHANGED THE COURSE OF OUR OWN DESTINY AND NONE OF IT FOR--
HENRY...
OF COURSE YOU WOULD LEAVE THE X-MEN! OF COURSE YOU--
HENRY...
...I'M QUITE FOND OF YOU.

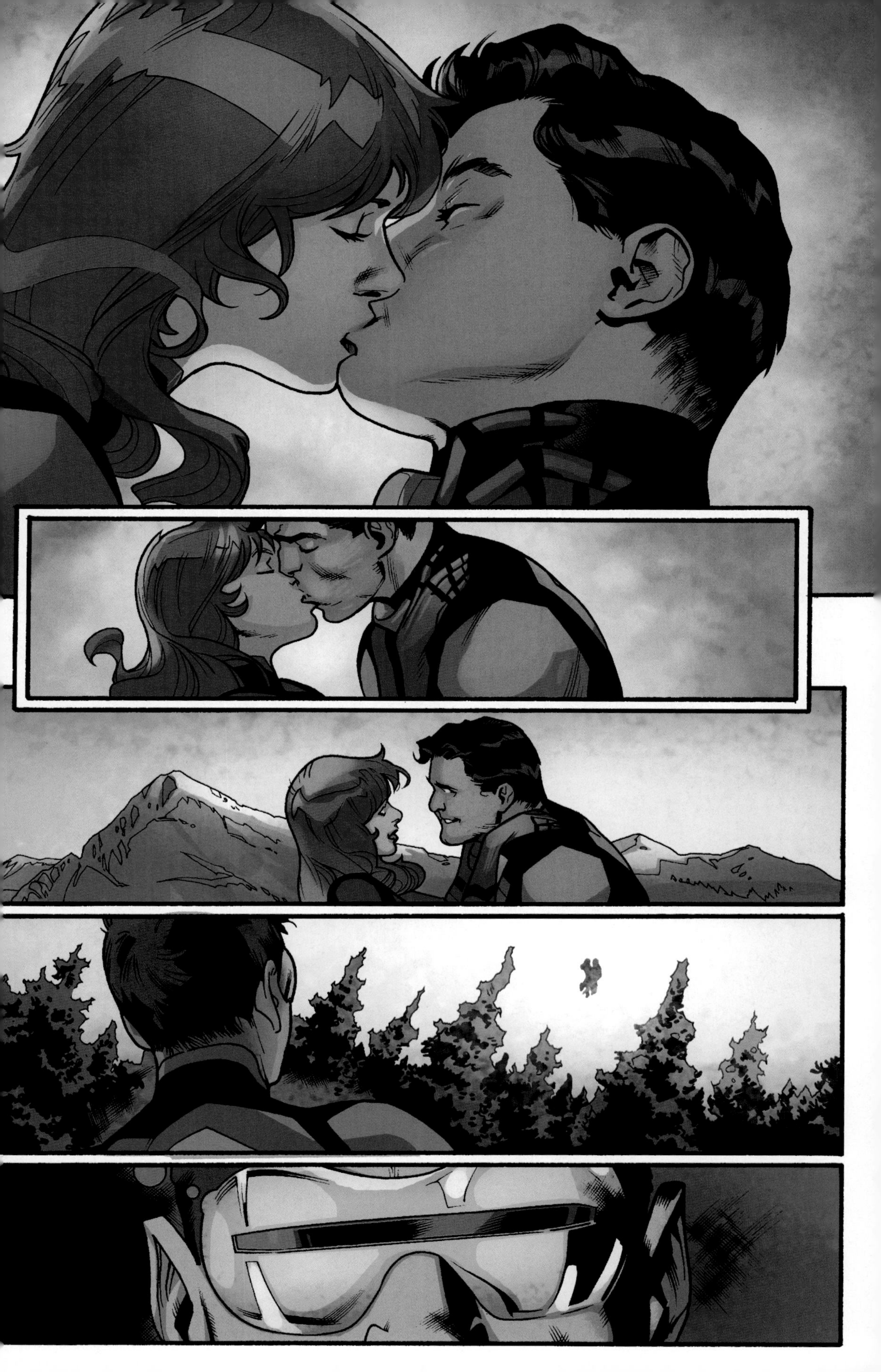

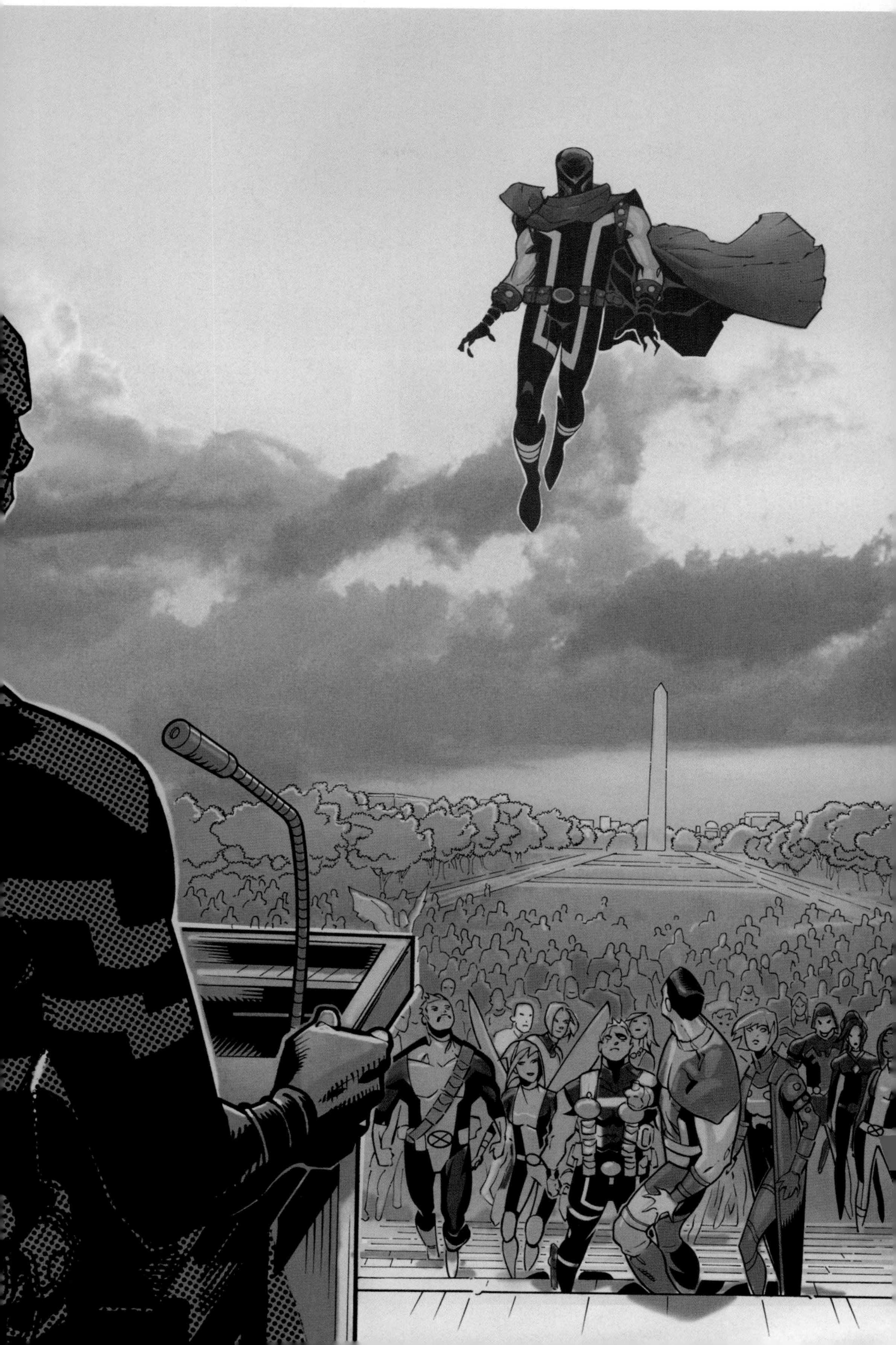

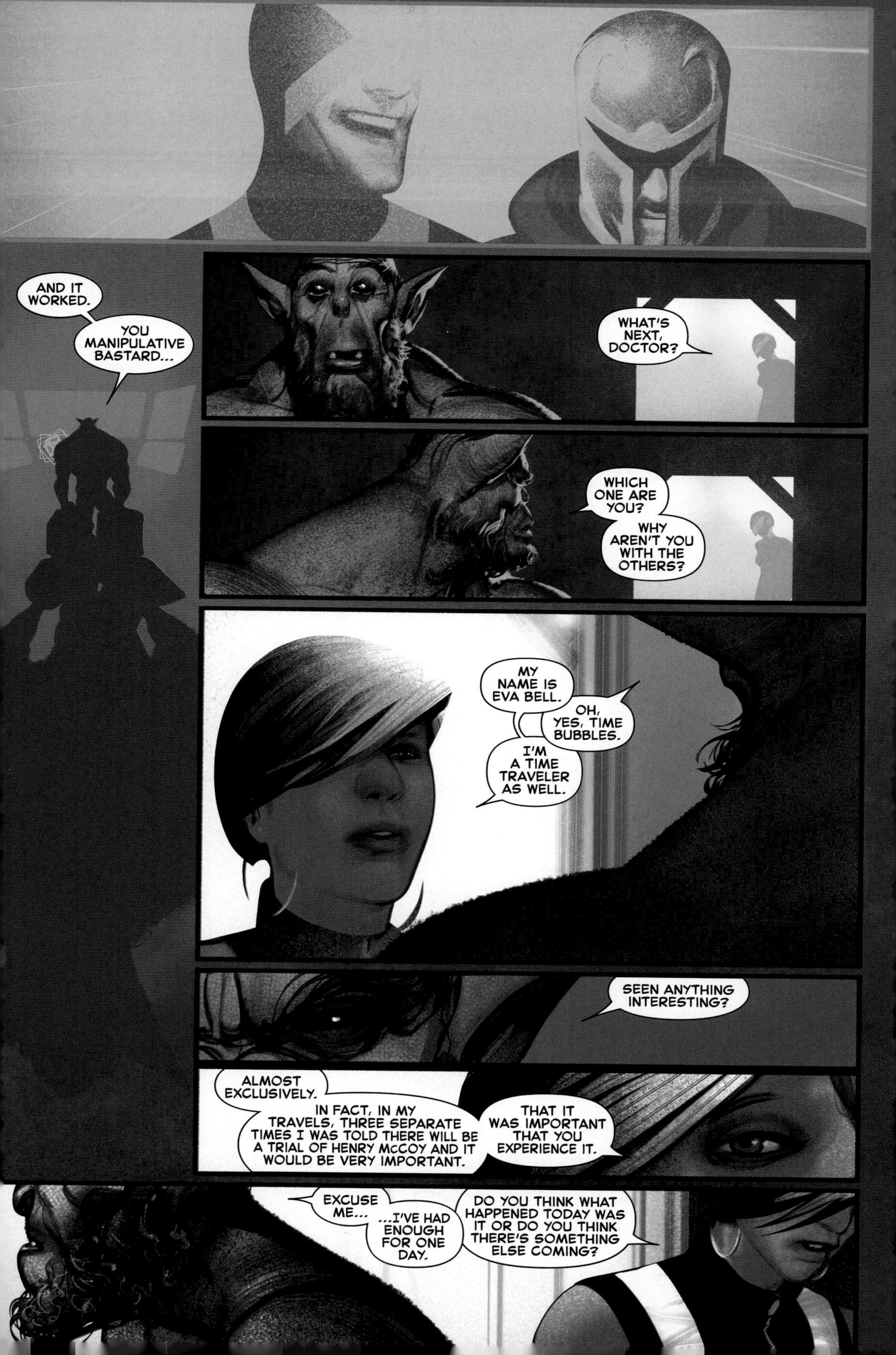

AND IT WORKED.
YOU MANIPULATIVE BASTARD...
WHAT'S NEXT, DOCTOR?
WHICH ONE ARE YOU?
WHY AREN'T YOU WITH THE OTHERS?
MY NAME IS EVA BELL.
I'M A TIME TRAVELER AS WELL.
OH, YES, TIME BUBBLES.
SEEN ANYTHING INTERESTING?
ALMOST EXCLUSIVELY.
IN FACT, IN MY TRAVELS, THREE SEPARATE TIMES I WAS TOLD THERE WILL BE A TRIAL OF HENRY McCOY AND IT WOULD BE VERY IMPORTANT.
THAT IT WAS IMPORTANT THAT YOU EXPERIENCE IT.
DO YOU THINK WHAT HAPPENED TODAY WAS IT OR DO YOU THINK THERE'S SOMETHING ELSE COMING?
EXCUSE ME...
...I'VE HAD ENOUGH FOR ONE DAY.

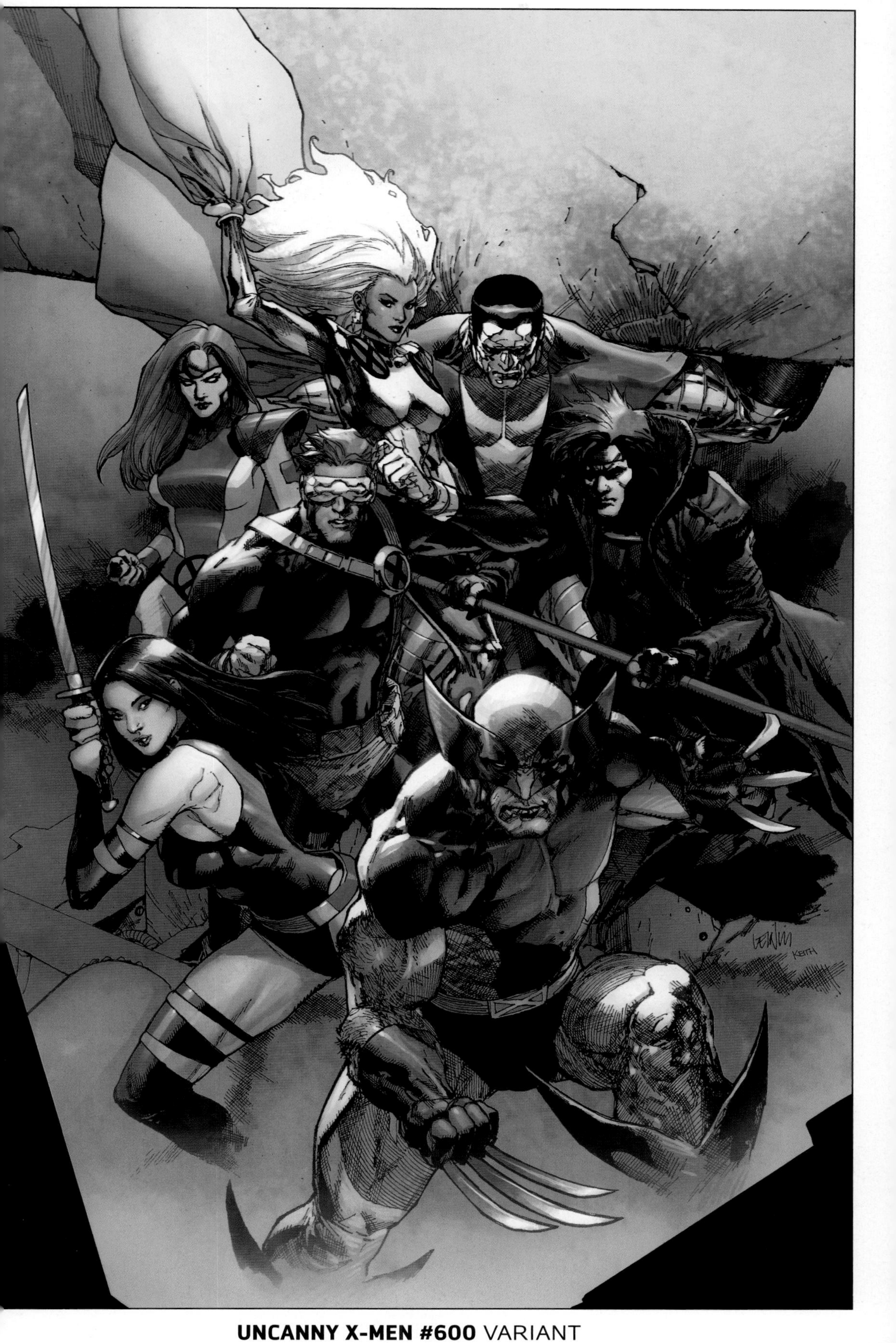

UNCANNY X-MEN #600 VARIANT

BY LEINIL YU & JASON KEITH

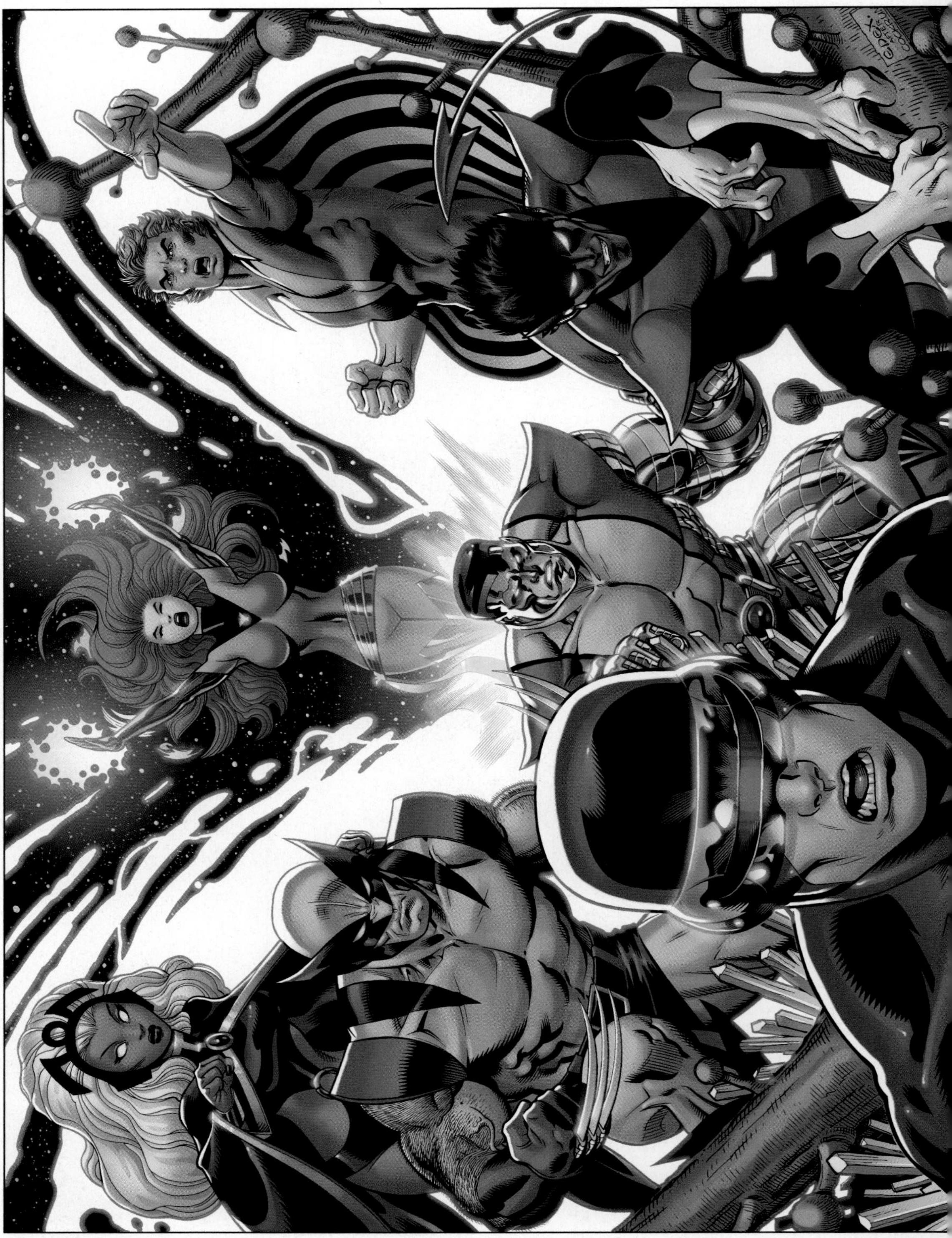

UNCANNY X-MEN #600 VARIANT

BY ED McGUINNESS, DEXTER VINES & VAL STAPLES

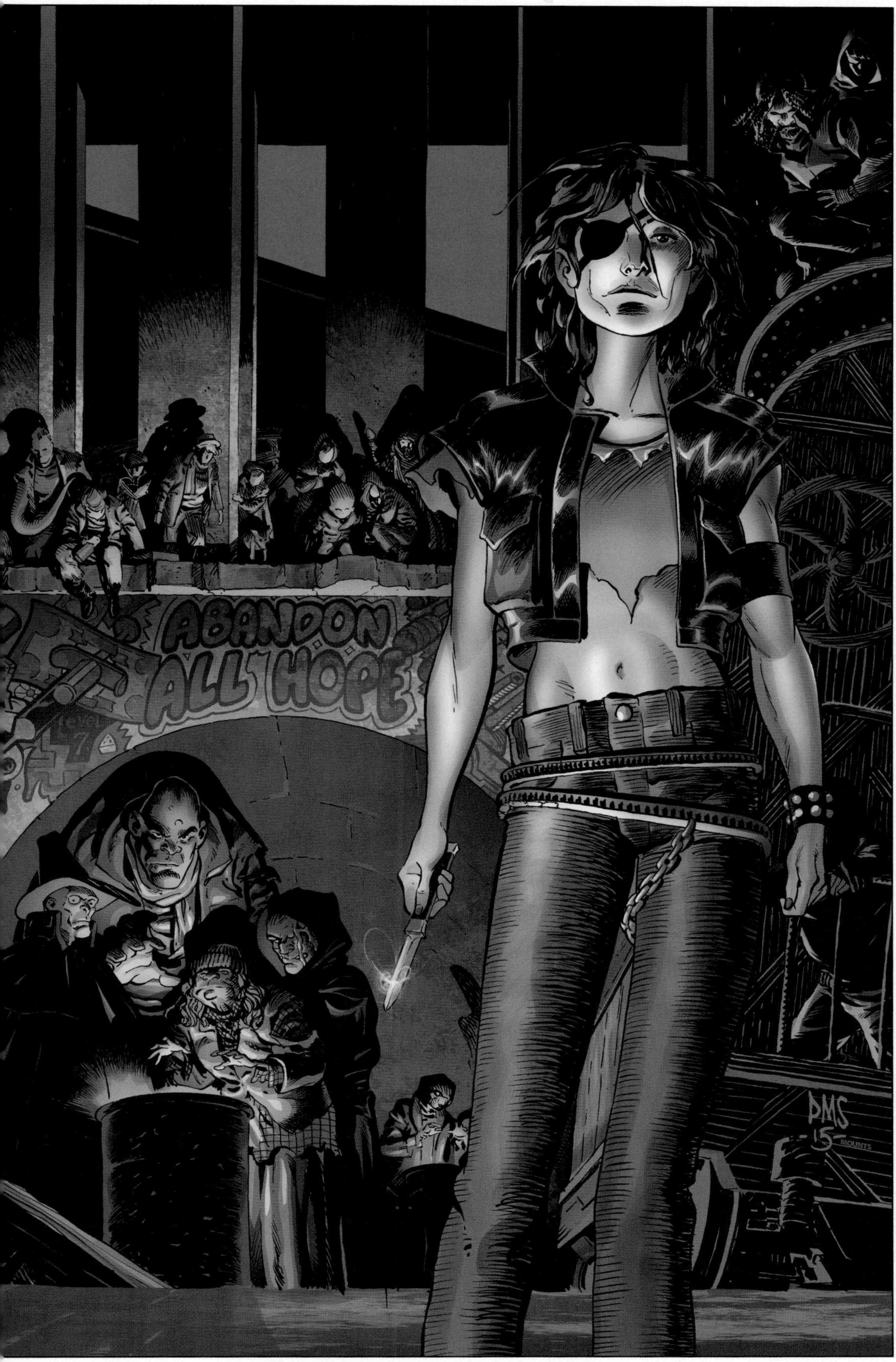
ABANDON
ALL HOPE
PMS
15
MOUNTS

UNCANNY X-MEN #600 VARIANT
BY PAUL SMITH & PAUL MOUNTS

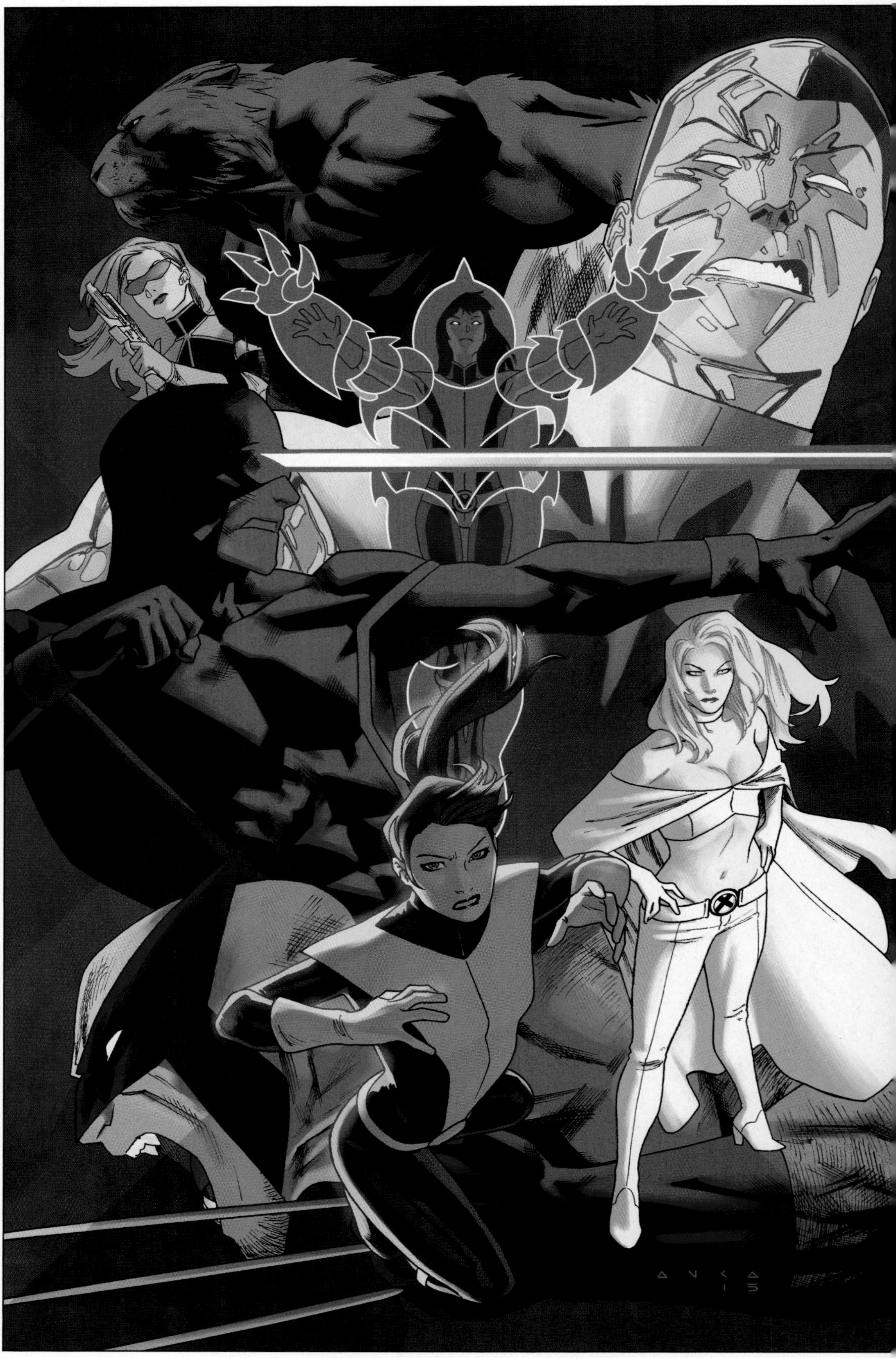

UNCANNY X-MEN #600 VARIANT
BY KRIS ANKA

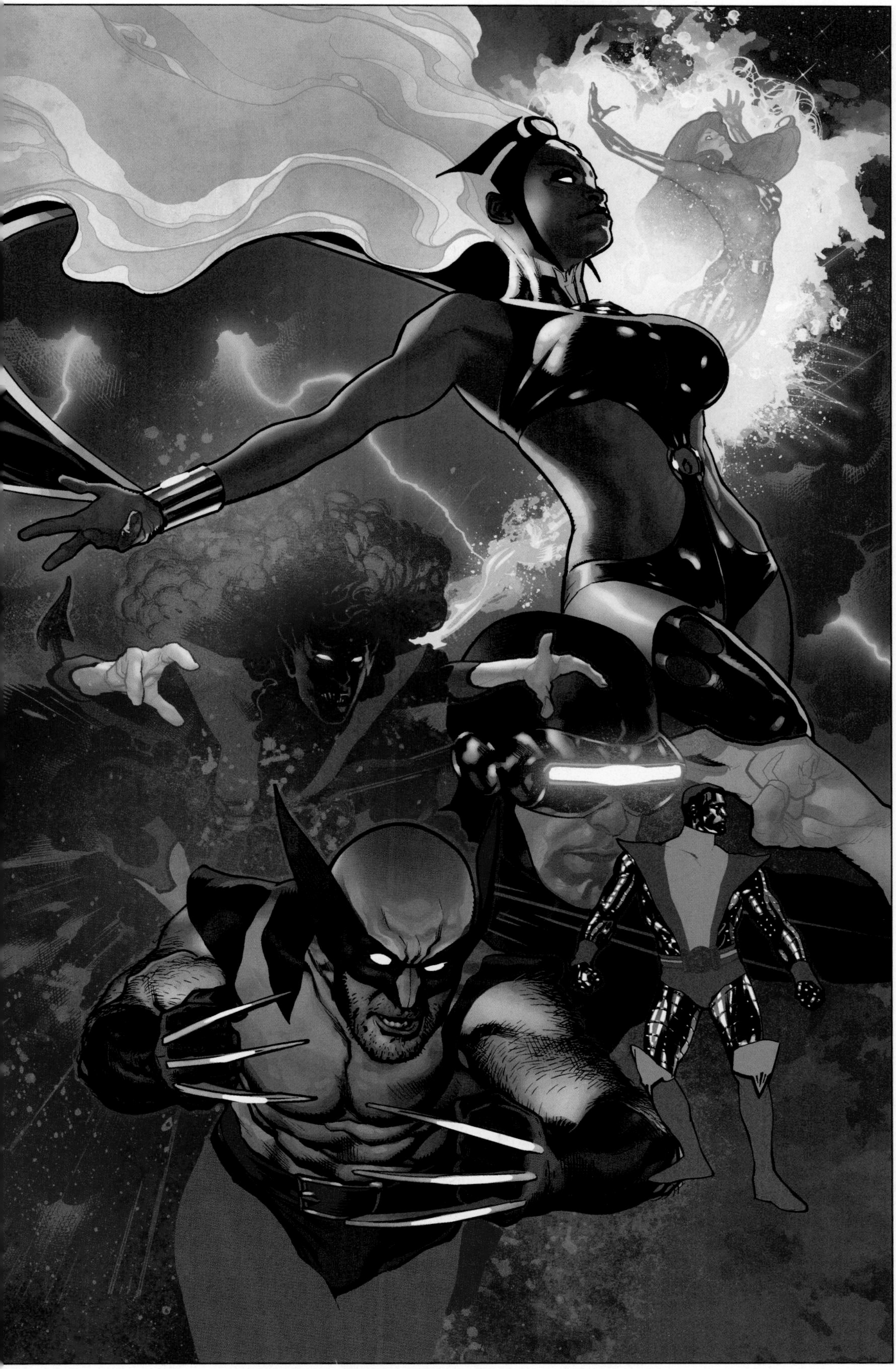

UNCANNY X-MEN #600 VARIANT
BY ADAM HUGHES

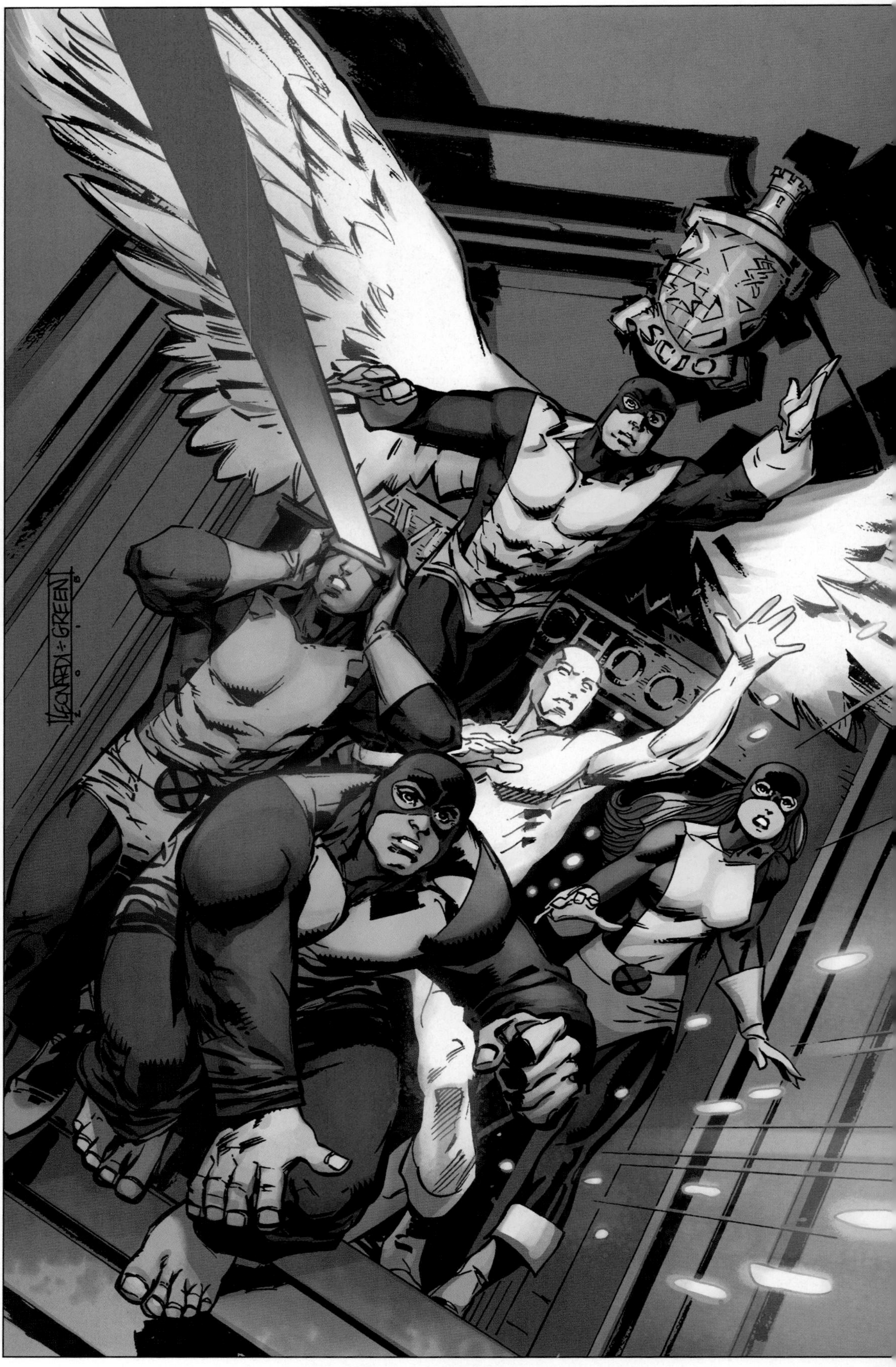

UNCANNY X-MEN #600 VARIANT

BY RICK LEONARDI, DAN GREEN & JASON KEITH

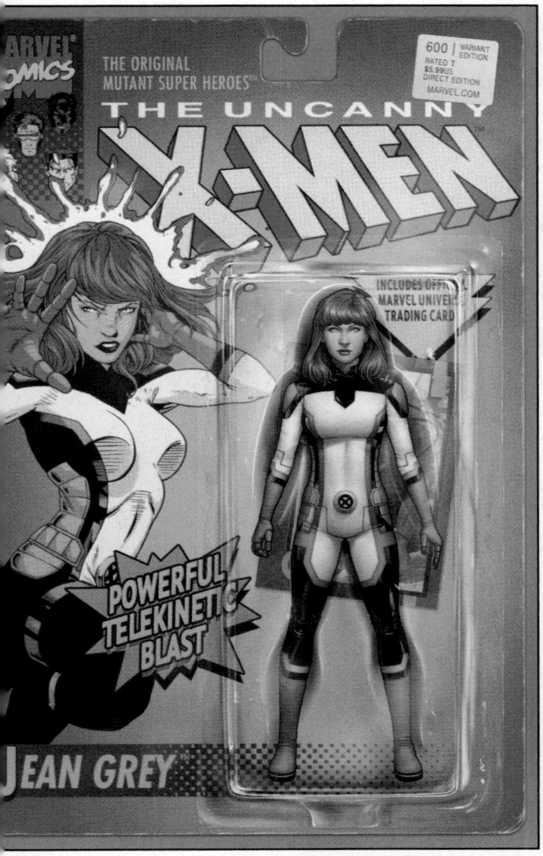
MARVEL COMICS
THE ORIGINAL MUTANT SUPER HEROES™
600 | VARIANT EDITION
RATED T
$5.99US
DIRECT EDITION
MARVEL.COM
THE UNCANNY
X-MEN™
INCLUDES OFFICIAL MARVEL UNIVERSE TRADING CARD
POWERFUL TELEKINETIC BLAST
JEAN GREY™

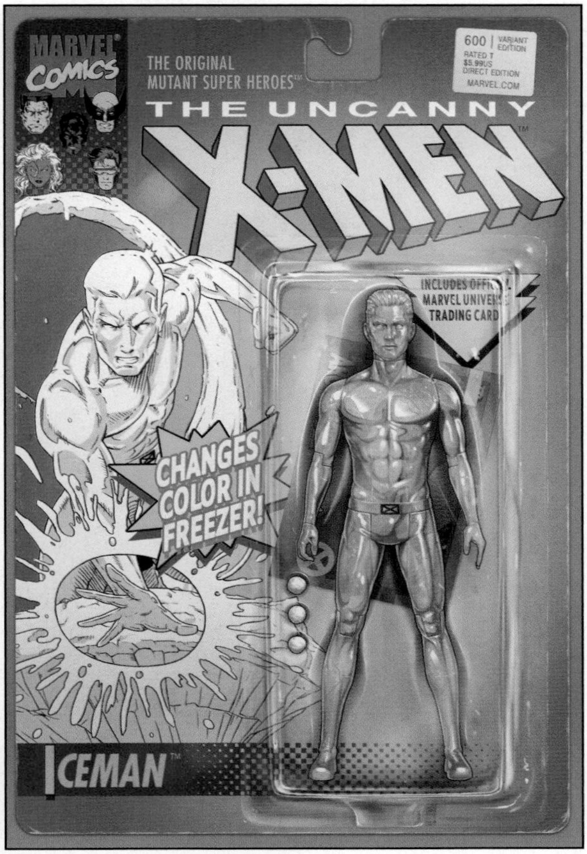
MARVEL COMICS
THE ORIGINAL MUTANT SUPER HEROES™
600 | VARIANT EDITION
RATED T
$5.99US
DIRECT EDITION
MARVEL.COM
THE UNCANNY
X-MEN™
INCLUDES OFFICIAL MARVEL UNIVERSE TRADING CARD
CHANGES COLOR IN FREEZER!
ICEMAN™

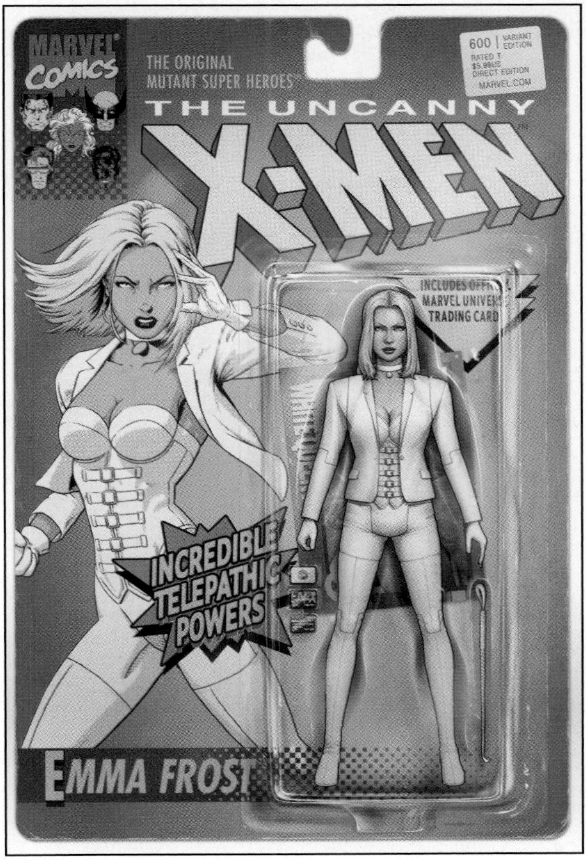
MARVEL COMICS
THE ORIGINAL MUTANT SUPER HEROES™
600 | VARIANT EDITION
RATED T
$5.99US
DIRECT EDITION
MARVEL.COM
THE UNCANNY
X-MEN™
INCLUDES OFFICIAL MARVEL UNIVERSE TRADING CARD
INCREDIBLE TELEPATHIC POWERS
EMMA FROST™

UNCANNY X-MEN #600 ACTION FIGURE VARIANTS

BY JOHN TYLER CHRISTOPHER

"Hold on to your hat because this is one heck of an X-Men book." – *IGN.co*

New York Times Best Seller!
"Bendis is off to a great start."
— ComicList.com
UNCANNY X-MEN
REVOLUTION
AR
BENDIS
MARVEL NOW!
BACHALO
IRVING

UNCANNY X-MEN VOL. 1: REVOLUTION

978-0-7851-6702-0 • DEC130777

"The setup and payoff will rock your socks, so hold on to them too." – *IGN.c*

MARVEL NOW!

MARVEL
FREE DIGITAL COPY OFFER
PEEL HERE TO REVEAL CODE

TO REDEEM YOUR CODE FOR A FREE DIGITAL COPY:

1. GO TO MARVEL.COM/REDEEM. OFFER EXPIRES ON 12/2/17.
2. FOLLOW THE ON-SCREEN INSTRUCTIONS TO REDEEM YOUR DIGITAL COPY.
3. LAUNCH THE MARVEL COMICS APP TO READ YOUR COMIC NOW!
4. YOUR DIGITAL COPY WILL BE FOUND UNDER THE *MY COMICS* TAB.
5. READ & ENJOY!

YOUR FREE DIGITAL COPY WILL BE AVAILABL

MARVEL COMICS APP FOR APPLE® iOS DEVICES

MARVEL COMICS AP FOR ANDROID™ DEVIC